Islands of Imagination

MĀNOA 26:2
UNIVERSITY OF HAWAI'I PRESS
HONOLULU

Islands of Imagination

VOLUME ONE

MODERN INDONESIAN PLAYS

FRANK STEWART

EDITOR

JOHN H. MCGLYNN

COBINA GILLITT

GUEST EDITORS

Steam geysers,
Kawah Kamojang,
West Java, 2011.
Jean Gaumy/Magnum

Founded in 1988 by Robert Shapard and Frank Stewart

Permissions are on page 241.

Mānoa is published twice a year. Subscriptions: U.S.A. and international—individuals $30 one year, $54 two years; institutions $50 one year, $90 two years; international airmail add $24 per year. Single copies: U.S.A. and international—individuals $20; institutions $30; international airmail add $12 per copy. Call toll free 1-888-UHPRESS. We accept Visa or MasterCard, and checks or money orders payable to University of Hawai'i Press, 2840 Kolowalu Street, Honolulu, HI 96822, U.S.A. Claims for issues not received will be honored until 180 days past the date of publication; thereafter, the single-copy rate will be charged.

Mānoa gratefully acknowledges the support of the University of Hawai'i Administration and the University of Hawai'i College of Languages, Linguistics, and Literature; and additional support from the National Endowment for the Arts, Hawai'i State Foundation on Culture and the Arts, Mānoa Foundation, and the Lontar Foundation. Special thanks to the Ministry of Education and Culture, Republic of Indonesia.

ART WORKS.
arts.gov

HAWAI'I
STATE FOUNDATION on CULTURE and the ARTS

LONTAR

manoajournal.hawaii.edu
uhpress.hawaii.edu/journals/manoa
muse.jhu.edu (Project Muse)
jstor.org

The Mānoa Foundation

CONTENTS

Islands of Imagination | **Volume One**

Modern Indonesian Plays: An Introduction

Sukma, Yogyakarta, 2011. Kurniadi Widodo

Early twentieth-century national theater in Indonesia, then known as the Dutch East Indies, was largely revolutionary in tone and intent, supporting the end of colonial rule. Productions were urban, performed on proscenium stages, and presented in what would be soon adopted as the Indonesian national language, rather than in one of the country's 350 local languages. However, by the 1930s, Indonesian theater had shifted its focus away from the independence movement and toward domestic dramas and psychological realism. This modern, Western style was preferred by the first national theater academy, Cine Drama Institut (later renamed Akademi Seni Drama dan Film Indonesia, or ASDRAFI), which opened in the Central Java city of Yogyakarta in 1948, three years after Indonesia proclaimed its independence.

The primary academy training was—and continues to be—Method Acting, developed in the United States by Richard Boleslavsky, one of Stanislavski's former students. Boleslavsky's 1933 book, *Acting: The First Six Lessons,* had been translated into Indonesian by Asrul Sani. Together with Usmar Ismail, Sani founded Akademi Teater Nasional Indonesia (or ATNI) in Jakarta, the nation's capital, in 1955.

This modern acting style focused on the internal struggle of realistic characters, frequently from the elite class, in domestic settings—so-called "living room" dramas. It was therefore the antithesis of indigenous Indonesian theater, which was characterized by music and dance and by stylistically conventional portrayals of character types, and which was based on local myths, historical legends, or ancient Indian epics.

Opening *Islands of Imagination* is a play representative of the style of the 1930s. Armijn Pané's *A Portrait of the Times* is a living-room drama in the literal sense. The play's four acts are set in the home of a model, Dutch-educated professional family. Trying to make their way in a struggling economy and changing society, the younger family members are faced with personal and professional decisions. *A Portrait of the Times* begins in the midst of a game of bridge being played by the family's son and two of his friends. Winning and feeling in control of his life, the son is confident and optimistic. As the action unfolds, however, he becomes drawn into the misfortunes of his sister's fiancé, Suparman. Although gender roles had begun changing in response to the struggling economy,

Suparman anguishes over his inability to fulfill a husband's traditional role of provider and head of household. Unemployed, he is deeply demoralized while his fiancée, whose salary could support them both, is optimistic about the changing times.

For fifteen years after Indonesia's first president, Soekarno, declared independence in 1945, national theatrical institutes and most performance communities continued to prefer modern dramatic forms over local performance traditions, regarded as backwards and provincial. Even plays that were written by Indonesians but followed Western playwriting conventions were rarely produced, because of the bias toward European drama.

Arrogating authoritarian powers, in 1959 Soekarno declared himself President for Life and instituted a policy of Guided Democracy. This policy mandated that everyone—including theater artists—work toward creating a national post-colonial cultural identity that rejected Western influences. The Institute of People's Culture (Lembaga Kebudayaan Rakyat), or Lekra, enforced the regime's policies. Founded in 1950 but most active between 1959 and 1965, this Maoist organization made sure that all works of art promoted Soekarno's ideal of "Nationalism, Religion, and Communism" (Nasionalisme, Agama, Komunisme), known as Nasakom. The government-funded Institute of National Culture (Lembaga Kebudayaan Nasional) was the regime's censor. Consequently, modern theater activity in Indonesia—except for Lekra-sponsored events—all but ceased by the end of 1963, even in the rarified world of the national theater academies. Journals that published plays, cultural essays, and other literary works were shut down. Outspoken artists were blacklisted and banned from performing publicly.

Because a young general named Soeharto promised political and economic reforms, many Indonesians welcomed the 1965 coup that installed him as president. Many in the artistic community were understandably elated when Soeharto's New Order regime (1967–1988) abolished the Indonesian Communist Party and its affiliated organizations, such as Lekra. They felt keenly that their work had long been co-opted and used for propaganda—first by the Dutch colonialists, then by the Japanese during WWII, and lastly by Lekra. Indonesia's artistic community believed there would finally be room to breathe. The playwrights soon found, however, that restrictions on free speech would not only remain, but become even more draconian.

Soeharto's New Order, like Soekarno's Guided Democracy, encouraged the development of a unifying Indonesian identity. But it did so by stressing indigenous cultural achievements. At the same time, the New Order did away with Soekarno's anti-Western ideology. Thus, a hybrid of traditional and Western art forms was created. Taman Ismail Marzuki (or TIM), a new complex in Jakarta, provided a venue in the nation's capital for indigenous traditional performances and playwrights, contemporary dramatic groups, and various forms of theater from around the world. Playwrights, inspired by both the new openness to the West and the appreciation of indigenous styles, moved away from living-room dramas and instead focused on the struggles of the common people, especially the downtrodden and destitute. In Iwan Simatupang's *No Address, No Name*, the characters are vagabonds and prostitutes living beneath a bridge. In *Ought* by Putu Wijaya, nameless workers fight among themselves over their rights and obligations when they are called upon to help individuals in urgent need. *Time Bomb* by N. Riantiarno examines the moral culpability of the privileged wealthy and the social predators who target and exploit the poor.

This effort to depict the lives of the "invisible," disadvantaged masses in a combination of traditional and modern styles might arguably have followed the regime's mandate to create an Indonesian cultural identity that embraced the country's vast ethnic and linguistic diversity. On closer examination, though, we see that many playwrights and directors fashioned works that took advantage of traditional performance styles to criticize—in a relatively non-confrontational way—inequality, poverty, and censorship.

Overall, the conditions that shaped theater during the New Order included the end of the previous government's edicts reining in the arts; the growing appreciation for exploring and employing rich traditional performance aesthetics as a way to create a theater of Indonesian national identity; the foregrounding of unrepresented and underprivileged groups; and the emergence of creative new ways to circumvent censorship in order to criticize the government.

Soeharto's government, over time, became more authoritarian, brutally crushing its opponents. At first, playwrights evaded censorship by writing allegorical fairy tales using wordplay and humor to obliquely criticize New Order policies. As anti-government sentiment spread in the general population, theater artists wrote and performed plays that called for direct political engagement and activism. Political activism in the theater not only mirrored the unrest in society, but eventually merged with the riots, protests, and street theater that successfully overthrew the Soeharto regime in 1998.

After Soeharto's ouster, the New Order was followed by a period of "reformation" in which many free-speech regulations, though not all, were lifted. During this time, contemporary theater activity slowed. So much creative energy and innovation had been channeled into opposing corruption and tyranny—and into direct protest and activism—that the writing and staging of new works took a backseat.

At the beginning of the twenty-first century, as democracy and the rule of law have taken hold, playwrights have begun to address topics that were previously prohibited or that had not seemed as urgent during the years of political turmoil, such as women's rights and the rise of conservative Islam.

Graffiti on Kewek Bridge,
Yogyakarta, 2011.
Kurniadi Widodo

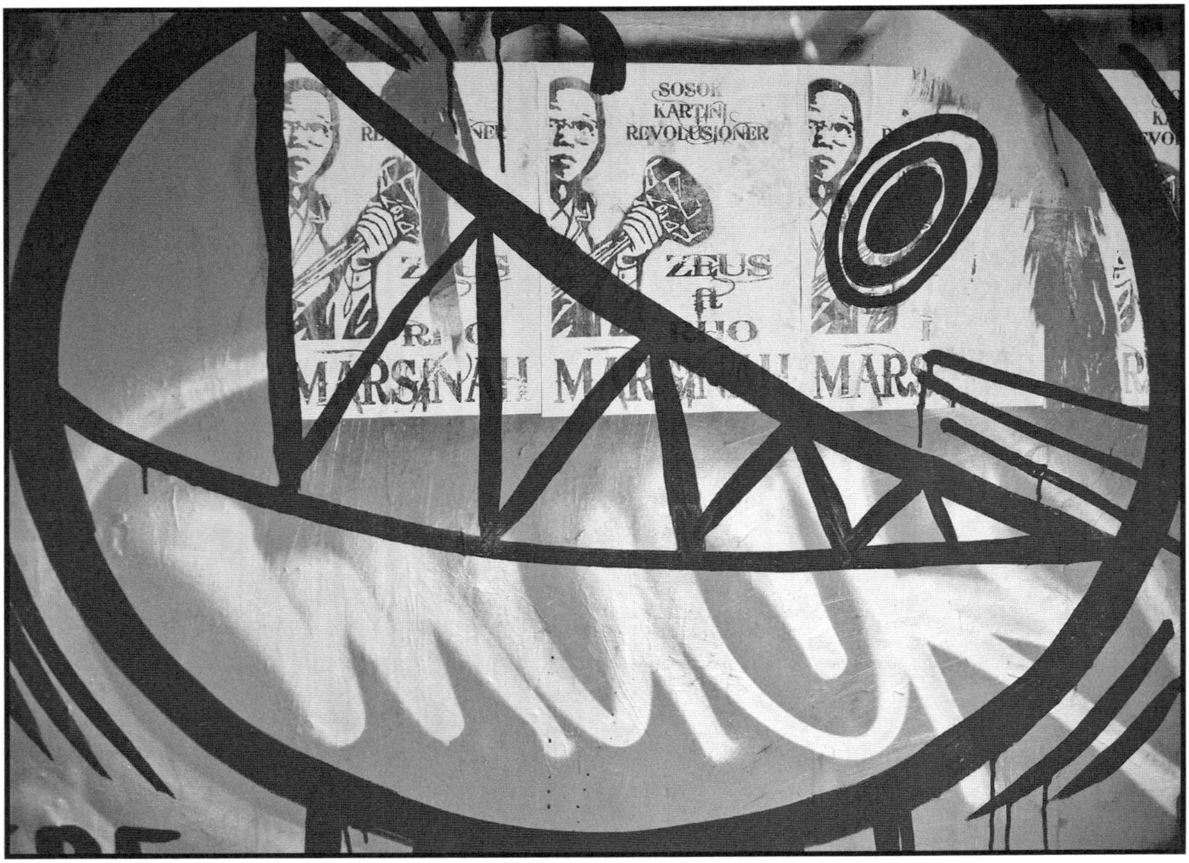

Some of these topics may have been neglected because the playwrights who were published and produced during the twentieth century were overwhelmingly male—but fortunately that has changed.

The three most recent plays in *Islands of Imagination,* all written by women, engage these new topics. In Ratna Sarumpaet's *The Prostitute and the President*, the abused, marginalized, and disempowered women in contemporary Indonesian society are finally able to confront their oppressors. *The Kitchen* by Luna Vidya concerns the ways that insidious political forces determine and thwart the personal and economic goals of three women. *Make Note!* by Rita Matu Mona depicts an idealistic young woman's attempts to challenge those who hold power over others and who enforce the conservative status quo.

The plays in this volume provide a record of Indonesian society in transition, finding its way among a number of powerful forces: the revival of indigenous Indonesian traditions, the struggle against repression, and the movement toward democratization. In their various ways, the playwrights in *Islands of Imagination* handle political and social issues with a high degree of dramatic and literary artistry, and present a fascinating portrait of Indonesia's ever-evolving national identity.

Cobina Gillitt
Assistant Professor of Theatre and Performance
Purchase College, State University of New York

Borobudur Temple,
Java, 1950.
Henri Cartier-Bresson/
Magnum

Male prostitutes on Taman Lawang, Jakarta, Java, 2010. Maximilian Norz/Corbis

ARMIJN PANÉ

A Portrait of the Times

Cast of Characters

Suparman, former student in Rotterdam; unemployed
Harsini, Suparman's fiancée; teacher
Kartono, Harsini's younger brother; student at the Netherlands Indies School for the Arts (Nerderlands Indische Artsen School)
Martono, volunteer at a government office
Suratman, graduate of Holland's Islands Kweekschool (Hoogere Inlandsche Kweekschool); unemployed
Sarti, Harsini's friend
Abu Talib, Sarti's husband
Puspohadi, father of Harsini and Kartono
Mrs. Puspohadi, mother of Harsini and Kartono
Sumardjo, Sarti's father; doctor
Manservant

Act One

The central room of a home. In the middle of the room but a little to the rear is a low table, around which are several matching chairs. The chairs are placed around the table so that none has its back to the audience. Seated in the left, right, and rear chairs are Martono, Kartono, and Suratman, playing a game of bridge. Kartono, who is playing the "blind," plays quickly, rapidly deciding which card to put down, his concentration focused solely on the game. Suratman's movements are slow. Martono takes a long time to think before playing, but then throws his cards down quickly. With his right hand, Kartono pulls the blind to the center, then looks at Martono and beckons with his index finger.

KARTONO — Now, where's your queen? I'm going to take her! [*Martono looks at his cards.*] Hurry up . . . I'll take her anyway. [*Suratman yawns, leans back, and stretches his legs.*] Your friend has yawned again.

MARTONO — [*Throwing down his queen with force.*] What can I do?

KARTONO — [*Putting down a king.*] I told you. [*Suratman looks at his

Putra,
Yogyakarta, 2011.
Kurniadi Widodo

cards for a moment, yawns, then plays his card.] What kind of a hand do you have?

SURATMAN I'm unlucky tonight. I didn't want to play, did I?

KARTONO Don't argue, look at this.

MARTONO [*After looking at the card that Kartono played, examines his own cards, then looks at the played card again.*] Let's go! Hit him with a good card! [*Suratman puts a card down.*] Ugh, it's really bad luck playing with you.

KARTONO [*Smiles, takes the cards already played.*] Here . . .

MARTONO [*Silent for a second.*] Well, what can I do?

KARTONO [*Puts down all of his cards.*] Four down! [*He writes it down. Martono examines Kartono's cards, looks at his own cards, repeats this several times.*] Well, how about it? Am I right or not? [*Martono lays down his cards. As Kartono speaks, Suratman also lays down his cards.*]

SURATMAN [*Looking outside.*] It's still raining.

KARTONO [*To Suratman.*] So, shuffle the cards. I'll deal. [*After the shuffling, he extends the deck of cards to Martono.*] Cut.

SURATMAN Let's just stop playing.

MARTONO Yes, that would be better. It's bad luck playing with you.

SURATMAN There's no end to this rain . . . Hey, it stopped. Let's go home.

KARTONO It's still early and you want to go home.

MARTONO What, this late and you say it's still early? Yes, it's time to go home.

SURATMAN [*About to get up.*] Ach, it's raining again. [*Sits back down.*]

MARTONO It's not going to end soon. We can use an umbrella. [*To Kartono.*] Do you have one?

KARTONO Wait a bit more, until the rain stops, alright? It won't be long.

[*Exits, then re-enters with an umbrella and raincoat.*] Here, the two of you can use this umbrella. But this coat is for you, Suratman. You're always complaining about the cold.

MARTONO [*To Suratman.*] You can hold the umbrella. [*Suratman takes the umbrella and raincoat from Kartono.*]

KARTONO Come again tomorrow night, Tono. Ni will be here.

MARTONO Sure, I'd like to come.

KARTONO [*To Suratman.*] Why don't you keep me company tomorrow? You don't have any work, do you? We could go for a bike ride. [*All exit.*]

[*Offstage, loudly.*] Look out, man, don't get wet!

Kartono enters. He collects the cards from the table and places the deck on a small table to one side of the room. He picks up the used cups and carries them offstage, then reenters with a pipe in his mouth and a thick book in his hand. He sits down, stretches his legs, and begins to read. Now and then he exhales smoke from his pipe. He looks up from his book. The sound of the rain has faded. Light from the moon fills the room through the left side of a window in the rear wall. Suparman enters slowly. Looking confused, he stops. He is thin and pale. Both the look on his face and his posture suggest he is feeling weak. His clothes are damp and disheveled. Kartono looks up from his book. Spotting Suparman, he immediately gets up and approaches him.

Hello! [*Extends his hand to Suparman. Suparman slowly extends his hand toward Kartono, who shakes it vigorously.*]

You look pale. Have you been ill? [*Suparman smiles weakly and shakes his head.*] Please, have a seat. [*Both sit down, Suparman in a chair on the left, Kartono in one on the right.*] You're wet.

SUPARMAN Yes, I was standing under the tree by the road, waiting for your guests to leave.

KARTONO Why didn't you come in? You know you can regard this house as your own. [*Smiling.*] Ni is coming home tomorrow. She's on vacation.

Suparman turns his face quickly toward Kartono but then turns away, staring into space. He grips the arms of his chair.

Have you been writing each other? Did you arrange to meet here? [*Suparman shakes his head.*] No? [*Looks at Suparman's clothes.*] Why didn't you just come right in?

SUPARMAN [*Smiling weakly.*] You had guests.

KARTONO So? You know them, too. It was Martono and Suratman. Surely they would have been happy to see you.

SUPARMAN [*Shakes his head.*] No, I didn't want to come in. I didn't want to bother you.

KARTONO [*Responding with a look of surprise, then shaking his head.*] You've changed...

SUPARMAN [*Nodding.*] I'm afraid of running into other people, especially old acquaintances.

KARTONO [*Surprised.*] Why?

SUPARMAN Well, I don't have...

KARTONO Don't have what?

SUPARMAN I'm worthless, different from other people! I know people look down on me. I feel empty.

KARTONO I'm shocked.

SUPARMAN [*Smiling weakly.*] I wanted to see you. I know that you won't look down on me, regard me as contemptible or lowly. I'm tired, worn out. [*Closes his eyes and leans back with his hands still gripping the arms of the chair.*] My heart is desolate.

KARTONO [*Slowly.*] You weren't like this before.

SUPARMAN Yes, but that was before. Times change, you know. Time has wafted me away. I'm like an old leaf, fallen from the branch, without energy. I feel as if I want to lose myself, to disappear. I used to want to be seen, to be noticed, to stand out, to be talked about by people... but now, now I just want to vanish, to disappear, with no one knowing where I am. Recently I've been thinking a lot... [*Seizing his head with both hands.*] No, not thinking really, but reflecting, until I was worn out, unable to continue that train of thought, wanting only not to think anymore, to forget, to forget myself. I feel alone in Jakarta; there's no one to whom I can express what I'm feeling...

KARTONO You used to be so strong willed, so good at restraining your emotions.

SUPARMAN That was before, when things were different. How many offices have I been to since then? Climbed the stairs, entered... and always, always they'd write down my name and tell me that if there were any openings I would be informed... I'm worthless. I'm ashamed. Before, I used to think I was worth something, that my ideals were as lofty as the heavens. [*A ray of moonlight falls upon his head.*] Several times I stood in the moonlight by the edge of the ocean at

Tanjung Priok—many people were there, enjoying themselves—but I just stood there, trying to estimate the depth of the water with my eyes, and thinking, What if I were to jump? I felt so desolate, but at the same time, I didn't dare . . .

KARTONO You're not well.

SUPARMAN [*Shakes his head, then speaks again.*] I'm weary . . .

KARTONO Tomorrow Ni is coming. What will she say?

SUPARMAN Tomorrow, tomorrow . . . She'll feel fortunate . . .

KARTONO Yes, because you are close to her heart.

Suparman shakes his head. He stands, goes over to the window, looks outside. In the distance, people can be heard singing a melancholic Javanese love song, "Tembang Kinanti." Kartono gets up, stands next to the chair Suparman had been sitting in, and looks out the window.

SUPARMAN [*Suddenly turns around.*] I can't bear to hear that song. Everything disturbs me; everyone has turned his back on me. [*The singing continues.*] Everyone talks about me behind my back: "Look, he doesn't have any work." They point at me. [*Quickly turns back to the window, looks out. Kartono sits on the arm of the chair.*]

I shouldn't be here when Ni comes.

KARTONO Why? I'm sure she'd be happy to see you.

SUPARMAN Happy? [*More slowly.*] I'm sure she'll be happy, but don't tell her I'm here. Please, don't. [*Turns back again.*] The rain has stopped. Yes, the rain has stopped. Now, I'll be going home . . . [*As he begins to leave, Kartono approaches him and grabs his arm.*]

KARTONO Where are you going? You can sleep here, just like you used to.

SUPARMAN Yeah, like I used to when things were different.

KARTONO It's already late.

SUPARMAN I'm used to walking about late at night. I like the night, to be hidden by its darkness.

KARTONO Promise you'll come by tomorrow.

SUPARMAN Tomorrow?

KARTONO Yes, tomorrow!

SUPARMAN — Better not tomorrow . . . [*Suddenly.*] No, Kartono, I will come! [*Exits. Kartono watches him, standing silently for a moment.*]

Curtain falls.

Act Two

The same central room. Puspohadi wears a sarong, a Chinese shirt, and a kerchief tied Javanese-style around his head. He sits, legs crossed, on a chair and reads a newspaper. After a moment, the Manservant enters carrying a covered cup. He sets the cup on the table, then exits. A moment later, Mrs. Puspohadi enters. Though she looks old, she is still healthy and strong. She sits in a chair on the right. She starts to sew a button onto a shirt. After a short while, Sumardjo enters. He is a little younger than Puspohadi.

SUMARDJO — Hello, anyone home?

PUSPOHADI / MRS. PUSPOHADI — [*Together, as they rise.*] Doctor Sumardjo, please come in! Take a seat. [*Sumardjo sits in a chair on the left. The Puspohadis take their seats again.*]

SUMARDJO — I've just come from visiting a patient near here, and I wanted to stop by for a bit.

MRS. PUSPOHADI — You certainly have a lot of business, Doctor.

SUMARDJO — Yes, if that was all I had to deal with, I'd be fine. [*Sighs.*]

PUSPOHADI — Um, what's that sigh all about?

SUMARDJO — How can I not but sigh when thinking of my children? Just imagine, Tartini is going to get married! [*Observes their faces as they look at him with full attention.*] Surprised? [*Laughs.*] So, you hadn't heard? Actually, I too only this morning heard it from her very own mouth.

MRS. PUSPOHADI — To whom?

SUMARDJO — To whom? I don't know.

PUSPOHADI — What, you don't know?

SUMARDJO — [*Laughs.*] No, I don't know. Isn't this the modern era? Old folks like us—there's no need to consult us for such things. Before you know it, they've already found a partner and all we can do is say yes. And not only that, apparently the young lad is still in medical school in Batavia. I don't know how many more years it'll be before he's finished. Just imagine who's going to have to support them.

MRS. PUSPOHADI — His wife . . . ?

SUMARDJO Exactly! She's supposed to be an attorney-at-law, a *meester in de rechtenn,* but just look, she's not working.

PUSPOHADI Didn't Sarti also marry a fellow who hadn't finished school?

SUMARDJO Yes, but she already had work as a teacher.

MRS. PUSPOHADI But once they wanted to have kids, she quit . . .

SUMARDJO And when he finished school and couldn't find work, they moved in with their in-laws and sponged off them—namely, me.

PUSPOHADI They say it's progress, but sometimes we go backwards, too.

SUMARDJO What do you mean?

PUSPOHADI Didn't it used to be like that for our fathers, too—marrying young and then living at their fathers' houses or those of their in-laws?

SUMARDJO [*Roars with laughter.*] True, true. So actually, we old folks are the modern ones. [*The Puspohadis chuckle. Suddenly Sumardjo points at the shirt on the table that Mrs. Puspohadi had been mending.*] Whose shirt is that? It's not Hadi's, is it? Doesn't look like the kind of shirt an older man would wear.

MRS. PUSPOHADI No, this is Kartono's.

SUMARDJO Oh, I just thought—

PUSPOHADI Yes. The kids spend more money than their father.

SUMARDJO That's nothing. Just the other day Sarti says to me, "Dad, buy a new car will you—a 1937 model? I'm embarrassed to be seen in a car like this." Just like that she thinks I'll go out and buy a new car!

MRS. PUSPOHADI My word, girls these days! They want everything big and new. It was different for us. Our wages were modest and so were our lives.

SUMARDJO [*Laughs.*] Now, even without any wages they want to live the good life. [*Laughs again.*]

PUSPOHADI To be honest, it's our fault, too. We brought them up to want the good life, so it's not easy for them to give it up. [*Mrs. Puspohadi nods in agreement.*]

SUMARDJO You put them through school, and when they're done and can't find work, you have to keep helping them out. And if we, their parents, don't send them to school, it's even worse. [*Takes out his watch, checks the time.*] But hey, it's getting late and I have one more patient to see. [*Stands up.*]

MRS. PUSPOHADI Bless me, I forgot to offer you something to drink!

SUMARDJO [*Laughs.*] Just one more sign of these modern times!

The Puspohadis see Sumardjo out. When they return, the two of them sit down again. Puspohadi reads his newspaper while his wife resumes work on her son's shirt. They sit in silence for a moment.

MRS. PUSPOHADI Why haven't you touched your drink? [*She takes the lid off the cup sitting before her husband.*]

PUSPOHADI Listen to this: there's another article about a girl who ran off with a young man. Their parents wouldn't give them permission to marry. It seems this is common these days.

MRS. PUSPOHADI [*Not looking up from her sewing.*] Whose daughter was it?

PUSPOHADI I don't know. All it says is some minor noble's daughter from Tegal. But I'd guess that it's the parents' fault, too.

MRS. PUSPOHADI [*Looks up from her sewing.*] Why their fault?

PUSPOHADI [*As though not paying attention.*] I suspect that if they had supported her a little, they wouldn't have had to suffer this embarrassment. No, it's the young ones themselves who know whom their partners should be...

MRS. PUSPOHADI My, my, you're really singing a different tune now. It's like you're becoming young again...

MARTONO [*Enters.*] Hello...?

PUSPOHADI Oh, it's you, Tono. Have a seat.

MARTONO [*Sits down, bowing slightly as a sign of respect. Sets his elbows on the arms of the chair and clasps his hands in front of him.*] What were you two making such a fuss about, ma'am? I could hear you outside.

MRS. PUSPOHADI My husband here seems to be entering his second youth. He wants to elope with somebody.

PUSPOHADI That's not it. There was an article about a girl who ran off with a young man, and I said their parents were probably to blame. [*Martono thinks this statement over. Puspohadi keeps talking.*] Don't you think I'm right?

MRS. PUSPOHADI Of course Martono is going to agree.

MARTONO [*Slowly.*] For the most part, young people don't know how to restrain their emotions. They want things right away, they want everything to come easily for them, they don't weigh things carefully. But there're also a lot of older folks who don't want to accept that times are changing. Nowadays, daughters are being educated freely. With more self-esteem, they know what they want.

MRS. PUSPOHADI Know what they want? These days it's the woman who comes to carry the man off! The world's been turned upside down. By the way, Martono, when is someone going to carry you away?

MARTONO [*Pauses.*] I believe, ma'am, that any young man who would take on the responsibility of supporting a young woman these days is crazy. It'd be disastrous for him, and even worse for his young bride. Times are so uncertain; life itself is uncertain. Most young men either don't have jobs or must manage on tiny incomes.

MRS. PUSPOHADI Now that you mention it, we lived on small incomes back then. Why can't young people these days do the same? [*Martono thinks.*]

PUSPOHADI Times are different, I suppose.

MARTONO You're right, sir, these are different times. Our education is different. We live on a grander scale . . .

MRS. PUSPOHADI Couldn't you scale things back?

MARTONO That is not so easily done. Not everyone has the strength and capability to change. And young ladies these days have high aspirations, so it's better not to bind a woman to you with promises. Promises are so easy to break, even without meaning to.

MRS. PUSPOHADI Young people today are so different.

MANSERVANT [*Enters.*] Madam, the young master is asking for his shirt. [*Mrs. Puspohadi gives him the shirt without looking at him.*]

MARTONO [*To the Manservant.*] Please tell Kartono that I am in here.

MRS. PUSPOHADI [*To the Manservant.*] Bring some tea.

MARTONO That's alright, don't bother; we'll be leaving soon. [*The Manservant exits.*]

MRS. PUSPOHADI Lots of young women are waiting, and meanwhile the boys are afraid to marry them.

PUSPOHADI That's true, exactly right; they're afraid.

MARTONO Afraid? I don't think so. They just don't have the opportunity.

KARTONO [*Enters.*] What are you talking about?

MARTONO — Your mother thinks that we're afraid to get married.

KARTONO — [*Laughs.*] Marriage seems dangerous! [*Pauses.*] It used to be easy, but not anymore. But this is too complicated a subject to discuss right now. [*To Martono.*] Come on or we'll be late. Ni will be upset if we're not there to meet her.

MARTONO — [*Stands.*] We're leaving. Ma'am, sir . . .

MRS. PUSPOHADI — [*Nodding.*] Be careful, Tono! On the way you just might meet some woman who will carry you off! [*Martono laughs.*]

KARTONO — No need to fear for me, Mom! But if it's Suratman, that would be alright. [*Exits with Martono.*]

Curtain falls.

Act Three

The same central room. Dressed as in the second act but with an open shirt, Kartono sits with Martono. On the table are fruit and several lidded jars full of cakes and snacks. The men are eating the fruit and cakes. A moment later, Sarti enters, dressed neatly and elegantly.

SARTI — Hello! It looks like you're enjoying the food!

KARTONO / MARTONO — [*One after the other.*] Hello! [*They rise.*] Please join us!

SARTI — Presents, I'll bet. Where's the person who brought them all?

KARTONO — In the back! [*Heads offstage, followed by Sarti. A moment later the voices of Harsini and Sarti can be heard.*]

HARSINI — Sarti!

SARTI — Ni!

The two women burst out in laughter. Pause. The two enter.

HARSINI — I haven't even had the chance to change clothes or bathe yet. But those things can wait for a while. [*The women sit.*]

SARTI — You've filled out nicely.

HARSINI — [*Laughs happily.*] And you are looking so nice! But where's your husband?

SARTI — He had other business. He'll come to pick me up later.

HARSINI — [*Pointing at Sarti.*] Just married and you're already going your separate ways?

SARTI It's been six months already, Ni!

HARSINI Sarti, you must try some of this fruit. [*Sarti reaches for a salak, a snake fruit, then peels it slowly with her fingers. Harsini notices Martono is about to light a cigarette. Addressing him.*] Had enough already? [*Tapping a large lidded jar with her finger.*] Have you tried this cake? [*Martono nods. Kartono enters and sits down.*]

SARTI Did you come with friends?

HARSINI I came alone. And do you know how I occupied my time? By reading! Try to guess what.

SARTI A novel?

HARSINI [*Laughs.*] No! The collected letters of Kartini!

SARTI [*Looks at Harsini, rather surprised, her expression questioning.*] Kartini's letters?

KARTONO You're just now reading that? Poor you.

HARSINI See, men always want to criticize. I'd read them before! I was just reading them again. Frankly, it's strange that no one has ever thought of her writings as a kind of novel about a woman's life. People don't see in them the struggle she undertook to achieve her ideals.

KARTONO Listen to my sister, the eternal teacher!

HARSINI [*Disregards Kartono's comments.*] Her sorrows, her joys, not to mention her struggles with herself... people don't pay enough attention to them. [*Notices a surprised expression on Martono's face.*] Yes, it's true; the essence of Kartini's struggle is her struggle with herself.

MARTONO Meaning?

HARSINI At first she wanted to be independent, to go to the Netherlands. So she got financial support from the government, but then decided against it because it wasn't a good time for her to go. Then she just wanted to go to Jakarta, but even that didn't work out, and then she married. She said that for a woman, it wasn't good to stand alone. Better to fight at the side of a man. A woman's soul would only find fulfillment if she were by a man's side! I think Kartini wasn't active enough; she was just a dreamer. She liked to dream, to be idealistic.

SARTI Have you read the new novel about that?

HARSINI Which one?

SARTI What's the name of it, Kartono? You were the one talking about it.

KARTONO You mean the one by Sutan Takdir Alisjahbana.

HARSINI [*Quiet for a second, trying to recall.*] Isn't he one of the Pujangga Baru, that new writers' group?

KARTONO That's him.

SARTI I've heard of the magazine *Pujangga Baru*. It's the one with modern poetry, right?

KARTONO Yes, that's the one.

SARTI And what's the name of that other writer involved in it?

KARTONO You mean Armijn Pané?

SARTI Yes, that's right.

HARSINI Armijn Pané? Isn't he the one who wrote the play that Indonesia Muda put on in Solo awhile ago? Him?

I think it's a strange magazine. And he is simply arrogant, acting like God, trying in his plays to bring to life people who couldn't possibly be real at all.

KARTONO What are you talking about? If anything is strange, it's your feminist ideas. Don't all of those people really exist? Only the names have been changed. He doesn't have a particular person in mind, because these are general problems. He's portraying the conditions of today's youth. He knows those problems are real; they're even discussed heatedly in the papers by all sorts of people—men and women.

MARTONO I read that play in the magazine. I felt as though I, too, were being portrayed, as though I were also playing a part in it.

KARTONO Of course, you're not the only one who felt that way; all of today's youth would surely feel as though they had roles in it.

HARSINI Let's talk about something else. What do these pseudo-writers matter to us?

KARTONO Women don't understand these things.

SARTI [*Smiles.*] Barely reunited and already quarrelling—a true mark of siblings.

MARTONO From afar, longing; when close, disagreement.

HARSINI Still a student and pretending to be a doctor.

KARTONO What are you talking about? Changing subjects like that only proves that women are totally illogical.

SARTI Now, how do you respond to that, Ni?

HARSINI Just ignore it; men are such children. By the way, I forgot to ask about Tini. How is she?

SARTI She wants to marry a medical student from the Geneeskundige Hoogeschool.

HARSINI Ah, so she'll stop working?

SARTI No.

MARTONO I'm surprised there are still people who dare to tie themselves down in these times.

HARSINI Why not? Men today are truly cowards.

MARTONO That's not it. They're hesitant to carry a woman into a life of poverty.

HARSINI What, don't you think we could endure poverty?

KARTONO Hmm . . .

HARSINI And what does that mean?

MARTONO Think of yourself for a moment. Would you like to try living off less than one hundred guilders, for example?

HARSINI Why not?

KARTONO Do all women today think like that?

SARTI Not all. I, for one, would find it difficult.

HARSINI But how could we not try to endure it if we really loved our man?

SARTI [*Laughs.*] Love alone isn't enough.

MARTONO That's how I see it, too. A relationship must also be based on the material situation.

KARTONO Just say it plainly . . . on money!

HARSINI You mean love that is bought. I once read a Jakartan saying . . . Oh, what was it? I've forgotten it again . . .

KARTONO If there's money, one's hubby is sweet, but if there's no cash, he's out on the street!

HARSINI Yes, that's it!

MARTONO That's not what I meant . . . [*Suratman enters.*]

HARSINI — Oh... [*Rises.*] Suratman! [*While shaking hands with him.*] How are you? Have you found work? [*Sits down again. Suratman takes a chair from the front.*]

KARTONO — He's waiting for an official appointment.

SURATMAN — [*Brings the chair over and puts it near the table. Sits down.*] Is there any need to hurry?

SARTI — [*To Suratman.*] Slow but sure, right?

SURATMAN — [*Nods.*] Have you read today's paper?

KARTONO — What about?

SURATMAN — The government is planning to expand the educational system, so they are going to be needing more teachers.

HARSINI — Well, then, luck is on your side!

KARTONO — As long as you get an appointment, that is.

SURATMAN — Why wouldn't I?

MARTONO — I don't know. Sometimes people's luck is not easy to guess.

SURATMAN — Yes, but then again, it looks as though things are getting better. The Depression is over. Good times are coming again.

HARSINI — I wouldn't be too quick to believe the newspapers.

MARTONO — I agree. Often, it's just rumors being printed. They take things out of context, too, and things that aren't true are broadcast far and wide.

KARTONO — They're fond of giving praise. They say the "friend" of so-and-so is bright, bold, because he or she knows the truth, is well liked by people, is always objective. Because you read that, you'd think they're all first rate. But in reality it's not true. It's like they're building castles in the air. They're only first rate in their own minds. If the friend of so-and-so isn't praised, he or she'll go public and tell the truth. Then the writer, Mr. X, will be exposed as someone who doesn't know anything except how to write long articles without rhyme or reason. Then it will be discovered that he used lots of foreign expressions, but apparently only because he took them from a volume full of "memorable quotations."

HARSINI — Yes, yes, our contemporary journalists.

ABU TALIB — [*Enters.*] What are you complaining about?

HARSINI [*Standing.*] Oh, it's you; you snuck up on us. [*Shakes hands with Abu Talib.*]

ABU TALIB [*Looking at Sarti.*] Is everything alright? [*Sarti smiles.*]

HARSINI Look at that: separated for just a bit and they're already missing one another.

ABU TALIB [*Sits in Kartono's chair, while Kartono exits to get another chair, then enters again.*] Yes, so it is with married people. They're of one word and one mind—don't you think so, Ti?

SARTI [*Smiles.*] When my man speaks, his words are sweeter than honey.

HARSINI Such men are common; don't pay attention to them.

KARTONO Hmm!

ABU TALIB Listen to that! There, she's starting again.

KARTONO It's the old story: a woman's mind . . . Don't pay any attention.

HARSINI [*Motioning to Abu Talib.*] Please, take whatever you like. Some fruit or cake?

ABU TALIB [*Taking a cake.*] Did you make these yourself?

HARSINI Of course!

KARTONO Of course?

ABU TALIB Yes, what do you mean, "of course"? What kind of woman goes into the kitchen these days? [*Sarti cuffs him on the shoulder.*]

HARSINI What? You mean Sarti never goes into the kitchen?

SARTI Why should I? We have plenty of servants.

HARSINI Men want for women to be their friends and all that and for women to take an interest in their work, but even so, a woman can't neglect her kitchen. And then, of course, there are the children, too.

SARTI But if we were to do everything men wanted, we'd never have any time for ourselves.

ABU TALIB [*Taking notice of Martono.*] I think Tono wants to say something.

Everyone looks in Martono's direction.

MARTONO I, for one, believe a woman should be in the kitchen.

HARSINI [*Moans with Sarti.*] Can you believe there are still men as old-fashioned as this?

MARTONO "Old-fashioned," "modern"—they're just terms. Think about it... What use is it for women to have jobs of their own? There's not much work as it is, and now women are competing with men. Take our office, for example. There are several young ladies working there. If they were to stay at home, their jobs could be filled by men. That way, the number of unemployed men would decrease.

HARSINI A typical male point of view! What you're actually saying is that you think women should get married, right?

You're forgetting that men these days are cowards. They don't want to get married. And so, if a woman is expected to sit around and wait for a man to propose to her, it could very well be that she won't get married at all. And if she's not going to get married, she has to be able to support herself, don't you think? [*While they are talking, Kartono gets up and begins pacing. He has been moved by thoughts welling up within him.*]

ABU TALIB This problem is not an easy one...

KARTONO [*Happily.*] That's right! Lots of men are unemployed, but women, too, have contributed to a decrease in available jobs. If a young fellow has work but is earning very little, it's going to be hard to share his income with a woman, much less support a household. At the same time, if a man doesn't want to start a household, where does that leave the woman? She is going to have to work, even if she is just waiting for a man to come along and propose. So, what happens is that the woman starts competing with the man even as the man is trying to get himself into a position where he can take care of the woman. But the woman is blocking his path because she herself has become his competitor. It's a vicious circle is what it is, and that's the tragedy of it.

HARSINI If today's men had the least bit of courage, it wouldn't be a problem.

KARTONO Didn't Ti just say that not everyone is like you? And it's also true that not all men are afraid.

ABU TALIB [*To Kartono.*] When you finish school, where will you go?

KARTONO I don't know; a *kampong,* a village, somewhere out of the city. I'll start a practice there and live like the traditional healers used to. You're laughing, but why not? In a small town, I could live according to the standard of the majority of the people there, become a part of that society. Ah, it's hard to explain.

MARTONO — I understand. You want to be on an equal footing with your patients, not above them.

KARTONO — [*Quickly, overlapping Martono's last word.*] And not live as an outsider!

SARTI — I'm sure Suratman might think differently.

ABU TALIB — [*Smiling, then looking at Suratman.*] But humanity has all kinds, doesn't it?

SURATMAN — [*Nods.*] That's right. And, anyway, what use is there to rush? If that's your destiny, you'll get there soon enough. [*Kartono has a mocking look on his face.*]

MARTONO — Only recently I discussed this very problem with a married woman who ridiculed me for not yet being married. So I asked her, What kind of young man is going to get married now? Let's say the man has graduated from high school and wants to marry a woman who is also somewhat educated—a graduate from junior high school or something of that sort. Do you think that woman is going to marry him? No! She's going to have her sights set on someone better: a university graduate, a lawyer, a doctor, an engineer, or someone like that—someone with a good income. And could you fault her for that?

And what about the young woman with a high school education? Well, her wishes are going to be even more grand. [*Smiling.*] And do you know what my woman friend said? She let slip the view that the peace of a household can be upset by that sort of person. Imagine the man who sees his wife getting older and then compares her with the many young ladies who are single and available.

KARTONO — If I think about that, I could agree with the idea of polygamy!

HARSINI / SARTI — Ugh!

ABU TALIB — Sometimes it's hard to tell if the world is progressing or going backwards.

MARTONO — That's true! Just imagine: in my office, the chief clerk is an unmarried woman—one who's a bit on the older side of maidenhood—whose salary is in the hundreds of guilders. Do you think she wants to get married?

HARSINI Why, of course!

MARTONO [*Smiles.*] No, she doesn't. She's happy standing on her own two feet. If she married, she would probably have to give up that job and salary and be made to feel dependent upon a man.

HARSINI You don't understand how a woman feels. Every woman wants to have children and a family of her own. I'm sure of it. That kind of feeling doesn't just go away.

ABU TALIB So you think a woman should stay at home?

HARSINI I would say that if a woman must choose between an office and the kitchen, she must choose the latter.

MARTONO That's not how the chief clerk thinks. She's happy; she can buy a new frock whenever she wants. In fact, that seems to be her only true pleasure.

SARTI All the men are probably too afraid to propose to her.

HARSINI That's right. What man would dare?

KARTONO [*Laughs.*] A widower, maybe.

The other men laugh. Sarti smiles while Harsini looks angrily at her younger brother. Pause.

MARTONO That's why I think it's not good for a woman to become overeducated.

HARSINI Look, more old-fashioned thoughts!

MARTONO Or too modern! There should be a quota, a *contingenteering* of sorts for girls who continue their education after junior high. Only a few should be given permission to go to high school.

ABU TALIB All I can say is that sometimes it's hard to tell if the world is progressing or going backwards.

MARTONO You're right about that. [*The Manservant enters, carrying tea for Suratman and Abu Talib. Martono continues.*] But there's another problem as well. Supposing we have a man who has no job but whose fiancée is working. Do you think they should marry?

HARSINI Well, of course! Aren't men and women equal?

KARTONO [*Seriously.*] But a real man would be ashamed to do that.

SARTI This conversation of ours is dragging on and there's likely to be no end to it. Besides, it's getting late. [*Stands.*] Not to mention that Ni must be exhausted.

[*Abu Talib rises, and everyone else follows suit. Sarti speaks to her husband while pointing at her purse.*] Would you be a dear and carry that for me? [*Abu Talib picks up the purse.*]

HARSINI Thanks for coming by.

SARTI You must visit our place. How about a game of tennis?

HARSINI That would be lovely. [*Walks with Sarti to the door. The others follow.*]

SARTI We've renovated our court. You really must come and try it out.

Curtain falls.

Act Four

The same central room. Kartono is reading the paper. After a moment, Suparman enters slowly. When he is several steps away from Kartono, he stops and smiles.

SUPARMAN A penny for your thoughts!

KARTONO [*Looks up, startled. Stands and happily shakes hands with Suparman.*] I've been waiting for you for so long I was in a bit of a daze. Have a seat!

Suparman slowly walks to the window.

[*Stands quietly, looking in Suparman's direction. Finally sits on the arm of his chair.*] You surprise me. Just a few months ago you were happy, strong willed, and active. But now? You've changed completely. What happened to your will, your happiness?

SUPARMAN You know, I actually didn't want to come here today. I don't know why it is, but I came anyway. I shouldn't have, but I was swept along in this direction, just like an old leaf blown along by the wind.

I used to be a young leaf, firmly anchored to a strong branch. This is what happens when a person loses his soul. A man's soul is his work. Work is his means of action. And if there's no work, there is no means of action. He becomes an old leaf, carried by the wind.

You have no idea of the emptiness I feel inside. Everything inside me has wilted, and nothing is left standing.

Think of a rice field after a windy storm: the broken stalks lying on the path between the paddies; people stepping on them as they hurry by . . . I'm like that. Yet there's not a single person who is merciful enough to stop and push me out of the way, much less help me stand upright again.

And how could they, when my stem is already broken? [*The two men are silent for a moment.*]

KARTONO But what about Ni?

SUPARMAN [*Smiles.*] She'll forget me in time, gradually overlook my existence. If Borobudur, a temple so large and magnificent, could be forgotten for centuries, how can you think that she won't forget me?

Human memory has its limits, Kartono, and what am I to Harsini? I was in Rotterdam for two years and have absolutely nothing to show for it. I traveled to Paris and to Berlin—my father had a lot of money then—and neglected my studies. I sailed my boat on the wave of politics and forgot about my classes and my future. I forgot that Harsini, who was waiting for me, had a right to a happy life, to a husband who could come back home with a degree in hand.

Now, look at me. I'm unemployed. From my clothes, you'd think I was a gentleman, but the fact is, I don't have a cent to my name and am living only on the charity of family.

KARTONO Lots of men are out of work and dependent on their families. That doesn't mean you have to be like this.

SUPARMAN [*Smiling, then speaking more slowly.*] So, it's not just me, huh? [*Louder.*] How many other young men are suffering as I am or are even more unfortunate?

KARTONO You know, this situation won't last. Things will get better. Why, I just read in today's paper [*points to the newspaper on the table*] that good times are coming. It's 1937, and the Depression is going to end. So it'll all be over.

SUPARMAN Good times are coming? And did you also hear that they're going to be starting a work-exchange program for young people? [*Bows his head. Pauses. Looks up.*] Well, even if the times do get better, that's not going to be true for people like me.

For several years now, the Depression has raged, and anyone who didn't find work during that time is not going to be considered for a job, even if good times do resume.

Just look at the number of young men out there! Did you read that advertisement for jobs with the post office? Postal inspectors needed, but no one over the age of twenty-one need apply! Obviously, they're looking for young people fresh out of high school.

And what about that announcement for jobs at the government pawn office? Two positions available, but no one over twenty-five years of age need apply!

People like me—men my age—don't count anymore. We're the dry hulls among the grain, to be culled for having no value. [*Mockingly.*] But, maybe, if there's a lot of chaff, you can at least still feed it to the chickens . . .

KARTONO Actually, the question was raised in the Legislative Council: allowing applications from people who finished their education four or five years ago.

SUPARMAN [*Smiling sadly, shaking his head.*] Forget it . . . We don't count anymore; the times have passed us by.

I heard that the resin trade in Palembang has begun to pick up again. An old friend asked me to go there with him. He said he had high hopes of us becoming successful traders . . . But I just can't; I'm broken, I don't have the energy anymore. Actually I— [*Stops, surprised upon seeing Harsini enter.*]

HARSINI [*Joyously.*] Par! Suparman! [*Approaches Suparman, stretching out her arms to him. Suparman takes his fiancée's hands in his own. He looks elated. Kartono leaves the room.*]

SUPARMAN You look good, so healthy and alive.

HARSINI But you . . . [*Pausing, studying Suparman's face.*] You look so pale, drawn. [*Starting to worry.*] Tell me what's wrong. Let's sit down. [*Draws Suparman over to a chair and makes him sit. She sits on the arm of the adjacent chair.*]

SUPARMAN [*With a depressed look on his face.*] If I knew you were here, I wouldn't have come over.

HARSINI [*Quickly bending, taking Suparman's hand.*] Why? What's wrong? [*He stands suddenly, paces back and forth.*] It's lucky I hadn't fallen asleep. I don't know why, but I suddenly thought of you. [*Tenderly.*] I've really missed you.

SUPARMAN [*Stops pacing, looks at Harsini.*] It's good that we're together after all. [*Pauses, then speaks with determination.*] I'd like to speak honestly, Ni. I've thought about this for a long time . . . I think it would be best if . . . we changed our old agreement.

[*Harsini looks at him with surprise, then laughs. Suparman speaks earnestly.*] You're laughing? Please listen, Ni. I'm serious. I want to tell you I don't have any hope . . .

HARSINI So?

SUPARMAN So, I think it would be best if we ended our relationship.

HARSINI [*Approaches him, speaking earnestly.*] Suparman, have you forgotten our agreement? What's yours is mine; what's mine is yours. I'm working; I can support us. What are you worried about? You won't be in these circumstances forever.

SUPARMAN [*Angry.*] Ni, I wouldn't be a man if I accepted your offer. It's shameful for a man to be supported by a woman. I'd rather die than live like that.

HARSINI Coward! Embarrassed to be talked about? Embarrassed to be pointed at?

You've forgotten what you used to say: that all the old customs and traditions have to be changed and that we shouldn't be afraid of being talked about.

I told you then that it was much easier for a man to change customs than for a woman. You laughed at me and told me that men and women are the same, that it's only people's perceptions that differentiate men and women, that women have to help change our traditions, too.

[*Sobbing.*] Why have you changed your mind? Are you afraid of public opinion? Is your shame greater than your love for me?

Don't you remember anything you told me? Were all your professions of love just lies? You once professed to wanting to be an important leader. But if you can lie like this to a woman, wouldn't everything you say to the people be lies as well?

For a woman there's nothing greater than her love. She lives for it. If she loses that love, she loses her rudder. She becomes a boat adrift upon the ocean.

Is that what you want for me? Think, Suparman, please! [*Her face hardens and she stops sobbing.*] And remember that I am a woman of these times. We have our own souls, our own needs, and our own wills. We know where we are going and have the courage to steer ourselves in that direction.

What—do you think I would let you go just like that? You love me and I love you. What do we care about others? As long as what we do is no sin in the eyes of God, what do we care if people talk about us? It would be different if you really didn't love me anymore.

In that case, what could we do but go our separate ways?

Harsini sits down. Suparman goes to the window and opens the curtain. The moon can be seen shining outside. The wind gently blows through his hair. A sad Javanese love song, "Tembang Maskumbang," resonates in the distance.

SUPARMAN What if I said I didn't love you anymore?

HARSINI [*Firmly.*] You'd be lying!

SUPARMAN [*Earnestly.*] It's true. You must believe me, Ni.

HARSINI You're looking for a reason to break off our relationship. I suppose that explains your letters these past few months. I had a feeling that's what you were getting at.

I used to think you were different from other men, but now I see you're exactly the same: sweet talking, making passionate speeches, but at heart a coward.

Why didn't I see this long ago—that you could talk big in front of others but lacked the courage to test your fate with a woman?

What can I say? You're not worth a cent, not even half a cent, Suparman. Really, you don't deserve to live.

Leave me! You're not good enough to even kiss the bottom of my foot! [*Slowly.*] You know something? I've wanted to break with you for a long time now, because there's someone else . . .

SUPARMAN [*Fiercely.*] Now it comes out! I've been hearing things for a while . . . I don't care about any of that. But there's one thing I won't forget: that you said only my words are daring.

Someday you'll see, Ni—you'll see that I'm not like you think I am. [*Sneering, he approaches Harsini and extends his hand.*] Good-bye, Ni! Let's shake hands.

Harsini turns her back on him and moves several steps away. Suparman laughs, then exits. She wheels around quickly, her face stricken with sorrow.

KARTONO [*Enters.*] What's all the noise about? And where's Suparman?

HARSINI [*Pretending to be cheerful.*] Gone, disappeared! [*Kartono is shocked.*] We've broken up. I called him a coward, then drove him away! [*Laughs.*]

KARTONO You're laughing? You drove him away? But he needed cheering up, Ni—to be made happy. Why did you do that?

HARSINI [*Laughs.*] What need do I have for a jobless man?

KARTONO [*Angry.*] Rotten woman! [*Calling out as he exits.*] Par! Suparman! [*His voice fades into the distance.*]

HARSINI [*Alone. Full of sorrow, she clenches her hands.*] If I hadn't hurt him, he might never have the chance to be happy, never regain the courage he used to have. Now, he might have the courage to start a new life in Palembang . . . even if it means that he is lost to me.

He hates me, thinks I was making a fool of him. And now that he's vanished, gone from my sight, my own hopes will surely die. [*Lowering her head and pausing.*] Lord God, we women know how to sacrifice . . . I drove him away because I love him. Nevertheless, I pray to you, dear God, to bring him back to me.

Curtain falls.

Translation by Michael H. Bodden

IWAN SIMATUPANG

No Address, No Name

Dedicated to Sri, Maiden of the Beggars

For there are many great deeds done in the small struggles of life. There is a determined though unseen bravery, which defends itself foot to foot in the darkness against the fatal invasions of necessity and of baseness. Noble and mysterious triumphs which no eye sees, which no renown rewards, which no flourish of triumph salutes. Life's misfortunes, isolation, abandonment, poverty, are battlefields which have their heroes; obscure heroes, sometimes greater than the illustrious heroes. *Victor Hugo,* Les Misérables

Cast of Characters

Gramps, man of about sixty
Pocky, man of about thirty-five
Gimp, man of about thirty
Ani, woman of about twenty-five
Ina, woman of about twenty
Ati, woman of about seventeen

Scene One

The play is set in a large city beneath a bridge, the home of people considered "of no consequence": vagrants, poor and jobless people, pedicab drivers, and prostitutes. It is late evening. Torn mats, old boards, broken furniture, empty butter and milk tins litter the site. Small kerosene lamps hang from makeshift huts. Two small cooking fires glow. Steam rises from the butter tins, used as cooking pots, that are perched on top of the flames. Beside one fire a man, Gimp, rests on his haunches; an older man, Gramps, squats beside the other fire. Two young women, Ani and Ina, dressed in faded lengths of batik cloth and colored brassieres, are busy putting on makeup. Each woman holds a cracked mirror in her hand. Trailer-trucks driving across the bridge make a thunderous noise. There is also a roll of thunder.

Slum dwellers,
Jakarta, Java, 2007.
Jonas Bendiksen/Magnum

GRAMPS Sounds like it's gonna rain hard.

GIMP [*Laughing.*] That's a truck, Gramps!

GRAMPS What?

GIMP A truck! That's a trailer-truck going by.

GRAMPS [*Shaking his head while stirring the contents of the butter tin on top of his fire.*] Another one! This bridge is going to fall down one of these days. I thought those things were banned.

ANI So?

GRAMPS So it's against the law. [*Ani laughs loudly.*] Well, what's the law for then?

ANI To be broken.

GRAMPS And if it's broken?

ANI That's the State's business.

Gramps stirs his food and shakes his head again. A roll of thunder.

GIMP Now that was thunder.

ANI [*Suddenly concerned.*] What?!

GIMP [*Laughing.*] Thunder, sweets. Thunder! You know, *varrrooom!*—which usually means it's going to rain.

Ani frowns, then walks to the edge of the shelter offered by the bridge and peers upward at the sky. She raises her arm and shakes her fist at the sky. Another roll of thunderv

ANI [*Angrily.*] Oh, shit! Ina!

INA What?

ANI You can stop getting ready.

INA Never know, it might not rain. [*Another roll of thunder.*]

ANI [*Irritated.*] What do you mean "might not rain"? What are you, a rain doctor? Clean the shit from your ears. The only thing that's not sure is how we're going to get something to eat tonight if it does rain.

GIMP [*Stirring his food.*] If it's your stomach you're looking to fill, this is almost done.

ANI [*Putting her hands on her hips, turns to Gimp.*] Thanks, but no thanks! I've had my fill of that squash you pick out of the garbage heap over by the market. Half-rotten squash mixed with half-rotten leeks, moldy cassava and corn. *Bleck!* I'm sick of it! No, not tonight. Tonight I want something good to eat: hot rice, spiced beef, an egg swimming in chili sauce, and a tall glass of sweet tea. And to finish it off, a large and golden-ripe . . .

As Ani speaks of her favorite foods, the others listen wistfully, repeatedly swallowing their saliva. When there is another roll of thunder, everyone looks sadly at Ani.

[*Hysterically.*] Oh no! It can't rain tonight. It just can't!

INA [*Approaching Ani.*] Take it easy. Rain or not, we're still going to go out.

ANI Are you joking? Who's going to want us soaking wet?

INA Never know. And who says we have to get wet?

ANI [*In a monotone.*] You go out in the rain, you get wet. That's usually what happens, isn't it?

INA Well, I for one . . . Why don't we take a pedicab?

GIMP You're going to strut your stuff in a pedicab, are you? Where's the fare going to come from? [*Ina cackles with laughter.*] You got a deal going with the pedicab driver, don't you?

Ina continues to laugh. Ani frowns.

[*Irritated.*] Damned pedicab driver!

INA What's it to you?

GIMP I know what you're up to. It's that driver you're after, that black-skinned one, isn't it?

INA [*Giggling.*] That's how I like 'em—black and sweet. So you know him, do you? [*Laughing again.*] What, are you jealous? [*Gimp suddenly kicks an empty can.*]

ANI What's got into you? Since when is Ina yours and yours only? [*Gimp frowns petulantly.*] Think about it! Who are you anyway? And what do you got to be jealous about? Son of a bitch! Men never know when they got it lucky.

INA Stop it, Ani.

ANI Stop what? I'm asking you, Ina, since when did you become his fiancée, his wife, or his mistress?

INA — I never—

ANI — The men around here always want everything for free.

GIMP — Who's talking free? I put my share in here, too.

ANI — What share's that? That half-rotten shit you eat all the time? God's sake, squash, leeks, rice leavings, and cassava—and all of 'em rotten or half rotten.

Do you think that brain of yours is half so good as a woman's body for keeping warm at night? Hmmm?

And what about Ina? What's she to you? What are any of us women to you?

GRAMPS — Stop nattering. Next thing you'll start talking about Kartini and women's emancipation.

ANI — [*Shooting Gramps a look of disgust.*] Come on, Ina. Let's get dressed. We got to go.

GRAMPS — [*With a touch of humor in his voice.*] A plate of rice...

GIMP — [*Adopting the same tone of voice.*] Spiced meat...

GRAMPS — An egg swimming in chili sauce...

GIMP — And a tall glass of sweet tea.

GRAMPS — And to finish it off, a large and golden-ripe...

GIMP — Banana!

ANI — [*As she finishes dressing.*] Yes, my dear sirs, I'm having them all tonight. I'll do whatever it takes to get them, just so long as I can have them tonight!

INA — [*To Ani.*] I'm ready.

A loud clap of thunder is followed by a flash of lightning. Seconds later, the sound of heavy rain.

[*Looking at Ani, then at the falling rain.*] What are we going to do?

ANI — No turning back! We're not made of salt, are we?

GRAMPS — 'Atta way, girls! Wet or dry, I hope you find what you're looking for tonight.

ANI — If mother luck is with us, we'll bring back something for you, too.

Ani and Ina grab a piece of tattered mat as a cover for their heads and run out into the rain. The rain falls harder.

Scene Two

As the rain continues to fall, flashes of lightning brighten the sky. Gimp and Gramps are eating their meals straight from their butter tins.

GRAMPS — Hot rice . . .

GIMP — [*Licking his fingers.*] Spiced beef, a peppered egg . . . What else did she say?

GRAMPS — [*Cleaning out his tin with his fingers.*] Sweet tea and a banana.

GIMP — You forgot the "large and golden-ripe." [*Throwing his tin to the ground.*] Shit!

GRAMPS — [*Hurriedly retrieving Gimp's tin.*] Hey! There's still some left. [*Cleans out Gimp's tin with his finger, eats what is left, and licks his fingers.*]

GIMP — I'm surprised you can still remember them.

GRAMPS — [*Still licking his fingers.*] Remember what?

GIMP — You know: spiced beef, eggs, bananas.

GRAMPS — [*Laughing.*] Why should I forget?

GIMP — After all the years of living like this?!

GRAMPS — [*Wipes Gimp's tin with his finger one more time, then turns it over on the fire.*] You got a butt?

GIMP — [*Shaking his head.*] You took the last one I had earlier.

GRAMPS — [*Laughing.*] That's right. [*Moves to sit beside Gimp on an outcropping of cement at the base of one of the bridge pillars.*]

Now you listen to me and listen good: that butt of yours I smoked this afternoon—I can forget that. But there's no way I'm ever going to forget hot rice, spiced beef, eggs, and bananas. No way! No more than I could forget the bed I slept in when I was a boy. Or the red-and-white porridge that my mother used to make for me when I was sick. Or the smell of my mother's hair after her bath, when she put me to bed and told me stories from the shadow plays about the warrior Gatotkaca, the goddess Sinta, and . . . [*Yawns.*]

GIMP — [*Moved by Gramp's recitation.*] Go to sleep, Gramps. You're tired.

GRAMPS — [*Laughing but trying to close his mouth.*] It's just that I got this lazy kind of feeling, the kind I used to get whenever my mother put me to bed. It's memories, you know. It's memories that make us sad and forever open our eyes to the rubble of our lives around us. It's memories that form the steel pillar within us that people—even you and me—mistakenly call self-respect.

But now I want to ask you, son: where is your self-respect here, beneath this bridge?

GIMP — It'd be all right if we were working or had something to do. We wouldn't have problems then. The memories and the self-respect you talk about are problems only for the likes of us: people who aren't able to use their bodies as they should be used, and people with cart-loads of free time on their hands.

GRAMPS — But you keep looking for work.

GIMP — Maybe so, but I never seem to find a job.

GRAMPS — Why do you think that is?

GIMP — Because people assume things about people like us.

GRAMPS — Who are these "people like us"?

GIMP — They all think that people like us—the jobless, the drifters—don't know how to work.

GRAMPS — What do they think we can do?

GIMP — At best, keep ourselves from dying by foisting hollowed-out coconut shells on passersby. They think of us as a race apart, as the lowest and meanest race.

GRAMPS — But if they knew what you could do . . .

GIMP — Don't make me an exception, Gramps. The both of us—you and me—would do anything, just so long as we could find a way out of this joblessness.

GRAMPS — But it doesn't seem that any of them are willing to give us that chance.

GIMP — Even the way we look is enough for them to throw their guard up. But what kind of face are we supposed to show them except the one we have? If we look down and out or unhealthy, is that our fault? Is it our fault that our bodies and our clothes reek of piss and the stench of the water beneath this bridge?

GRAMPS — That's what social law's about. If you're going to apply for a job, you have to put your best face forward.

GIMP | If I had a gabardine suit, leather shoes, and a silk tie, and my hair were slicked back with imported pomade, would there still be a place for me beneath this bridge? Would there, Gramps? What kind of vagrant would I be then?

GRAMPS | Where does it start and where does it end for people like us?

GIMP | The world of joblessness is a vicious circle, Gramps, which every day grows more fearsome and strong. The only thing left that can help us is good fortune—luck!

GRAMPS | That's all we do here, every day: wait for the chance to have a good future.

GIMP | We long for the impossible. We're dogs howling at the moon, and one by one we end up floating facedown in this foul river. And coolies, working for the city, carry our half-rotted corpses to the public hospital, where tags are tied to our toes with the words "Name Unknown." With no name, no address, we're buried without ceremony. Hospital coolies do the work. If we're lucky, our corpses are used for research by medical students.

GRAMPS | Well, that's not so bad. I mean, maybe it's only our corpses they want, but in that way—through the dissection of our cadavers by medical students—we can still become unsung heroes for the human race. What would become of humanity if it weren't for people like us?

Scene Three

The rain has stopped. The sounds of cars and trucks passing by on the bridge overhead become louder. A man and a woman, Pocky and Ati, enter.

POCKY | Aren't you asleep yet?

GIMP | You're back late.

GRAMPS | You got a butt?

POCKY | [*Laughing.*] Hold your horses, Gramps. Fact is, I got me a real cigarette, a whole pack of 'em. And I got me here four pre-packed meals with rice and all the trimmings.

GRAMPS | You didn't rob someone, did you?

POCKY | [*Laughing.*] No, Gramps, I haven't sunk that low.

GIMP | They say a vagrant is as low as you can get.

POCKY | [*Emotionally.*] Who put that pearl of wisdom into your head?

GRAMPS [*Laughing.*] Patience, patience! Where's the food? You said you had four.

POCKY Yeah, and all of 'em for you guys. I—I mean *we*—have already eaten.

Gramps and Gimp suddenly notice Ati.

GRAMPS I see we have a guest.

GIMP [*Coughing.*] Where did you pluck that one? And what about Ani? Have you thought about that?

POCKY [*Angrily.*] Watch your mouth, will ya? This here is Ati. I found her crying outside the entrance to the harbor, looking for her husband. I walked halfway 'round the harbor with her, but we still didn't find him.

GRAMPS Maybe he got on one of the ships.

POCKY Could be.

GIMP Is he a deckhand?

POCKY [*As if insulted.*] It's not only deckhands who get on ships.

GRAMPS I'm just trying to picture the situation is all. I see a guy telling his girl to wait for him at the harbor entrance. He then goes inside but disappears out another gate.

POCKY And for every story you come up with, I can make up one, too.

GRAMPS But an old man's hunches are usually right.

POCKY Is this intuition or experience we're talking about?

GRAMPS Both. I was a deckhand once.

GIMP [*Laughing.*] A girl in every port, huh, Gramps? And wherever you went, you left behind a new bride with promises of the moon and the stars.

POCKY [*Apparently offended.*] Shut up!

ATI He promised he'd take me with him when he left. He took my suitcase with my clothing and jewelry, and then he vanished.

GIMP *Tsk, tsk, tsk*... He must have been quite some guy, that one. But was he really a sailor?

ATI He said he was.

Out of patience with Gimp, Pocky pounces on him and begins to strangle him. Gramps manages to break Pocky's grasp as Ati screams in fright.

GIMP [*Gulping air.*] What the hell's gotten into you?

POCKY Ever since I got here, you've been trying to get my goat.

GIMP And I'm supposed to keep my mouth shut? Is that it? Why is it every time I speak, you think I'm trying to pick a fight?

GRAMPS Enough said already. Where's the food? [*Ati hands the parcels of food to Gramps.*]

POCKY Where's the other two?

GIMP Where else? On duty.

POCKY Duty? In the rain?

GIMP Horniness knows no season!

To this remark Pocky says nothing, but with a weary look on his face, he sits down on the concrete outcropping around the base of the bridge pillar. Ati hesitates momentarily, then sits down next to him. Gimp and Gramps begin to wolf down the food.

GRAMPS [*Excited.*] Hey, there's an egg in here!

GIMP [*Excited.*] And spiced beef! Looks like your strong-arm methods worked for you today.

POCKY [*Tired.*] No strong arm today. I got my advance.

Gramps and Gimp look at Pocky in surprise.

GRAMPS Did you say "advance"?

POCKY [*Lightly.*] Yeah, like in "advance wages."

GRAMPS [*Approaching Pocky.*] So, they took you?

POCKY Yeah.

GRAMPS Which means you'll be leaving us soon? [*Pocky bows, not answering.*]

ATI What's going on? Who took whom? And who's leaving?

GIMP So he hasn't even told you about it?

ATI Nobody's told me anything. [*Stares nervously at Pocky.*]

GRAMPS [*Pointing at Pocky.*] Well, it looks like he got a job as a deckhand. He applied for the job a long time ago but must have got accepted today. Which is why he was given an advance—you know, part of his wages upfront. That's normal on a ship. And . . . [*swallowing*] with the money he bought us this here food. [*As if about to cry.*] Now is it clear to you?

Gramps, unsteady on his feet, looks like he's going to fall. It appears there is something caught in his throat, and he is unable to continue eating. He rewraps his parcel of food and puts it away in a corner near the base of the bridge. He coughs, then retreats in haste to a dark corner of the bridge.

POCKY Here's that cigarette of yours, Gramps. [*Gramps shakes his head.*]

ATI [*To Pocky.*] Take me with you!

POCKY Where?

ATI Wherever. I want to sail away.

POCKY A deckhand can't take a woman along. Put that out of your mind. They wouldn't even allow you on board.

ATI You could hide me in your cabin.

POCKY You'd get caught for sure, and then the both of us would be dropped at the nearest port, without provisions. I'd end up being what I was before I left: a bum, jobless, with a mountain of problems.

ATI We could look for work together.

POCKY [*Shaking his head.*] A guy like me, who's lived without a job this long, ain't going to be so easily persuaded to go back to unemployment—not once he's succeeded in leaving it. You don't know what being without a job is like.

ATI [*As if about to cry.*] I don't know, and I don't want to know. I only know that I'm still young and that I have the right to a little love and a taste of happiness. [*Begins to cry. The only sound is that of her sobs and, occasionally, the traffic passing overhead.*]

GIMP "A little love and a taste of happiness." You can rest assured there's not much chance you'll find that here, underneath this bridge.

ATI [*Emotionally.*] Who said I came here for that?

GIMP [*Sympathetically.*] If I were forced to answer that, I'd have to say that it was just to find a place to stay for the night.

But would it end up being for one night only? What about tomorrow?

POCKY I'm warning you just once more not to stir up trouble.

GIMP [*Pulls himself into an upright, threatening position and faces Pocky.*] If what I just said is enough to cause a fight, then come on, let's fight! Maybe you'll beat me—thin as I am, and crippled besides. You're strong; you got the body of a deckhand. You could even kill me, bury my body in the mud over there. But now, for the last time, and for your own sense of honor [*screaming*], you answer me this: what is it you have in mind for this poor young woman? Come on, tell me! Tomorrow morning, when the sun comes up, what is it you're going to do? What are your real plans for her? Come on, tell us. Don't build up her hopes, for God's sake! You could commit no greater sin against her.

Pocky looks thunderstruck. Without further word, he sits down beside Ati.

[*To Ati.*] It might be good for you to hear this. Pocky got his advance. That means he's going to sail soon, maybe even tomorrow. [*Turning toward Pocky.*] Isn't that right? [*Pocky nods.*] Tomorrow! So tomorrow we'll say good-bye to him, maybe for the last time, never to meet again. After our good-byes have been said, he'll go off to the open sea and we'll come back here, which is where the most important question will arise for you, for all of us: what is going to happen? What am I to do?

The stillness of the night is interrupted by Ati's sobs.

ATI I want to go along.

GIMP That's impossible. He told you that already.

Ati cries harder.

Don't take offense at my suggestion but, for the sake of what's left of your self-respect, might it not be better for you to go home to your family in the village?

ATI [*Wiping the tears from her eyes.*] What about if I ask you—yes, all of you—why you don't go back to your villages?

Gimp says nothing. He and Pocky stare at each other for some time.

POCKY [*Thoughtfully.*] Yeah, why don't we all go back to our own villages?

Scene Four

A pedicab bell rings, following which Ina enters looking cheerful and carrying a package.

GIMP	Ina.
POCKY	Where's Ani?
INA	Ani won't be coming here anymore. She had a bit of good luck. This old Chinese man, one of her customers—guess what he said at the police station? He said that he wanted to marry her! And she said yes.
POCKY	Why were they at the police station?
INA	[*Gives her package to Gramps, who has just emerged from his dark corner, then notices Ati.*] What do we have here? A new resident? It's almost as if you knew that Ani wouldn't be coming back. [*To Pocky.*] Is she yours?
GIMP	She's just staying overnight. She's going back to her village tomorrow.
INA	Then why is she here? A state visit or something? [*Still looking at Pocky.*]
GRAMPS	[*Inspecting the package that Ina brought.*] More food! Look at this: spiced beef and a peppered egg, too! And look, a bunch of bananas! That Ani is too much.
INA	She just wanted to keep her promise to you.
	From the corner of the bridge, Gramps retrieves his unfinished food.
GIMP	Here, look at this—another parcel, with spiced beef and eggs, too.
INA	[*Surprised.*] Where'd that come from?
GIMP	[*Pointing at Pocky.*] He got lucky. He'll be sailing tomorrow.
INA	[*Surprised.*] Sailing? You mean you got the job?! [*Pocky nods, and Ina hugs him happily.*]
	I'm so happy for you. For you and for everyone here. Are you really sailing tomorrow?
POCKY	If nothing comes in the way, I am. Midday, at the latest, I'm supposed to be on board. We sail in the evening.
INA	[*Cheerfully.*] Where to?

GRAMPS Who cares? What's important is that he's sailing! Away, and far from here. Anyplace has got to be better than here, beneath this bridge.

POCKY Tell me what happened to Ani.

INA Oh yeah... But why aren't you eating the food she sent? You don't even look hungry.

GRAMPS [*Laughing.*] I don't know what the gods were thinking. Twice now, in one night, they've sent us food that we vagrants haven't been able to even dream about for years. The stars up there in the sky—the spirits of our ancestors—seem to be making fun of us tonight. And to heighten the comedy of this rare event, we're not the least bit hungry because, for this great fortune, we have had to pay with the news [*looking at Pocky*] that he's going to leave us. That he's going to sail off tomorrow, and that Ani is not coming back here. I don't know about you, but I'm feeling that this food is like my last meal before I'm dragged away to the hangman's post.

POCKY [*Laughing.*] Oh, Gramps, you are something. Is it as bad as all that?

GRAMPS The loneliness of parting is sometimes more painful than death itself. Why are we—us vagrants—supposed to pretend that it's not so?

Stillness hangs in the air. Only the occasional sound of a vehicle passing by on the bridge is heard.

INA [*Sitting down.*] When we left earlier, that pedicab driver we know happened to pass by.

GIMP [*Sneering.*] "Happened to pass by"? He was probably out there waiting for you.

POCKY [*To Gimp.*] Why are you breathing so hard?

GIMP You probably don't know that all this time they've been working with that pedicab driver, operating what you might call the complete pedicab.

POCKY "Complete pedicab"? What's that? I was just reading something in the paper about the "complete patriot."

GRAMPS [*Amused.*] What with everything so complete these days, why do I get the feeling that everything is getting less and less!

POCKY And what's this "complete pedicab" supposed to be?

GIMP — A pedicab, complete with a woman, for a night. To make it even more complete, the pedicab driver takes care of finding and renting a place to spend the night, the cost of transport, and so on. The point is, after everything's finished, the client has to pay only one fare—the complete cost in one set sum.

GRAMPS — When I was working as a deckhand, we called that kind of system "all in." Everything was included! The cost of the room, the food, the liquor, the woman, the taxi that took us back to the ship the next morning so that we wouldn't be late.

POCKY — And who gets the money?

GIMP — The pedicab driver, I just told you. He gets the biggest share. That's why he sets the price that the woman charges.

POCKY — Is he fair?

GIMP — That depends on the driver. But keep in mind there are times when the stuff he's peddling doesn't sell—and I'm not talking about his pedicab—even after peddling 'round for hours. When that happens, he usually has to lend the woman some money. And if he doesn't have any set aside, it's nothing to eat for them.

POCKY — That's normal.

GIMP — But I know a pedicab driver who's become really rich that way. He's got a string of ten or twenty women, all operating at the same time. And he's got close connections with hotel workers. He's a veritable pleasure-tour operator. He owns a car now and a big house in the village. Not too long ago, he built himself a big fancy place in the city, too. And next month, I hear, he's going to make the pilgrimage to Mecca.

GRAMPS — But his money is ill gotten.

GIMP — Ill gotten or not, the point is he can afford to make the pilgrimage. And when he gets back, if he wants to, he can wear a pilgrim's shawl. So tell me, is he a real pilgrim or not?

GRAMPS — That turns my stomach.

GIMP — Turns your stomach or not—ill-gotten, dirty money or not—he's still going to be Mr. Pilgrim, the man who went to Mecca. Period. So will the people who address him as such be wrong?

GRAMPS — There should be some kind of law to prevent people like that from going to the Holy Land.

POCKY — But that wouldn't be right either: trying to stop a person from fulfilling his religious duty. Whether his money is unclean or not, that's for him and God to work out—not the Pilgrimage Organizing Committee. God, I suspect, sees it this way: the man has sinned for his ill-gotten gains, but by making the pilgrimage, he's performed a virtuous deed. Does the one balance the other? Which is better? Only God knows, and He's sure not going to tell us. So, for that reason, who are we to pass judgment on the wily pedicab driver who's gone on to become a pilgrim? If we run into him on the street, what's wrong with saying, "Good evening, Mr. Pilgrim"? And if he offers me a cigarette, am I supposed to refuse it just because there's a little voice telling me, "Don't! He may have bought that cigarette with unclean money"? No! I'll take the cigarette, and if it tastes good, I'll enjoy it. If it doesn't, I'll throw it away. Period. That's how I see the problem.

GRAMPS — The same way a butcher would see it! This is meat, so keep it. This is fat and gristle—yeah, there's some use to that—so set it aside. But what's this? It ain't meat and it ain't fat or gristle, so throw it in the garbage bin. We got no use for intestines here . . .

POCKY — [*To Gramps.*] We're getting too far off the subject. [*To Ina.*] Back to what you were saying, Ina, about Ani.

GRAMPS — Is there more to tell? I thought—

INA — Well, anyway, one of Ani's johns, a regular—the fat Chinese guy who owns the noodle factory—was already waiting for her.

POCKY — What do you mean a "regular"?

INA — A regular, you know. They've been getting it on regularly for about three months now. I guess he has the hots for Ani. He said that Ani looks just like his dead wife.

POCKY — God in heaven . . .

INA — He's even been trying to get her to come and work for him.

POCKY — Work?

INA — Yeah, work. You know, like help take care of him and his kids.

POCKY — How many kids does he have?

INA — Sixteen, I think.

POCKY Sixteen? Ani's had it now!

INA And do all the housework besides!

GRAMPS [*In a pitched voice.*] The complete servant!

Gimp and Pocky break out in laughter. Ina glares at them with irritation.

And he calls that "help." He's no dumb cluck, that guy.

GIMP They usually aren't.

GRAMPS That's a case of—what is it the newspaper calls it? What's the phrase? *Ets . . . etsel . . .* whatever! Point is, after that you got the word *loopoorloom.*

POCKY [*Laughing.*] I think the phrase is *"L'homme est un loup pour l'homme"* or *"Hommo homini lupus."* But that's how it is when you only read scraps of newspaper. And then, only if the wind happens to blow them to the side of the road and we happen to pick them up. Do you know what those words mean?

GRAMPS If I'm not wrong: "man oppressed by man."

GIMP Ace in the pocket!

GRAMPS Hey, don't think a former deckhand don't know anything.

GIMP [*Amused.*] And what does the future deckhand think?

GRAMPS [*Looking at Pocky.*] That he's the happiest creature in the world.

POCKY Go on with your story, Ina.

Gramps smiles and bends toward Ina.

INA To make it short, when they were, uh—

GIMP [*Interrupting.*] "Amusing themselves"?

INA Yes! Well, at the place where they usually amuse themselves, there was a raid.

GIMP A raid?! [*Immediately repeated by Gramps and Pocky.*]

INA Yeah, a raid, by the police! Those of us who were outside got away. But Ani and her john got caught red-handed. We saw them herded onto an open-back truck together with some of the others. Judging from past experience, we guessed they'd be taken to the police station, so the pedicab driver and I went there.

POCKY Why?

INA 'Cause he was going to tell the police that he was Ani's husband.

POCKY What for?

INA Because the police only release a woman if they've got a guarantee from her husband.

POCKY But since when's the pedicab driver been married to Ani?

INA The complete pedicab comes with marriage documents, too!

GIMP That's the kind of service the complete pedicab offers.

POCKY So, an emergency husband, in case of raids!

GRAMPS [*Screaming.*] That means he's a "bust man"!

INA [*Ignoring Gramps.*] But this time the driver didn't have to offer his service. There, in front of the police, Ani's john proposed to her. And she said yes!

Pocky, Gimp, and Gramps are surprised.

I for one was real glad Ani said yes. Maybe the guy is fat and a little sleazy. Yeah, maybe Ani could have been more choosy, but at the very least, she's got a steady position now. She's going to have a permanent address and [*crying*] even an identity card!

Everyone is moved and impressed by this news.

[*Wiping her tears.*] And I have something else to tell you. [*Beginning to cry again.*] I've decided to [*sobbing*], to accept the pedicab driver's proposal.

GIMP [*Surprised.*] The pedicab driver?

INA [*Wiping her tears and looking at Gimp.*] I know you don't like him, but supposing I were to put myself and my life in your hands, what could you offer me except, maybe, a place here under the bridge?

GIMP It won't always be like this. Who says I'm going to be here forever?

INA You keep talking about the future and about your dreams and happiness. But I've never seen a single shred of evidence that you really want to put your words into practice. I'll tell it to you straight: I've always respected you for what you have to say. It's all so deep. And the words you use and the way you use them make you—I don't know—different from all the others. On those nights that I've slept beside you [*Gramps coughs*], I've been able to let my fancies float to worlds unknown. Supposing, just supposing, that all those beautiful words that you, a man I admire so much, say were true, I would be the happiest woman in the world. If only they were true.

But right now my heart is nearly broken. Day in and day out, experience has shown me that your words are always going to remain just that: words. You've got this gap between attitude and action. You're afraid to do anything. You're a daydreamer, a man of words only, a complete foreigner to the world of muscle and sweat, dirt and noise.

I once held inside me the secret hope that one day you would express yourself as a writer. You don't know how disappointed I felt when I saw you throwing away the outlines of your work in petty conversation, in trite and boring stories, here, in this place, under this bridge. This place here, under this bridge, has killed and buried the writer in you.

But I'm just an ordinary vagrant, haunted by needs, pursued by bad memories. I can no longer swallow your words as I once was able to. And now you have become for me an odd and alien man. No more, no better, no less than a parasite.

And just because I accepted the pedicab driver's proposal doesn't mean that I love him. In fact, deep down, I'm still drawn to your words and their meaning. But I must choose certainty and reality, the facts of life. I'm not unaware of the kind of life that the wife of a pedicab driver must have. Heck, I might not even be his only wife. I might not see him for days on end. Maybe he won't always be able to give me shopping money. Maybe, in not too long a time, I'll even end up having to nurse him because he's throwing up blood and doesn't have the strength to drive his cab anymore. But I'm willing to accept that—just to have an identity card!

[*Crying.*] An identity card means the end of uncertainty, the end of the fear of being chased all the time, the fear that at any time the police are going to swoop down and drag us away in their open-back trucks to a hell which the newspapers call "a helpful lesson for the unemployed."

They print big pictures of us, seated in the back of the

trucks, but the newspapers say nothing about how we're treated in their holding tanks. Of course we try to escape, but only to be caught again in places like this.

No! Starting now, I want to sleep in peace and not be woken up with a start, my body damp with cold sweat.

The bell of a pedicab rings repeatedly. Suddenly, Ina's demeanor changes. She stands and looks around slowly, examining all the corners beneath the bridge.

I'll leave all my things here. Keep them if they are of any use. Throw them away if they're not. [*The pedicab bell rings again. She sobs and hugs Pocky.*] Good-bye and happy sailing. I hope [*pausing, almost unable to continue*], I hope you'll forgive me if I've ever done anything or said anything you didn't like.

POCKY [*Emotionally, in a hoarse voice.*] The same for me, Ina.

INA [*To Gramps.*] And Gramps, I hope that we never see each other again.

GRAMPS [*Laughing.*] You hate me that much, Ina?

Ina shakes her head. She hugs Gramps and cries.

[*His voice cracking.*] I hope that one day I'll see you pass by on your husband's pedicab with a batch of happy and healthy kids. Good-bye, little one.

INA [*Now standing in front of Gimp.*] And you, good-bye. I hope that you're able to understand my decision and forgive me.

Unable to say anything, Gimp nods his head slightly. The pedicab bell rings again.

GRAMPS [*To Ina, laughing.*] Looks like you've got an itchy one on your hands! Hurry now or that husband of yours is going to vanish!

INA [*Laughs and turns to Ati.*] And to you, last of all, I ask you to forgive me if I offended you earlier. If you'll let me, I'd like to give you one piece of advice: take a good look at those of us who are here under this bridge. Look at us one by one, and then look at the situation here. Then, tomorrow morning, go straight back home, to your village. [*She opens her handkerchief and takes out some money.*] Take this. If you're careful, this should be enough to get you home and to eat along the way. [*Ati takes the money.*] Go home, as fast as you can. Don't breathe this air. Once you've taken a breath, you won't be able to release yourself from the tentacles of the octopus that lives here.

POCKY [*As if just awakened.*] And to make sure that you go back to your village, I'm going to ask Gimp to take you there. I can take care of his fare there and back. [*Pulls out some money from his pocket and gives it to Gimp.*] There, that's the rest of my advance. [*Laughing.*] Oh well, so what?! I don't need anything more. No need for money on a ship!

The pedicab bell rings again, this time very loudly.

INA [*Looking offstage, toward the sound of the bell.*] Good-bye, my home of no address. Good-bye, my home of no name. [*Her eyes glisten.*]

Wiping her tears, Ina runs out from beneath the bridge. A short while later, the sound of a pedicab bell fades in the distance.

Scene Five

ATI [*After a long silence.*] Why does he have to come back after taking me home?

GRAMPS [*Suspiciously.*] What do you mean?

ATI What would be wrong with him staying and resting in my village for a while? Who knows, he might be able to find some work he can do there.

GRAMPS [*Nudging Gimp's side with his elbow.*] You're right! I couldn't agree more. He can stay there and rest—that is, as long as your parents don't object.

ATI I think my folks will agree.

GRAMPS [*Cheerfully.*] Hooray! Even with his gimp leg, he could still work.

ATI Sure, in the rice field.

POCKY [*Heartily.*] Hooray! And, who knows, after your parents see his potential as a farmer, maybe, just maybe, they'll think of taking him on as, uh, a son-in-law!

ATI [*Blushing.*] Maybe.

GIMP [*Surprised.*] What? Son-in-law?

GRAMPS [*Smiling.*] What's wrong? Don't you have enough strength to be a son-in-law?

GIMP A son-in-law to whom?

GRAMPS Good God, think of what Ina just said. The time has come for you to keep her words in mind—at your age especially. You've got to stop confusing yourself with dreamy immaterial stories. Starting now, you have to go for it: put your words into action! The opportunity is there in front of you. Act! Do something! Isn't that what Ina told you?

So, tomorrow at dawn, you will go with Ati to the train station. Make sure that she arrives safely at her parents' home. And there, play your role as best you can, just as we have outlined it for you. If you haven't done anything wrong and your prospective in-laws still kick you out, then you can be assured your life will be a most difficult one from that time on! And that it will be mostly of your own doing. At that point I don't think even the angels in heaven will be able to help you.

Gimp appears confused by Gramps's words. He looks like he wants to shout, but gradually he begins to grasp the meaning of what Gramps has told him.

[*After a long pause.*] Tonight, with all of us so wrapped up in our own emotions, I suspect that none of us will be able to sleep. Even so, we should try. It's late, and in the morning the sun will take us to distant places. One of us has to sail, in fact. So let's gather our strength so that our steps tomorrow are light—not heavy—and we walk upright and on the proper path. [*Yawns.*] Have a good rest! [*Pinching Pocky's arm and nodding toward Gimp and Ati.*] Let them be. [*Pointing his head toward the corner of the far side of the bridge.*] We can sleep over there.

POCKY [*Laughing.*] Of course. [*To himself.*] Dumb cluck.

Ati blushes, embarrassed. Gimp suddenly bolts upright, angry.

GIMP Wait just one second! Where are you two going?! And just what kind of dirty little secret are you laughing about?

POCKY [*Laughing.*] We just mean well.

GIMP [*Yelling.*] I won't have it!

GRAMPS Won't have what?

GIMP I mean that I'm not going to start off this relationship with any funny business. Or were you just trying to make fun of me?

POCKY My God, who's making fun of you?

GIMP [*Shrilly.*] If you really do want me to start a new life, a life like the one you suggested, then by God, why won't you have me start out on the right foot?

GRAMPS Who's telling you to start it on the wrong foot?

GIMP [*Emotionally.*] You are—the two of you—with your shameful suggestion!

POCKY Shameful?

GIMP Don't play innocent with me. What did you mean by moving off to the corner over there and leaving the two of us alone?

Pocky and Gramps stare open mouthed at Gimp for a moment, then burst out laughing.

POCKY Oh, sorry, forgive us. Praise God if you really do want to start off on the right foot.

GIMP I've made up my mind to try to start everything the right way, the good and proper way. Tomorrow I'll take Ati home, but without the thought of becoming a son-in-law. What right do I have to even think that her parents might accept me? Maybe they will, but it's also within their right to refuse me. So it would be best to keep that in mind right from the start. Yes, I'll go, but only with the original goal in mind: to work.

I want to work, to feel and control the movement of my body beneath the heat of the sun, with the knowledge that the drops of sweat that pour from my body are my payment for a rightfully earned plate of rice.

As for becoming a son-in-law, as for marriage and love—for the time being, I suspect, it would be better not to think about that. I intend to bury the "outline" that Ina spoke of, at least for now. I want to get back my former zest for life, which through my own fault I lost, who knows how many decades ago. I hope that Ati and her parents will not regard me as anything more than an applicant for work, an applicant for a life that offers a way for me to return to what I once was. [*Inhales deeply and speaks in a lowered voice to Ati.*] But of course you have the right to refuse my proposal . . .

Silence. Gimp's words have greatly impressed the others. Gramps and Pocky stare at him for a long time before Gramps, unsteady on his feet, approaches Gimp and hugs him. Gramps begins to cry. Pocky hugs Gimp, too. Ati wrings her hands and starts to weep. Her sobs convey a mixture of emotion and respect—the seeds of true love. She takes Gimp's hand and kisses it. Gramps looks weary and makes his way back to where he had been standing.

GRAMPS — [*Yawning.*] I really am tired. [*To Ati.*] Come here. I'm going to sleep over here. You can sit nearby and, uh, watch over me.

Ati goes to where Gramps has lain down and sits beside him. He turns his head toward Pocky and Gimp.

And there might be some good in you getting some rest, too. Go to sleep, if you can. Remember all that you have to do tomorrow. [*Yawns again.*]

Pocky and Gimp go to the other corner of the bridge and lie down. Only Ati is still sitting. Nighttime sounds from the city are heard, as are the chirps of crickets and calls of frogs. The sound of the river flowing beneath the bridge and the traffic passing overhead are also heard.

ATI — We'll all be leaving tomorrow. What about you?

GRAMPS — [*In a drowsy voice.*] Me? Where am I supposed to go?

ATI — You can come along with us, to my village.

GRAMPS — Go along with you? I'm too old to follow anyone anymore, especially now. With all of you gone, what would happen to this place under the bridge—this home of no address and no name, as Ina called it?

Hearing Gramps speak, Pocky and Gimp sit up. They look on him with sympathy.

ATI — Well, if this place has no address and no name, it means that no one owns it and that you, too, can leave it behind.

GRAMPS — Oh, but you don't know what meaning this place here under the bridge has in my life. I've used up a good part of my life here. This place is owned by anyone who comes here for having nowhere else to go. Its owners are those with nowhere to turn, whose thoughts are upturned, who don't know what to do with their hopes and dreams, who have failed to latch on to the rhythm of their place in time. [*Yawns again.*] Everything I say is jumbled up inside me, one thing on top of another, in layers, with the outermost growing harder. Yes, I am getting older! And the older we get, the slower we become and the more we find ourselves outside the main current of life. And finally, without work—jobless—life itself is taken from us. We become the burden of the government coolies who cart our corpses to the hospital. And if we're lucky, just a little lucky, our corpses and our skeletons can perform a service for medicine and we can be unsung heroes of humanity. [*Yawning.*] But, oh, I say good night.

Ati attempts to respond, but Pocky stops her by putting his index finger to his lips. She looks wistfully at Gramps, whose chest rises and falls easily. Weeping silently, she covers him with her small sash. Wiping away her tears, she strokes his white hair. She looks at Pocky and Gimp, who have lain back down and are asleep. Gimp begins to snore. Ati laughs nervously. Soon thereafter she, too, lies down. From overhead comes the sound of cars and then a pedicab bell. Ati turns over on her side. In the distance, a dog releases a long howl. She draws a deep breath. The curtain falls slowly.

Translation by John H. McGlynn

Homes of garbage recyclers,
Jakarta, Java, 2007.
Jonas Bendiksen/Magnum

N. RIANTIARNO

Time Bomb

For my son
Bangkit Sentosa
who came, then left
as a ray of light
shunning the world
to choose eternity, instead

Cast of Characters

Jumini, woman who has lost her husband and child
Roima, good-looking young tough
Julini, transvestite, Roima's "girlfriend"
Kumis, civil defense guard
Bleki, civil defense guard
Abung, mad philosopher who lives in a tree
Tarsih, pretty and popular prostitute
Kasijah, prostitute
Turkana, Jumini's companion and admirer
Tibal, young villager newly arrived in the city
Tuminah, Tibal's sister
Sawil *and* ***Bilun,*** pair of dreamers and schemers
Subdistrict Head, government bureaucrat
Secretary, subdistrict head's secretary
Singer
Prostitute 1
Prostitute 2
Other Prostitutes
Diners
Beggars
Guards

Opening Scene

Night. A bright moon shines. Beneath a well-lit bridge, a row of huts stretches along a river and into the background. The slum's inhabitants dream of a better life.

Jumini stares at the moon. Abung is perched on a chair and appears to be deep in thought. At the window of a cheap hotel, a would-be Singer practices. On a higher level, above this panorama, is a fancy restaurant. Five Diners, people of apparent wealth, are seated at a table. Statue-like, they eat their dinners without speaking.

JUMINI — You smile down every night. Why don't you come here? Come to me. I know you miss me. I miss you, too, constantly. On a bright moonlit night like tonight, I know you must be out, playing. And your father, lying on the bench in front of the house, is singing Javanese songs and thinking of me. [*Pauses, while Turkana enters without a word.*] Smiling down every night... What news would you bring if you came down to meet me? No, please don't bring me bad news. I don't want bad news. Who would?

Abung looks up at the sky. The Diners greedily eat their dinner. The Singer prepares to sing.

But you never come. Never. I wish I could cut you down from your hanger in the sky, if only for a moment, to hold you in my lap and ask you about my little boy. Would you tell me that he's fine? I don't want a sad answer. Who would? But all you do is smile. Every night, just smile...

ROIMA — [*Suddenly emerges from the hut he shares with Julini. Angrily.*] You're ugly, Julini, and mean! You don't care about me anymore. You're used up, worn out!

JULINI — [*Comes out of the hut in pursuit of Roima.*] As if I care! Take my bra, my hairpiece, my ass...

ROIMA — And I'll throw them in the river!

JULINI — You wouldn't dare! Thief!

ROIMA — Putting me off like that... why shouldn't I be angry?

JULINI — Well, what with you trying to force me like that when I'm tired. Who'd put up with that? My bra, my hairpiece, my ass...

ROIMA — I swear I'll burn them.

JULINI — You're a sadist. I'm clearing out.

ROIMA — I'll take a razor to them!

JULINI — I'm going, I tell you, I'm going.

ROIMA — Big deal. You think I can't find me another slut? Hell, there's a warehouse full of sluts like you in the world.

JULINI — Is there really?

ROIMA So go if you want.

JULINI Honestly?

ROIMA It's up to you.

JULINI Is that it?

ROIMA [*Even angrier.*] Every night, it eats me up: my heart, my soul, holding in my feelings, pacing up and down like I've nothing to do, swallowing my spit . . . When can I spit it out? Every night, I feel my blood rising. My muscles tense—medicine don't help—my hands begin to itch and tingle, just waiting for someone to punch. Shit! [*Julini goes back into the hut.*] They say that the more tired you are, the hornier you get. That the harder you work, the more you think of a nice bed with a mattress and pillows. But washing the sheets every morning and night—it wears them out. And soap's expensive. Shit! Coconut oil's expensive, too.

JULINI [*Comes out of the hut with a bundle in her arms.*] I'm going! I got my bra, my hairpiece, and my ass. That's my capital. Don't try to follow.

Swinging her hips as she walks, Julini disappears behind the pylon of the bridge. At first Roima just stares, stunned that Julini would actually leave him. But then he grows even angrier.

ROIMA Son of a bitch. Alone again! And lonely again. And single again. She's left me again. Julini's gone. She's gone. Help! Julini's gone!

Roima breaks down and begins to cry uncontrollably. Abung stares upward. A cloud covers the moon. A group of Beggars, the slum's inhabitants, crawl out of their huts. The would-be Singer begins to sing in semioperatic style, his voice clashing with Roima's moans.

SINGER [*Keeps repeating the same phrases.*]
In the sky, so many stars
And a sliver of moon, peeking
Like a young girl's breasts
On her wedding night

JUMINI [*Angrily.*] There's never any peace around here. Roima and Julini—a cheap love story if there ever was one. A gutter romance, as filthy as they come. To hell with your love-making. I hope your bum swells and your whozee-what's-it bursts with boils. When will I get some peace? [*Going into her hut.*] If you died and went to hell, who would care?

The Subdistrict Head enters with his Secretary and bodyguard. They stand beside the bridge, looking at the hovels.

SUBDISTRICT HEAD What an extraordinary sight this is. My dear friends, why must you suffer such a fate? To have to live like pigs in dirty hovels along the river. Who must take responsibility for your fate? There is little I can do. I can only survey the scene. I can only look. [*To the Secretary.*] Handkerchief!

Your suffering must end. These awful hovels must be replaced with buildings, apartments, and hotels. I will report to the District Head, to the Governor, to the President, if need be. [*To the Secretary.*] Tissue!

It's extraordinary. This sight is extraordinary! My friends, I swear that I shall fight for you to be able to live a proper life. Secretary!

The Beggars gather around, like dogs.

SECRETARY Yes, sir.

SUBDISTRICT HEAD Write this down. This area must be cleaned up, and soon. Everything dirty and disgusting must be swept away. We'll pull everything down. Yes, we'll raze the entire area. Fix me a time to see the Governor.

SECRETARY Yes, sir.

SUBDISTRICT HEAD [*With trembling voice.*] It's extraordinary, an extraordinary sight. If those people up there can close their eyes to your fate, I, your Subdistrict Head, cannot. I will do something. I will pull everything down. We will knock this all down. [*To the Secretary.*] Towel! [*Weeps into his towel and exits, followed by the Secretary and bodyguard.*]

BEGGARS [*In chorus.*] Extraordinary! Extraordinary!

The Diners continue to eat their meal, undisturbed. Turkana enters. The squatters, darkened shapes, scramble out of their huts. They mumble and mutter, but it's not clear what they are talking about.

ABUNG [*Stares at the sight below him and begins to sing.*]
Compare one hundred rupiah
For a plate of rice
With five million for a birthday gift

Compare five thousand a month
For a monthly wage
With one million from a ten-percent kickback

My land, my country
That I love

Compare a hut on the riverbank
With a shining palace
In which no one lives

And feelings of fear, pain, and apprehension
With the laughter of victory
After the general elections

My land, my country
That I love
The future—what will it bring?

Suddenly there is the sound of gunshots. The Beggars scream, fall to the ground, and rapidly disperse. The Singer stops singing and closes his window. Abung looks tired, weary of it all. More gunshots ring out, this time closer. The Diners continue eating, oblivious to the commotion below. Kumis and Bleki appear, intending to disperse the crowd, but the Beggars have already disappeared.

KUMIS Get out! Scram!

BLEKI They've gone . . . [*Lights a firecracker.*]

KUMIS From a distance I thought there were lots of people. Judging from the commotion, ten thousand or more. If anything happens here, it's me who gets the blame. It's me who cops the anger and gets the demotion. The security of this area is totally my responsibility. [*The firecracker that Bleki lit explodes with a sound like gunfire.*]

[*Running, looking for a place to hide.*] Get out of here! Go!

BLEKI [*Chuckling.*] Hey, it was only a firecracker.

KUMIS A firecracker?

BLEKI Yeah, you know.

KUMIS I thought it was gunshot. What are you doing, scaring me like that? Damn you!

BLEKI Might as well go, sir. Seems safe around here. They don't usually have demonstrations at night.

KUMIS You never know. The enemy can sneak in from any direction, catch you unawares, if your eyes aren't peeled. These huts would make an easy hiding place.

BLEKI The most you find here at night is crazy Abung up there in the palm tree. Maybe he stole a cassette or something, and all the racket you heard was from that. Let's wake up Sawil or Bilun and cadge a cigarette.

KUMIS — Nah, we'd better go.

BLEKI — Yeah, I suppose.

Kumis and Bleki exit. The stage is silent.

ABUNG — [*Looks down on the sight.*] So many problems. So many problems. You can't choose one and leave the rest. You have to find solutions for all of them. But which one first? I can't work on them all at once. I'll have to think about this, think hard . . .

As Abung counts silently on his fingers, the lights slowly dim.

Scene One

Night. A prostitution complex on the riverbank. Only the poles that support the huts are visible. One of the prostitutes is teaching an English class. Her pupils are her colleagues—the other Prostitutes. They appear to be listening to the lesson, if only halfheartedly.

TEACHER — [*Loudly.*] One way to improve your standard of living is to study a foreign language and culture. You don't want to be satisfied with just being a whore. Who says we can't dream of good fortune coming our way? Why can't we dream of being the wife of a big shot or an official?

FIRST PUPIL — You mean the seventh wife, Teacher?

TEACHER — Seventh wife is still a wife. Your welfare is guaranteed. Now, let's go over yesterday's lessons.

[*Slowly intones the vocabulary items. The pupils slowly repeat the words, with a strong Indonesian accent.*] *Ini sa-pi.* This is cow.

PUPILS — *I-ni sa-piii.* Ndis is coowww.

TEACHER — *I-tu sa-pi sa-pi.* Those are coowws.

PUPILS — *I-tu sa-pi sa-piii.* Ndose ar kow-wes.

TEACHER — *I-ni monyet.* This is monkey.

PUPILS — *I-nii monyeet.* Ndiss is mongkiii.

TEACHER — *I-tu ko-dok.* That is frog.

PUPILS — *I-tuuu ko-dooook.* Ndat is prooooog.

TEACHER *I-tu ba-bi.* That is pig.

PUPILS *I-tuuu ba-biii.* Ndat is pig.

TEACHER *I-ni kursi. Itu kursi.* This is chair. That is chair.

PUPILS *I-niii kursiii.* Ndis is cheer. Ndat is cheeer.

From a distance comes music. The pupils start to get up.

TEACHER Hey, hey, where are you going?

SECOND PUPIL We're tired, Teacher.

One of the Prostitutes begins to sing. Another joins in and is soon followed by the rest. The Teacher seems to be at a loss.

PROSTITUTES Butterflies flying by night
Shimmer in the light of the moon
When the sun appears
They turn into filth.

JULINI [*Enters, grumbling to herself.*] Shit! I've had it. I've had it up to here.

PROSTITUTE 1 It's Julini. Julini's here.

PROSTITUTE 2 That's funny. She's usually parked down at the night market.

JULINI My heart feels broken. What the cure is, I don't know.

PROSTITUTE 1 [*To the others.*] It's Julini. Julini's here.

The Prostitutes emerge, like crickets from their holes.

JULINI Is Tarsih with a client?

TARSIH I'm here. What is it, Jul?

KASIJAH Why do you ask only after Tarsih? Don't you ever think about me?

JULINI [*Sympathetically.*] How could I forget about a friend who shares my own fate?

[*Begins to sing.*]
Forget the wounded heart
Forget the tortured soul
Seeing ourselves mirrored in each other's eyes
We send our cry to the sky

TARSIH The sky does not care
The night remains dark
And daylight blinds our eyes

KASIJAH But the stars and the moon
Are faithful friends
In times of loneliness

TARSIH And the night wind
Forever begs us
For our body and our soul

JULINI Let the sky be dark
Or blindingly light
Forget the wounded heart
Forget the tortured soul
When we see ourselves mirrored in each other's eyes

They laugh in agreement.

TARSIH Have you been quarreling with Roima again?

KASIJAH You always come running over here when you're having problems with Roima.

JULINI Where else am I to run to if not here? I'm all alone. I have nowhere else to take my troubles. I am but a dried flower carried by the wind into the ditch water. When will I find a man whom I love and who loves me, who doesn't desire me only for my services? There's more to life than a mattress.

KASIJAH A bed, you mean.

JULINI Well, a bed has a mattress, hasn't it? Roima has never understood that I am a very sensitive person. My love for him is as soft as snow. But he's forever hurting my feelings. He knows that I cannot escape his grasp. That whenever I run away, I shall surely return to his arms. It's fate, just fate . . .

TARSIH Is Roima so special?

JULINI Listen, there's no other man who can plow like my Roima. He is rough but gentle, forceful but giving. He might have a ready fist, but he also has an easy caress. If you speak of water, Roima's a waterfall. Of wood he is teak, of fruit he is a mango. In short, he's the best. Oh, I miss him so. I thrill at the thought of him. I must go back. [*Exits hastily.*]

KASIJAH She's mad.

TARSIH She's in love.

Kumis and Bleki enter the complex, intending to find Tarsih, but she spots them before they see her.

TARSIH [*To Kasijah.*] Oh, it's them again. They want the lot but never want to pay. Say I'm booked up.

KASIJAH Who is it? Kumis and his dog?

TARSIH Who else? Tell them, will ya? [*Hurries off.*]

KASIJAH [*Addressing the audience.*] In this game you'll find many people who demand a lot but who don't want to give a thing. Parasites is what they are. Fine looking perhaps, but dangerous.

PROSTITUTE 1 [*To Bleki.*] Inspection, love?

PROSTITUTE 2 Coming down to look us over, love?

BLEKI Have there been any problems? Have you heard of any trouble?

PROSTITUTE 1 It's all quiet here. It certainly ain't raining money tonight.

BLEKI Raining money? Crap!

PROSTITUTE 2 Not crap, doll. But there is a distinctive smell.

PROSTITUTE 1 Maybe it's just Galunggung erupting again.

BLEKI Joking with officials, are you? Always playing around, never serious . . . What do you think this is? A picnic? When I ask you a question, I expect a straight answer. If we took you in to headquarters, then you'd know.

KUMIS [*Softly, to Bleki.*] Stop beating around the bush. Ask for Tarsih, stupid. You're wasting time with your yapping.

BLEKI Yes, boss! [*To Kasijah.*] I'm looking for the flower among flowers. The flower whose perfume spreads for thirty kilometers, the flower far more radiant than the light of the moon—

KUMIS [*Grabbing Bleki.*] Cut the drivel! Ask them about Tarsih. Don't squirm about like a goddamned worm.

BLEKI Yes, boss. [*Turning back to Kasijah.*]

KASIJAH You looking for Tarsih?

BLEKI [*Surprised.*] Yes. Is she here?

KASIJAH She just went off with some gents in a limo. She told me that she was booked up.

BLEKI [*Angrily.*] When the boss wants her, she's supposed to be here. Who's the ape who pinched Tarsih tonight? Who's the toad who picked her up? Tell me! [*Kumis pulls him away.*] Who is it? Whoever it is, he's had it, trying to compete with a uniformed official. [*As Kumis pulls him offstage.*] Yes, sir. Sorry, sir!

As Kumis and Bleki disappear, the Prostitutes burst into laughter and then begin to sing.

PROSTITUTES — Butterflies of the night
Shimmer in the light of the moon
When the sun comes up,
They change to filth

A cloud covers the moon. The lights slowly fade.

Scene Two

Morning. Beneath the bridge. Jumini is mending clothes. The Diners above relax at their tables, enjoying coffee and desserts. The sun glows gently. Turkana is sorting cardboard. Roima, who is still angry, approaches Julini and pulls her by the ear.

JULINI — Don't, Roima. Please? Don't do that to my ear. *Owww!*

ROIMA — Where were you last night? Tell me.

JUMINI — You're always so mean to Julini. How can you treat your girlfriend like that?

ROIMA — You keep out of it. This is a private matter. [*To Julini.*] Where did you sleep last night? Tell me, bitch, or I'm going to—

JULINI — [*In pain.*] *Ow!* Give me a chance! You don't have to hit me.

ROIMA — Tell me then.

JULINI — I didn't sleep anywhere. I was at the station, walking up and down. I feel stiff all over from the cold air and the night wind. I'm sorry, Roima. I'll make it up to you. Let me kiss your lips . . .

ROIMA — Who do you think you are, staying out like that? And coming back here, like some rich bitch, thinking everything will be fine. Well, up yours, whore!

JULINI — Don't say that. I'm not a whore. I'm not a wanton woman who likes to wander and stray. I'm just a poor, wretched woman. Oh God, take pity on this poor soul who is all alone in the world! [*Jumini starts to laugh.*]

ROIMA — It's not funny. [*But starts laughing, too.*]

JULINI — [*Happily.*] You see. I do know how to keep you entertained! Love me, Roima! Love me with all your heart.

ROIMA — How am I supposed to love you when you're off peddling your ass?

JULINI Don't joke around. I'm not just a piece of merchandise. I'm a PTS graduate, you know, with a diploma to boot.

JUMINI PTS? What's that? A Private Technical School?

JULINI No . . . A "Purveyor of Tenderness and Satisfaction"!

ROIMA So with me, too, it's just a trade?

JULINI Not with you, Roima. With you I've found true love. Only with you have I no interest in trade. Only with you am I carried away on a sea of passion.

ROIMA Bullshit! Get out of here. You sound like a trashy novel. All I'm saying to you is that if you come back, don't run off.

JUMINI In any relationship it's not unusual to have bedroom problems.

ROIMA Get out of here!

JULINI Don't you want a kiss first?

ROIMA [*Pulls Julini to a concealed spot.*] Come here . . .

Jumini smiles. The lights change. A spotlight shines on Abung, who is dangling his legs. He looks around him, then crawls from one position to another. The only sound is that of the Prostitutes learning English.

TEACHER *Ini monyet.*

PUPILS *I-nii monyet.*

TEACHER *Itu mo-nyet mo-nyet.*

PUPILS *I-tuu mo-nyet mo-nyet.*

TEACHER This is monkey, that are monkey.

PUPILS Diss is mongkiii, dat ar mongkii.

TEACHER *Ini babi, itu babi-babi.*

PUPILS *Ini babii, itu babi-babiii.*

TEACHER This is pig. That are pigs.

PUPILS Diis iss pig. Dat ar pigesss.

TEACHER *Ini kursi.*

PUPILS *Iniii kursiiii.*

TEACHER This is a chair.

PUPILS Diss is a cheeer.

TEACHER *Itu kursi-kursi.*

PUPILS *Ituuu kursi-kursiii.*

TEACHER That are chairs.

PUPILS Daaat ar cheeer-es.

TEACHER Remember: chair. Remember: chairs.

PUPILS [*Voices fading.*] Remember chair, remember chairs.

ABUNG [*Addressing the audience.*] During the day, our problems turn into sweat and evaporate in the sun. At night, beneath a blanket of moonlight, they become more complex and intertwined. And sleep is not a constructive escape, but, rather, a postponement of the burden we must bear. What in fact are our problems, our difficulties, the things that stand in our way? They're ubiquitous, lurking in every corner, ready to stab us as we go by. It's no wonder we feel confused and helpless.

The spotlight on Abung fades. The lights change again. Julini emerges from the place where Roima pulled her. Her clothes are disheveled.

JULINI That wasn't a kiss—that was rape! That man! He has no sense of time or place. He just goes wild. I'd have thought he'd want something else to eat in the morning!

JUMINI My husband was like that, too.

JULINI But Roima's a real man, I'll give him that. If I compared him to a farmer, I'd say his tilling is skillful and exact. That's what makes me love him to distraction. The only trouble is, he doesn't want to marry me legally.

JUMINI But can he? Is it allowed?

JULINI No barrier can stand in the way of true love. [*Sighs.*] Oh, this is my fate: to be a mere object of desire.

JUMINI Don't let it get you down. Just keep on trying.

Sawil and Bilun appear, busily counting their imaginary profits.

SAWIL One kilogram of meat is two thousand rupiah. Cooking oil and kerosene, another five hundred...

BILUN Wouldn't it be better to use wood?

SAWIL There's too much waste, and the smoke gets in your eyes. That might put customers off. So how much was that—one thousand five hundred? The oil will last for two or three days. Then there's vegetables, onions, chili, and noodles... Let's say an outlay of five thousand for the lot. But that's not counting the initial capital for the stove, benches, plates, and cups. How much do we charge per bowl? A hundred?

BILUN At least.

SAWIL Okay, a hundred. But we should have a two-hundred-fifty portion, too.

BILUN Yeah, with two pieces of tofu and five meat balls. And thick noodles instead of thin ones.

SAWIL We could make nine thousand in a day.

BILUN That's if we sell out...

SAWIL Well, at the very least, seven thousand. That's a two-thousand-rupiah profit! But that's the worst case. Let's say two thousand five hundred... How much is that a week?

BILUN Seven days to a week, so two thousand five hundred times seven is...

SAWIL [*Scratches the figures on the ground.*] Two thousand five hundred times seven is—seventeen thousand five hundred! And per month?

BILUN Multiply by thirty—eh, I mean four.

SAWIL Times four is... seventy thousand!

As Bilun and Sawil do their calculations, they move farther and farther away from Jumini and Julini.

SAWIL A year?

BILUN Multiply by twelve.

SAWIL Twelve times seventy thousand... Seventy times twelve is eight hundred and forty, with three more zeros... That's eight hundred and forty thousand. [*Exiting.*] Almost a million!

BILUN We could buy rice land.

SAWIL Rice land and a car. In a year, two years, three years if we save carefully, we could...

Their voices fade away. For a moment the stage is silent.

JUMINI Every day, all they do is count...

JULINI And dream of selling noodles...

JUMINI Dreaming, constantly dreaming.

JULINI And tomorrow they'll have a different dream. Buying land in Lampung, maybe, and selling cloves. The day after, they'll be dreaming of something else: trading in building materials. And the next day, opening a coffee shop. The following day, selling off the gold from the National Monument. They're crazy!

JUMINI They never stop.

JULINI Even though they don't have a cent to their name.

JUMINI They're sick.

The lights change: Jumini is left in shadow. The restaurant where the Diners are eating remains bright.

JUMINI Smiling down, every night... Why don't you come to me? Come down. Please... How long must I wait?

What's he doing now? Asleep already? Surely by this time he must be sleeping soundly. I hope his father hasn't forgotten to cover him and to light a mosquito repellent coil before he goes to sleep. His skin will be eaten up by mosquitos if his father has forgotten. Smiling away up there... Have you taken note of everything that's happened? What do you have to tell me? I want to know everything about him, and about his father, too. When are they going to come and get me? Didn't he tell you? Why not? Of course... He has lots of work to do, especially if he's getting ready to come and fetch me. I'll be so happy when he takes me home. But you never say anything. All you do is smile. [*Angrily.*] What are you staring at me like that for? Why don't you say something? Do something!

Looking on, Turkana says nothing. The lights fade.

Scene Three

Same location. Jumini is sewing. Turkana is sorting cardboard. By their tone of voice, they appear to have been talking for some time.

TURKANA I keep telling you that remembering what's past is useless. You've said yourself that daydreaming is like being addicted to drugs. It can make you sick. But what do you do every day?

JUMINI I wait for Sueb and my boy to come home and get me.

TURKANA Jumini, Jumini... Sueb and Tole are dead. I brought the newspaper, you saw the news. Their ship sank. Lots of passengers drowned.

JUMINI: [*Angrily.*] Sure, lots of them drowned, but I didn't see a picture of Sueb and Tole. They weren't there! They're in Lampung, growing cloves and rice. And when they have enough money saved up, they're going to come and get me.

TURKANA: There's a list of the dead. Where is that paper? You still have it, don't you? I'll show you their names.

JUMINI: Sueb and Tole are common names. You don't know if it's Sueb my husband, or Tole my boy.

TURKANA: They're dead, and it's just our bad luck that we weren't able to see their remains.

JUMINI: They're alive! Don't talk about their "remains" like that!

TURKANA: I'm sorry, but I have to. Otherwise, you're going to spend your whole life in a daze. I don't want you to end up like Abung, sitting up there in a tree every day, dangling his legs, made crazy by his own thoughts. I don't want you to be like Bilun and Sawil, who can do nothing but count. Why, they'd count the hairs in their armpits if they could. And then there's Roima, and Julini, who dreams of becoming a woman. I want you to see the truth. Sueb and Tole are dead! [*Pauses, waiting for a response from Jumini, but she remains as still as a statue.*]

[*Continues wearily.*] For almost a year, I've been screaming for you to come to your senses. But it doesn't seem to do any good. [*Hopelessly.*] Oh well, do what you like . . . [*Exits. The lights change again.*]

JUMINI: You're still smiling. Do you see what I want to see? Sueb and Tole miss me, don't they?

The Diners greedily eat their food. The lights fade.

Scene Four

The local guardhouse. Kumis and Bleki have two visitors, Tibal and Tuminah, who have just arrived from a village.

KUMIS: Life in Jakarta is hard.

BLEKI: It's not easy.

KUMIS: Even those with jobs have trouble getting by.

BLEKI: Not to mention those who don't have work.

KUMIS It looks easy, sure. There are lots of jobs waiting, everywhere. And you can make money as long as you're willing to use your brain a bit, exert your muscles.

BLEKI Do whatever you can.

KUMIS But to survive in Jakarta? Hmmm...

BLEKI You have to be able to take hard knocks.

KUMIS Don't sell yourself too high.

BLEKI Cut your prices.

KUMIS Do whatever you can, just so long as it brings in money.

BLEKI If you're in a spot, you can steal—as long as no one catches you.

KUMIS [*Nodding at Tuminah.*] What's her name?

TIBAL Tuminah.

BLEKI Pretty, eh?

KUMIS She's your sister?

BLEKI Your real sister?

TIBAL Yes. It says so in the letter from the village chief, if you don't believe me.

KUMIS We believe you.

BLEKI Sure, we believe you.

KUMIS [*To Tuminah.*] Have you ever been to school?

BLEKI State, private, or religious?

KUMIS [*Exasperated.*] Shut up, you fool! I asked her, not you. Go sit in the corner over there and shut your mouth, permanently if possible. You just can't let anyone else talk. [*Bleki shrinks at the rebuke. Kumis paces the floor.*]

TIBAL This is how it is, sir. We have a letter from our village chief, and we have letters from the ward chief and the neighborhood head giving us permission to cultivate some of the unused land alongside the river. We're hoping to grow vegetables, but the ward chief and the neighborhood head told us to speak to you first. So, whatever you say is fine with us. As for the profits... those can be divided, too, however you say. Maybe four ways: between you, me, the ward chief, and the neighborhood head...

KUMIS So you want to be...

BLEKI — An urban farmer! [*Kumis moves toward Bleki as if to strike him.*]

[*Pleading.*] Don't, please don't. I'll be quiet.

KUMIS — Good! [*To Tibal.*] Good! You are like the morning sun, full of light and hope. Jakarta is becoming barren, and all we can see these days are shacks, rubbish, trees, skyscrapers, and monuments. But vegetables? You only see vegetables in the market. Here, amid the snarling traffic of this city, you want to become a farmer? Why not a bus conductor, a parking attendant, or a night watchman?

TIBAL — I only know how to farm.

KUMIS — Well, that's good—a noble profession. Most of us come from the village, and most village people are farmers, so most of us are farm children. We often forget it, though. Keep on with your plans, keep on. [*To Tuminah.*] And what's your name again?

TUMINAH — Tuminah.

KUMIS — And you want to be a farmer, too?

TUMINAH — I'll do whatever my brother does.

KUMIS — You don't want to be a waitress, a sales clerk, or a nightclub hostess?

TUMINAH — [*Demurely.*] All I know is the soil.

KUMIS — The soil . . . From earth we come and to earth we shall return. So, keep on with your plans. My prayers go with you.

BLEKI — Amen. [*Titters.*]

Suddenly, a hotel window is flung open.

SINGER — [*Sticks his head out and begins to rehearse.*]
In the sky, so many stars
And a sliver of moon, peeking
Like a young girl's breasts
On her wedding night

Kumis covers his ears, trying in vain not to hear the discordant singing, but the Singer keeps repeating the phrases.

KUMIS — [*Angrily.*] Bleki, where did that creature spring up from? Shut his trap. This is the age of the atom, the Rolling Stones, the Beatles . . . What's he singing that kind of crap for? Plug his mouth. That noise gives me a headache.

BLEKI [*Throws a rock at the hotel window.*] Shut up, you old crow. Shut up!

SINGER [*Offended.*] Primitive savages. No idea of art. [*Disappears from sight, slamming the window shut.*]

KUMIS Art? You call disturbing the peace art? Shit! You've got no shame.

SINGER [*Reappears at the window.*] With art, the more disturbing the art, the higher the quality. Didn't you know that? [*In Dutch.*] *Ben je gek?* [*Disappears again, slamming the window even more loudly.*]

KUMIS What the hell did he say?

BLEKI It was Dutch, sir. He said you're mad.

KUMIS [*Angrily.*] What? I'll have the neighborhood chief close down that hotel, that den of iniquity. I'll burn it down myself if I get the chance. Swearing in Dutch! Are we still a colony? I intend to report this to the Subdistrict Head, the District Head, the Governor! [*Falls back, exhausted.*]

TIBAL Sir, sir...

BLEKI He's out of it. Just let him be...

Tibal, Tuminah, and Bleki stare at the recumbent Kumis. The lights fade.

Scene Five

Late afternoon, a few days later. Turkana is counting his cardboard boxes. Jumini is serving food while Roima and Julini are smooching. Abung moves, apelike, from one tree to another. Up above, the Diners enjoy their meal.

ABUNG The world is getting more and more full of crazy people. And they're the ones who succeed! Those who aren't crazy never get anywhere. If you want to be part of the act, you got to be crazy or stoned. But however fortunate the crazy ones may be, the pious are still better off.

JUMINI [*To Abung, loudly.*] If everyone were mad, the word "mad" wouldn't exist. Come down out of that tree, Abung. You're going to turn into a bird if you stay up there much longer.

TURKANA You're wasting your breath. He doesn't understand anything. He does not hear anything, and he does not see anything.

JUMINI Like the moon, which night after night can only smile.

TURKANA Don't start that again.

JUMINI I started so long ago. I can't stop now.

Turkana keeps silent. Jumini says no more.

JULINI They're always fighting—just like us—even though I know that Turkana loves Jumini. He loves her to distraction. Supposing he were asked to jump down a well for her, he'd do it. Oh, if you were like Turkana, how happy I would be.

ROIMA You're not satisfied with me?

JULINI Completely satisfied. You're everything to me. If you're Zeus, I'm Leda. We will go everywhere together, traverse hell if that's—

ROIMA Stop! Your blather gives me a headache.

Tibal and Tuminah enter, returning home from their field.

JULINI Are you just getting home?

TIBAL Yes.

JULINI You must be tired.

TIBAL Yeah . . .

JULINI I bet you'd like a massage.

TIBAL If it doesn't cost anything, sure.

JULINI I'm good at massage.

ROIMA [*Slapping Julini's mouth.*] You rotten flirt!

Tibal and Tuminah go into their hut.

JULINI Now what's the matter?

ROIMA Your talk, that's what! You go too far.

JULINI They're good neighbors. What's wrong with being friendly? We're all newcomers here, trying to make a living in a strange land.

ROIMA Friendly is fine, but you don't have to advertise. [*Pulling Julini's ear.*] Want this?

JULINI Ouch!

ROIMA Or this?

JULINI Ouch, ouch!

ROIMA Everything's for sale! Prices will be slashed. Or maybe you want this . . .

JULINI — *[Runs toward her hut, followed by Roima.]* It's still daylight, Roima! People will see us.

ROIMA — Shut up, slut. All your yelling, people are going to hear.

Inside the hut, Julini begins to giggle. A short while later, the hut is silent.

SAWIL — *[Enters, followed by Bilun.]* Ten rupiah times . . . Well, say at worst, ten tins. If one tin holds twenty liters, that makes two hundred. So how much is that?

BILUN — That would be ten times two hundred.

SAWIL — Two thousand! So in a week: two thousand times seven. That makes fourteen thousand. A month—fourteen thousand times four. And for a year, multiply by twelve. Hmmm, that's not very much.

BILUN — I told you, there's not much profit in selling kerosene. A lot less than selling noodles.

JUMINI — *[To Sawil and Bilun.]* Hey, you two. What are you counting every day?

SAWIL — Profits.

JUMINI — You want to go into business? Do you have any capital?

BILUN — I said, why don't we see how much we can make from selling rolls? There's no hassles in that. You have your profits, plus a commission and monthly wage from the bread factory.

SAWIL — Okay . . . One roll costs . . .

BILUN — Two hundred at least. That's a fifty-rupiah profit. There's four hundred rolls in a load, so if you finish two loads in one day . . . Well, you work it out.

JUMINI — I asked you, do you have any capital or not?

SAWIL — *[Does his calculations on the ground.]* Fifty times four hundred times two . . .

BILUN — Plus five hundred a day for commission and fifteen thousand a month for salary . . .

Sawil and Bilun gradually make their way toward the riverbank.

SAWIL — Five hundred times thirty is fifteen thousand. With another fifteen thousand, that's thirty thousand. And if you . . .

Sawil's voice fades away, but Jumini continues to speak to them as if they were listening to her.

JUMINI [*Irritated.*] So do you have any capital or not? [*To herself as much as to Turkana.*] Those two drive me mad.

TURKANA You're never going to get an answer from them. You're just wasting your strength. Why don't we leave this place, Jumi? We can go back to the village. I still have two squares of rice land there. We could cultivate that. Better that than waiting here, getting nowhere and fooling ourselves.

JUMINI Everything makes me sick. Everything! Those two. You, too. You say you love me, that you want to do what I want, that you want to help, that you won't ask me to go back to the village before I've tired of this game of ours. You say this and that... Why can't you be patient?

TURKANA All right, Jum, all right.

JUMINI You say you accept the situation, that you won't ask for anything, that you'll look after me until I die, that you don't care what I do as long as we're together... Have you forgotten all that?

TURKANA But we've been lying to ourselves. We'll go mad if we go on like this.

JUMINI I don't care, as long as you don't betray me. [*Goes into her shack.*]

TURKANA Listen to me, Jum. I haven't finished yet. [*Tries to follow Jumini into the hut, but she pushes him back out.*]

JUMINI You try coming in here one more time and you'll never see me again. [*Turns her back on Turkana and goes inside.*]

TURKANA [*Angrily.*] What do you want me to do? Keep begging on my knees forever? Do you think I can stand that? Damn, damn, damn!

The lights fade.

Scene Six

Night. The prostitution complex. The Prostitutes are having an English lesson. A number of the Prostitutes are transvestites. In the restaurant, one of the Diners' chairs is empty. Julini, who is sitting in on the English lesson, plays with a large doll, a duplicate of the missing Diner, during the lesson.

PUPILS Dat are piig.

TEACHER This is *kerbauuu.*

PUPILS Dis is *kerbauuu.*

TEACHER English is a language of communication, an international language. We as workers in the field of social services must serve all nationalities and races, without distinction. It is important that we know English so that we don't get cheated. Isn't that right?

PUPILS Yes, Teacherrr.

Out of sight, behind the embankment, Tarsih can be heard arguing with Kumis.

TEACHER Now try to sing the song I taught you yesterday. Ready?

PUPILS Baa, baa, black sheep
Have you any wool?
Yes sir, yes sir, three bags full

One for my mother
And one for my dream
But none for the little girl
That cries in the lane

Tarsih's quarrel with Kumis grows louder.

TARSIH Promises, nothing but promises! Do you think I can live on promises?

KUMIS It's just for tonight. I'll give you four times the price tomorrow. I don't have any money now.

TARSIH Tomorrow . . . always tomorrow! How many tomorrows have there been already?

KUMIS Why don't you trust me? It's me, Kumis!

TARSIH I've had enough!

The sudden noise of something breaking is followed by the sight of Kumis scrambling up the embankment in nothing but his underwear. He ducks into an alley and is followed by Bleki, who scurries behind him with his uniform.

BLEKI Wait! You can't run about naked like that. People will think you're a thief. Your uniform. I got your uniform. What do you want me to do with it? Sell it to the ragman? [*Follows Kumis into the alley. Tarsih appears.*]

TARSIH [*Angrily.*] You come here again and I'll cut it off!

KASIJAH [*Giggling.*] I didn't hear you complaining before.

TARSIH He caught me; I couldn't get out of it.

KASIJAH That is our lot. If you're not lucky, you're really out of luck.

TARSIH / KASIJAH [*Singing.*]
One loaf of bread is all you got
Bite off a little today
But leave some for tomorrow
My mouth is very strong
My tongue knows how to dance
Get drunk, forget it all

I am a goddess with night for a shawl
My lipstick, the light of the moon
Hoping that the stars will fall
On the canopy of my bed

I am a goddess without hope
The mist which instantly disappears
The rainbow screened by the sun
The foamy waves, a loaf of bread

Take a little bite, just one bite
But leave some for tomorrow

JULINI [*Playing with the doll.*] One night I saw him, a god descended from the sky. He waved his hand, supple but strong. I went up to him and . . . It was truly amazing! What woman would not have fallen in love with him? My eyes swam just looking at him. "Do you want me?" I asked. He smiled. "Are you so special?" he asked. "Try me," I said. "Is it real or only plastic?" he then asked. "Is it important?" I asked in return. "What's important is pleasure, " I told him. "It is an art," I convinced him. And we went off. Drinking, dancing cheek to cheek . . .

[*Embraces the doll and sings.*]
Oh devour the night
Turn out the lights
And time becomes glue
Fusing love and desire

Pleasure—isn't that what we seek? Money is secondary. [*Moves the doll, then begins to dance.*]

To find a real man in the course of life
Is to seek a needle in the grass
So if you ever find him
Dare not, never let him go

But as soon as he is satisfied, he leaves. It's always like that. They come and go like dandruff.

Music plays as Julini dances a farewell dance with the doll.

When the dance is finished, she throws the doll up to where the Diners are seated. One of the Diners catches the doll and places it in the empty chair. He then returns to his own chair and continues his meal, as if oblivious to what has just happened. Below, Julini cries as she sings.

Good-bye pleasure
Once and for all
Hello pain and loneliness
My greetings as we meet again

The lights change, leaving Julini in darkness. A spotlight shines on Tarsih and Kasijah.

TARSIH Julini is right. We never get anything out of life. It's our lot always to give. But how long can we go on giving? Even the sea can run dry.

KASIJAH But what else can we do?

TARSIH [*Shakes her head, but then looks up. She seems to have discovered something.*] Why not? What makes us different from those people up there who do nothing but eat? And don't want to do anything else, even though they could? What makes us different from those who have eyes but who cannot see? From those who have mouths but will not talk about our fate? Who have brains but will not use them to think? Who have power to change their surroundings but are content to sink in their own mire?

KASIJAH Are you all right, Tarsih?

TARSIH I'm fine. I just want us to be able to do something to change our lot.

KASIJAH How? Take up weapons? The only weapon we have is our honor.

TARSIH Honor? When we spend our whole lives wallowing in the gutter, how can we talk of honor? The longer we go on, the less of it we have.

KASIJAH Everyone wants to be happy—I know that. Everyone wants a proper life. I know that, too. Who wants to live like us? No one—that is, if they have any choice. But everyone knows, too, that we're one part of something immoral. To talk of changing the situation, that's nonsense. The only thing that's going to change the situation is a miracle.

TARSIH A miracle, Kasijah. That's it. Why can't we make a miracle with our own hands? I can. I can.

[*Singing.*]
Rise up, maggots!
Why let yourselves be tied to dreary days?
Don't give up, maggots!
Why let your burdens weigh you down?
In the sky, the stars and the moon
Their light shining in the distance
Shall become our guide
Don't let yourselves be wounded, maggots!
Why are you willing to suffer?

We really are maggots, Kasijah, born in filth.

Runs off toward the main road, followed by Kasijah in swift pursuit.

KASIJAH Tarsih! Tarsih! Tarsih!

The lights fade quickly.

Scene Seven

Night. Jumini is arguing with Turkana outside her hut. Abung moves from one tree perch to another. The Diners, in their places, resolutely enjoy their dinners.

TURKANA Why don't we go back to the village? Sueb's land is lying idle. Mine, too. No one is working it. There's no purpose to us living here. What are we waiting for?

JUMINI What are we waiting for? What am I here for? Why? Who, oh who? Who is he? Who am I?

TURKANA I just don't know what to do anymore.

ABUNG Thrown up here with no explanation at all, what am I supposed to do? What am I? A character? A character with no discernible role. What tale shall I enact? When should I perform and when should I rest in the wings? [*Angrily.*] I'm tired, so tired, but I can't stop. So many people are allowed to live without any preparation—none at all. Their souls cry out. They bump into each other. Some are wounded and bleeding. People queue up to find out what they think can make their lives happy.

But the queue doesn't move, even as more and more people step into line. A demon creditor presses for payment of our debts.

TURKANA Answer me, Jumini, answer me! You don't want me to leave you, do you? When I ask you outright, you won't answer me.

Sawil and Bilun suddenly appear.

SAWIL Who would want to go it alone? In business, partners have to go along with the agreed policies, even if the venture goes bankrupt. That's the risk of the trade. If you're not lucky, then you're unlucky.

BILUN I only said, how about if we stopped counting? If you don't agree, fine, we'll keep on counting.

SAWIL Well praise be, if you really understand. Shall we start again?

BILUN Fine.

SAWIL Where were we?

BILUN A chicken costs a thousand rupiah.

SAWIL Which we can sell for twice as much. At a busy market we could sell, maybe, fifteen a day. How many is that in a week?

BILUN Multiply by seven.

SAWIL Fifteen times seven is one hundred and five. In a month—four times one hundred and five is four hundred twenty.

BILUN Less transportation, meals, bribes . . .

The two slowly move offstage as Sawil does his calculations in the dirt.

SAWIL Four hundred twenty . . . Two meals a day, to economize. One meal is four hundred, so two people makes eight hundred. Times thirty . . . plus zero, zero is twenty-three—

BILUN Is twenty-four.

SAWIL Twenty-four thousand! And transport costs? [*Their voices fade.*]

TURKANA Look at them, Jum. Look at what they're doing. What do Sawil and Bilun want? They count things that don't even exist. Sure, Sueb and Tole are alive. Sure, they've gone to Lampung, but—

JUMINI Shut up, Turkana, shut up! I don't want to hear what you're saying, not anymore. Go wherever you like, and don't bother me.

The hotel window suddenly opens.

SINGER [*Singing.*]
And a sliver of moon, peeking

Like a young girl's breasts,
On her wedding night
[*Just as suddenly closes the window.*]

TURKANA [*Exploding in anger.*] This place is a torture worse than hell. This isn't the place for us. I'm amazed that you can stand it at all. [*Exits angrily.*]

JUMINI [*Looks up at the moon in the sky.*] Smiling again, are you? Forever smiling. Tonight your light is especially bright. But starting tomorrow you'll begin to shrink and, gradually, fade away. And I'll have to wait another month to look into your face and to ask about Sueb and my boy. On nights when it rains and the sky is covered by clouds, you don't appear and I cannot help but be upset. Even so, I know that you'll be back to smile at me.

The moon clouds over. The lights slowly fade.

Scene Eight

Same night. In the opposite corner of the stage from Jumini's hut, Julini is massaging Tibal. Tuminah is seated beside Julini.

TIBAL [*In pain.*] Ouch, not so hard. It hurts, you know.

JULINI Well of course it hurts. If it's pleasure you want, don't come asking for a massage. Ask for something else.

TIBAL Hush. Ah, there, that's where it hurts. I must have pulled a muscle.

TUMINAH [*To Tibal.*] I can do that for you.

TIBAL That's all right. You must be tired. Why don't you go to bed?

Tuminah rises and enters their hut.

JULINI My, she's an obedient thing.

TIBAL I know. She never talks back. I'm her mother and father—two in one. It's hard looking after a young inexperienced girl.

JULINI You mean, she's never even . . .

TIBAL I tell you, when she gets married, I'll feel the loss. I hope she finds a good husband. He doesn't have to be rich, as long as he's responsible. That's enough for me.

JULINI How are your crops? They must be big by now.

Bus conductor,
Jakarta, 2012.
Kurniadi Widodo

National Monument Park,
Jakarta, 2012.
Kurniadi Widodo

TIBAL In another few weeks it will be time to harvest. We should be able to make a tidy profit.

Tuminah peeks out of the hut.

TUMINAH You'll buy me a nice dress, won't you?

TIBAL Yeah . . . And if there's enough, we'll put aside some for your marriage.

TUMINAH No need for that. Buy me a necklace or earrings. If we're out of money, we can sell them.

TIBAL It's late. Go to sleep. Otherwise you'll wake up late. The middlemen who are going to buy our crop said that they'd be here first thing in the morning.

Tuminah goes back into the hut.

JULINI How much are you bribing Kumis?

TIBAL Not bribing—*sharing the profits.* That's the arrangement.

JULINI Don't trust Kumis. He only looks after himself. Be careful.

TIBAL Yeah, yeah . . . . Ouch!

JULINI Oh my God—it's standing up!

TIBAL What?

JULINI It's stiff.

TIBAL What are you talking about?

JULINI It's going up and down.

TIBAL Shhh . . .

JULINI I know a place where we can go. Do you want to? It's nearby.

TIBAL I don't have any money.

JULINI Money's secondary. What's important is pleasure.

Julini and Tibal sneak off to a darkened corner. A moment later, Tuminah appears and gazes in the direction they have gone. Roima appears.

ROIMA Jul . . . Julini! Where has that whore gone? Jul, where are you? Turning tricks, I bet. You said you wouldn't do it today. [*To Tuminah.*] Have you seen Julini?

Tuminah nods in the direction Julini and Tibal have gone, then enters the hut and shuts the door.

Hey, don't go in yet. Tell me where she went. Who was she with? Say something, idiot! [*Walks off in the direction indicated by Tuminah.*] Juul . . .

Tuminah reappears at the door. The lights slowly dim.

Scene Nine

Night. The prostitution complex. The Subdistrict Head, his Secretary, Kumis, and Bleki are conducting a surprise inspection of the area. The Prostitutes are preening and showing themselves off.

KUMIS — No need to worry, no need to be nervous—our Subdistrict Head doesn't take advantage of people. He's a wise official with the people's interests at heart, especially those of the little people, the underdogs. He's here because he wants to learn about your line of work. When he interviews you, please give honest answers. The information he gathers will be forwarded to his superiors. As this is not an official visit, you're not being asked to behave officially. Our Subdistrict Head regards this prostitution complex as the most orderly in the area. So it's appropriate for him to visit.

Some Prostitutes whistle; others giggle.

BLEKI — Quiet, quiet . . . Be polite. This man's a government official. [*To Kasijah.*] You, step forward. Yes, you.

PROSTITUTE 1 — [*Whistles.*] Kasijah's got a booking!

KASIJAH — Hush.

BLEKI — The Subdistrict Head would like a few words with you.

KASIJAH — Fine by me.

BLEKI — Go ahead, sir.

SUBDISTRICT HEAD — What's your name?

KASIJAH — Caroline.

PROSTITUTE 1 — [*Whistles again.*] Rubbish, she's making that up.

PROSTITUTE 2 — Her name is Kasijah, sir.

KASIJAH — Hush . . .

SUBDISTRICT HEAD — How long have you been working here?

KASIJAH — I'm just in from the village—just three months ago.

PROSTITUTE 1 — [*Laughing.*] Hell, she's the oldest whore here.

KASIJAH — [*To Prostitute 1.*] Don't spill the house secrets. Don't be a pain in the ass.

SUBDISTRICT HEAD — And how did you come to be like this?

KASIJAH — Like what, sir?

SUBDISTRICT HEAD — Well, like this...

PROSTITUTE 1 — Being a whore is hard work.

KASIJAH — [*Losing her patience.*] Damn you, slut. You smell like the gutter, with a drain for a mouth. I'm going to scratch your eyes out, pull out your hair till you look like Kojak. [*Goes to strike Prostitute 1 but is stopped by Bleki.*]

BLEKI — That's enough. I'll shoot you if you don't calm down.

Kasijah and Prostitute 1 calm down, but their mutual hostility remains apparent.

SUBDISTRICT HEAD — Try another one, Kumis.

KUMIS — Another one... Hmm, which one? [*Trying to choose.*]

SUBDISTRICT HEAD — [*Notices Tarsih and whispers to Kumis.*] I like that one... She's really pretty.

KUMIS — [*Nervously.*] She's the star, sir.

SUBDISTRICT HEAD — All the better. What's her name?

KUMIS — Tarsih.

SUBDISTRICT HEAD — Call her over here.

KUMIS — [*To Tarsih.*] Hey, you, come over here. The Subdistrict Head wants to talk to you.

TARSIH — [*Swinging her hips as she walks toward Kumis.*] Want some action?

KUMIS — [*Taking Tarsih by the hand.*] Sshh, be a bit respectful.

TARSIH — Take your dirty hands off me. If I start talking about what you're up to, then you'll know about it.

KUMIS — Little bitch.

SUBDISTRICT HEAD — Do you want to be this kind of woman, Tarsih?

TARSIH — Hey, you know my name!

SUBDISTRICT HEAD [*Embarrassed.*] Yes, er, yes I do.

KASIJAH Read it in the newspaper, I suppose.

TARSIH Well I guess we are pretty well known.

PROSTITUTE 1 [*Laughing and pointing at the Subdistrict Head.*] He's the Subdistrict Head, so don't go pulling his willy . . . I mean, his leg!

TARSIH Stop that—you're embarrassing the man.

SUBDISTRICT HEAD But seriously: don't you think about your future, Tarsih?

TARSIH [*Resentful.*] I don't have a future. Everyone knows we don't have a future. It's only people of your sort who have futures. [*In declamatory style.*] Prostitutes of Jakarta, unite!

SUBDISTRICT HEAD Do you really think that's true?

TARSIH Yeah, it's true. You work hard, and you might get a promotion. But us? The older we get, the fewer clients we have. We pay taxes, too! We work our guts out, rocking this way and that, while Kumis here and people like him keep demanding *payments* in kind. And if we say we want to quit, what are we going to do?

SUBDISTRICT HEAD There are plenty of other types of work. In factories, in offices . . . A pretty woman like you doesn't have to work like this.

TARSIH And supposing we weren't here, how would people like Kumis get their rocks off? Men like that . . .

KUMIS [*Muttering.*] Me again, me again. What have I done wrong?

TARSIH I was told to tell the truth. Now I answer truthfully and you get offended.

SUBDISTRICT HEAD All right, all right. [*To Tarsih.*] Can you speak English?

TARSIH If I could, do you think I'd be in this place? With English I could charge more, maybe work out of a fancy hotel. It'd be heck of a lot nicer, a lot less hassle, than it is here. That's for sure. Around here you and your kind are always picking on us—those of us without power, the weak, people without connections.

SUBDISTRICT HEAD I'll make a note of that. Your plight will be looked into. Just be patient—

TARSIH [*Angrily.*] So what's the use of you coming here, inspecting us? Give us a proper job, and you're damn right we'll stop being whores. But don't just talk and make inspections. It's noted, you'll look into our plight . . . Bullshit, all of it!

KUMIS — We'd better go, sir. It's getting a little hot here. If anything happens, I'll get the blame.

SUBDISTRICT HEAD — Your plight will be looked into . . .

The Subdistrict Head and his party leave. Whistles accompany their departure. A spotlight falls on Tarsih.

TARSIH — [*Begins to sing.*]
They always come here
Pretending to care
While waiting for their chance
They keep on coming,
But only make wider
The gap that separates us
For what do they come?

Lights return to normal.

KASIJAH — Don't let it get you down. We did our best and said what we wanted to say. Maybe it won't work, but at least we got our feelings off our chest.

TARSIH — It just makes me so mad.

KASIJAH — Mad? You aren't mad. You're just doing what you have to do.

TARSIH — But I don't feel right.

KASIJAH — [*Sympathetically.*] Don't worry about it. You'll be yourself soon. [*Two veiled figures enter and approach.*] Look at those guys, Tarsih. They're probably looking for you.

VEILED FIGURE 1 — [*Approaches Tarsih.*] Got some time?

KASIJAH — What's it to you if she does?

VEILED FIGURE 1 — I'm talking to her, not you.

KASIJAH — Well I'm speaking for her.

VEILED FIGURE 1 — What are you? Her pimp?

KASIJAH — Get out of here.

VEILED FIGURE 1 — If you're not, keep your mouth shut. She can answer for herself. [*To Tarsih.*] Are you available or not? If you are, my boss here wants you. And if he's satisfied, you won't have to worry about how much he pays.

TARSIH — [*Proceeds down the riverbank, swinging her hips as she goes. Looking back.*] Come on.

Veiled Figure 1 whispers something to Veiled Figure 2, who nods and follows Tarsih. Veiled Figure 1 then squats on his haunches at a slight distance from Kasijah.

KASIJAH And what about you?

VEILED FIGURE 1 Leave me alone.

KASIJAH What are you anyway, a nurse, wearing a veil like that?

VEILED FIGURE 1 One more word and I'll punch you.

Kasijah restrains her temper and lights a cigarette, but then approaches Veiled Figure 1. When Veiled Figure 1 is not looking, she whips off his veil. Both Kasijah and Veiled Figure 1 are surprised.

KASIJAH It's you, the Subdistrict Head's secretary. And the one who went down there is—

SECRETARY I'll get you!

Kasijah starts to run away, followed by the Subdistrict Head's Secretary.

KASIJAH If you're the secretary, the other one must be . . . the Subdistrict Head!

SECRETARY Damn you, I'll get you!

Scene Ten

Same night. Different place. Julini and Tibal are cuddling.

JULINI A sliver of moon in the sky, smiling at us, as if to bless our newfound love.

TIBAL You're so romantic.

JULINI There are no clouds, only stars. The water of the river gleams like gold. Nothing can disrupt our intimacy.

TIBAL It's like poetry.

JULINI Our love will be eternal, united like the moon and its beams. You're the first real man I've met. You know what I want. You're my Gatotkaca, my Arjuna, my Superman. Our love will shine forth forever.

TIBAL But look at the moon. It's dark now, covered by a cloud.

JULINI A cloud?

Roima creeps along in the darkness toward Tibal.

TIBAL Maybe it's going to rain.

JULINI Don't leave me. I'm afraid of being alone. If you were to leave, to whom would I turn? Roima is iron, but you are gold. Roima is a nasturtium, but you're an orchid. Roima is a vulture, but you're an eagle.

ROIMA [*Unable to listen anymore, jumps out of his hiding place.*] Well, the vulture is here, looking for dead meat. Where's the corpse?

JULINI [*To Tibal.*] God help us! Your feeling was right. [*To Roima.*] Forgive me, Roima, forgive me. Don't hurt him.

ROIMA Who said anything about hurting him? I want you to go home.

JULINI No way, not if you're going to be so rough.

ROIMA Now, girl, go! I've been looking all over for you.

JULINI Only if you promise you won't hit him.

ROIMA Why should I? The one on the make was you, not him.

JULINI So you're going to beat me up?

ROIMA Not here.

JULINI Well then, I don't want to go home. I'm still free to do as I want. We're not husband and wife yet, are we? We're not bound to one another. If you want to find another guy, or another girl, I won't object.

ROIMA Then what do you want?

JULINI Marry me, and I'll be faithful forever.

ROIMA We'll talk about it at home.

JULINI But what do you think about getting married?

ROIMA I told you, slut, we'll talk about it at home. And if you won't walk on your own two feet, I'll drag you there. It'll make a nice show for the kids around here.

JULINI No, I won't go.

ROIMA You've got to. [*To Tibal.*] And as for you, slimeball, don't try moving in on Julini again. She's not yours to move in on.

TIBAL Whose is she? Yours?

ROIMA That's none of your business, bastard. Do you want to fight about it?

JULINI — Stop! I'll come home.

ROIMA — That's better.

JULINI — [*Exits in panic, muttering.*] Damn the luck, having a thug for a boyfriend.

ROIMA — [*Shouting.*] One more time, and I'll show you what trouble is. [*Exits.*]

Tibal sits, thinking. Tuminah enters.

TUMINAH — Tibal . . .

TIBAL — Oh, you're here.

TUMINAH — I was worried that something might have happened to you.

TIBAL — Been here all along?

TUMINAH — Mmmm.

TIBAL — Let's go home.

Tuminah and Tibal exit. The lights slowly dim.

Scene Eleven

Night. The prostitution complex.

KUMIS — You're always saying no. Do you have a new boyfriend?

TARSIH — What business is it of yours?

KUMIS — I've got money now. I can pay my old debts twice over and give you whatever price you ask.

TARSIH — I don't need your dirty money.

KUMIS — How do you know it's dirty?

TARSIH — Because it's from the sweat of other people's labor, that's how. You've no right to it. You sit twiddling your thumbs all day and rake in the cash.

BLEKI — Just take her, boss. What's she going to do about it?

TARSIH — If you try to force me, I'll report you to the Subdistrict Head.

KUMIS — Oh, so he's one of your clients now, is he? How can I possibly compete?

KASIJAH — That's right. How indeed?

BLEKI — Shut up when the boss is talking.

TARSIH — And supposing he is, what're you going to do about it?

KUMIS	I wouldn't doubt that he is. Just look at his wife, the old witch. After having a taste of you, he's not going to go back to that. [*The Subdistrict Head and his Secretary enter in veils. Kumis, ignoring their presence, continues to talk.*] The Subdistrict Head... Tell me, can he keep it up like me? Two or three minutes at best and he's snoring. And he has a bad heart, you know. If he had a heart attack, you could find yourself charged with murder. [*Veiled Figure 1 coughs.*] What are you coughing about? I'm in charge of security here. If I've got business with this woman, you stay quiet. Or come back later, when I've finished. [*Veiled Figure 2 approaches Kumis and lifts his veil to reveal his face. It is the Subdistrict Head. Kumis steps back in astonishment.*] Yes, sir.
SUBDISTRICT HEAD	I'll see you at my office.
KUMIS	Yes, sir.
SUBDISTRICT HEAD	Now clear off and don't make trouble.
KUMIS	Yes, sir. Come on, Bleki. It's time for our rounds.
BLEKI	Who was that, sir? Do you want me to beat him up?
KUMIS	[*Pulling Bleki along.*] Don't argue, idiot. Come along.

Kumis and Bleki exit, accompanied by whistles from the Prostitutes. The Subdistrict Head and Secretary take Tarsih by the hand and lead her to her hut.

Scene Twelve

Night. On the bridge. Kumis and Bleki are engaged in conversation.

KUMIS	Shit! Blast it! Damn it to hell!
BLEKI	What's wrong? Do you need my help?
KUMIS	What am I going to do now? My head feels like it's been hit by a bomb and blown to pieces.
BLEKI	Just tell me who did it. I'll smash in his face.
KUMIS	Maybe I should kill myself—jump off this bridge.
BLEKI	Wait a minute, sir. It can't be that bad. Tell me what the trouble is. And while we're at it, who was that veiled man? You looked, well, you looked...
KUMIS	Scared shitless? You bet I was. That was the Subdistrict Head.
BLEKI	Lord Almighty!

Scene Thirteen

Night. Abung is crouched in his tree.

ABUNG — I am everywhere, present in every event. But what role am I playing now? Am I the lead or just a bit player, present to make the suffering more complete? I know what's going on, but not what to do about it, because that's not in the script. I feel myself outside events. And after a while, it's no fun being a spectator. [*To the sky.*] Who must I turn to? Where? Tell me. Shit, shit, shit!

Abung moves from one tree to another. The lights fade.

Scene Fourteen

The Subdistrict Head's office. Kumis and Bleki have come to report to the Subdistrict Head.

SUBDISTRICT HEAD — [*To Kumis.*] Send your guard dog off to the other room. His face gives me the creeps. This is a matter between me and you as my subordinate.

BLEKI — [*Angry but helpless.*] All right, I'm going. [*Starts to leave.*] Such is the fate of a subordinate, to always be at the bottom. Come to think of it, being a "sub-ordinate," what hope do we have of getting on top? [*Finds a place to sit and gets ready to sleep.*]

SUBDISTRICT HEAD — These are my orders, which you will carry out whether you want to or not. On the first of March, three months from now, the Governor is going to inspect this area. He'll be coming here with the District Head and the Mayor. I've been ordered to clean up this area, and now I am ordering you to clean it up, without fear or favor. Get rid of the squatters' huts, the prostitutes' shacks, and the gambling dens. Raze them to the ground. How you do it is your own affair. If you do your job well, you might get a promotion, a raise. That's all I have to say.

KUMIS — Yes, sir, but Tarsih's beat is in that area, too, sir.

SUBDISTRICT HEAD — The whole area, I said. Don't talk to me about Tarsih. She's not the same Tarsih any longer. She has a whole new outlook on life because of me.

KUMIS — What do you mean, sir?

SUBDISTRICT HEAD — That is none of your business, Kumis. You just carry out my orders. Give the people a couple of months to prepare for the move. Any building without a permit is to be torn down. Understood?

KUMIS Yes, sir. Um, why is the Governor inspecting the area?

SUBDISTRICT HEAD Because it's an important state task. Because . . . Oh, how do I know? What I do know is that he's going to make an inspection. Full stop. That's it.

KUMIS Yes, sir.

SUBDISTRICT HEAD So when can I expect you to begin?

KUMIS As soon as the funds for the operation come through, I'll start right away. There'll have to be a feasibility study first, and how much that will cost is hard to calculate . . .

SUBDISTRICT HEAD Nonsense. You are to get going within a week at the latest. Next Monday I will have your report.

KUMIS Yes, sir. I'll start at once, sir.

SUBDISTRICT HEAD Then go. Talking to you makes me feel like I'm on a battlefield, even though all you've got for a weapon is an old handgun. Off with you.

KUMIS Yes, sir. [*Leaves the Subdistrict Head's office and finds Bleki sleeping outside.*] Wake up, you idiot.

BLEKI Yes, sir. Ready, sir. Where to, sir?

KUMIS You do nothing but sleep.

BLEKI Yes, sir. But I wasn't asleep, sir.

KUMIS Well, what were you doing?

BLEKI Meditating, sir.

KUMIS We're going to . . . Gad, I get tired of talking to you. It's like being on a battlefield. All that military respect and crap, even though you don't even have a blunderbuss. All you got is a worn-out stick. Let's go.

BLEKI Yes, sir.

KUMIS And shut your trap.

BLEKI Yes— [*Stops himself from saying more.*]

Kumis and Bleki exit. The lights fade.

Scene Fifteen

Night. One week later. Roima and Julini are talking in front of their hut.

ROIMA We haven't spoken to each other for a week. I've had it. I want to find out what it is you really want. This is wrong, that's wrong . . . I can't seem to do anything right. Do you think it's fun for me living under the same roof with a walking statue?

JULINI If I'm really like that, why do you want me? I told you long ago to give me some kind of commitment. That's all. Do you think I want my fate to hang in the balance like this forever? For you I'm just a picnic basket that you take wherever you go. There's food in that basket, but you never want to eat it. If you leave it too long, I'm telling you, it's going to go bad.

ROIMA Talk straight, would you? Your metaphors give me a headache.

JULINI But if I tell you what I want, you won't want to do it, so what's the use of telling you what I want?

ROIMA Before you've said what you want, you're telling me what I won't want. Come on . . .

JULINI But you won't want to, I know you won't.

ROIMA Tell me.

JULINI You won't marry me, will you?

ROIMA Who said I won't?

JULINI Then you will?

ROIMA Of course.

JULINI You won't be ashamed?

ROIMA No.

JULINI Really?

ROIMA I swear.

JULINI Then when?

ROIMA It's up to you.

JULINI [*Emotionally.*] Oh, Roima, that's the most romantic thing I've ever heard you say. It's like a voice from heaven. You're not fooling me, are you?

ROIMA Make the arrangements. Choose an auspicious day.

JULINI [*Excitedly.*] I'm going to get married! Jumini, Turkana, Sawil, Bilun! I'm getting married! The moon has come down to greet me. I've won the lottery.

Julini's shouts wake all of the area's inhabitants. Wedding music starts to play. People put on their best clothes. Julini is suddenly dressed in a Betawi-style wedding outfit, as is Roima, who dons a fez and all the trimmings. Roima also sports dark glasses, a gold waistcoat, and a crown, as well as a gold belt and sword. The music accompanying the ceremony is a combination of tanjidor, gambang kromo, disco, and dangdut music. The scene is lively as the guests enter to greet the bride and groom. Julini looks extraordinarily happy, but Roima seems gloomy. Tarsih comes forward to sing.

TARSIH

A drop of happiness
Dissolves without a trace
In a wallow of filth and pus
What meaning has a drop of happiness?

The sky is full of hate
The sun strikes and attacks
The moon and stars are but distant friends
What meaning has a drop of happiness?

We are moths in the lamplight
Trapped by the certainties of Fate
Which laughs as we flutter and struggle
What meaning has a drop of happiness?

This song of mine is a tuneless song
A song of the rejects
The hopeless and hungry beggars
The bird who pines for the moon

My song is a tuneless song
Tuneless, tuneless, tuneless

[*The crowd joins in.*]
Tuneless, tuneless, tuneless.

Fireworks explode. Kumis and Bleki appear. The wedding party continues gaily, spontaneously, until Kumis and Bleki step forward.

KUMIS — Stop it! Stop the party now! I've got good news. Stop the music.

BLEKI — [*While bustling about.*] Hey, stop the music. Stop the dancing. I'll shoot you if you don't stop.

The merrymaking finally ceases. Everyone looks at Kumis and Bleki.

KUMIS — It's good luck that you're all gathered here, because I have some good news. The Governor is going to visit this area. So, as usual, he wants the area cleaned up. He wants your huts cleared. As long as you have a building permit, there's no need to knock it down. All the rubbish around here has to go. Everything stinking or rotten must go. There will be no compromise, because this order comes from the highest quarters!

As the protector of this area, I will try to act kindly. I don't want you to have to move out of here in a panic. I don't want any of the old folks here worrying so much that they keel over from exhaustion. We have to work together and help one another. You have a month to clean this place up. That's reasonable, isn't it? You can tear down the huts gradually, piece by piece, if you want. Where you move is up to you. The main thing is that I've passed down my orders. The rest of it you can work out for yourselves. Understand? Whether you understand or not, do it! Remember: one month. Don't forget. So, go on with the party.

JULINI [*To Kumis.*] Are you going to let me get married or not?

KUMIS Oh, this is a wedding party, is it? Who's getting married? You? Who to? This man? Are you all mad? A man marrying a man? Where's the minister? Do you have a marriage license? Hmmm, how very modern. I could take you in for this, you know. You could be charged with creating a disturbance. [*Changing his attitude.*] But not to worry, not to worry, as long as there's something to, how shall we say, smooth things over. [*Chuckling.*] But after that, get out of here. If there's a check from up above, I could get in trouble.

Bleki is given cigarettes and money. He and Kumis help themselves to the food, after which they leave.

JULINI [*Fed up.*] The bastards!

BLEKI [*Suddenly appears again.*] Remember: one month! [*Exits.*]

One of the Diners leaves his place at the table to urinate in the public lavatory below. Julini and Roima sit in dumbfounded silence. The lights change.

JULINI This could be a bad omen. Just when I start to taste happiness, we're told to leave.

ROIMA Omen or not, our luck's never going to change.

JULINI This marriage of ours... Maybe it's not for the best. You've looked sour about it from the start.

ROIMA It's just that I realized that, no matter what, you're always going to be a man. Even with a sex change, you'd still be a man. Can your organs be made into a womb? We'll never have children.

JULINI — I know that. But what's the use of tormenting yourself? You're still young. Maybe we shouldn't marry.

ROIMA — Maybe that would be better.

JULINI — So we should separate?

ROIMA — Yes, better to follow our own paths.

Julini begins to cry.

There's no need to be sad. That's the way of the world. Nothing is eternal.

JULINI — I know, I know...

The lights change again. The Diner, having finished urinating, climbs back up to his place in the restaurant. He appears completely oblivious to the happenings around him. The people under the bridge watch his every move. The lights slowly fade till blackout.

Scene Sixteen

Night. At the guardhouse. Tibal and Tuminah have come to see Kumis. Bleki, who is supposed to be keeping watch, is nodding off.

TIBAL — You're saying we can't stay here any longer. That's it, isn't it?

KUMIS — That's not what I said. I said the place has to be cleaned up.

TIBAL — Then what about my field? It won't be ready to harvest for another two months.

KUMIS — [*As if not hearing what Tibal has said, picks up a wad of money.*] So this is the deposit? It's all there, no tricks?

TIBAL — Everything is written down. You can check my records if you want.

KUMIS — No, I trust you. [*Handing the money to Bleki.*] Count it.

BLEKI — What's this?

KUMIS — Just count it, don't ask questions. You'll get your ten percent.

BLEKI — Yes, sir. Right away, sir. [*Counts the money.*]

TIBAL — [*To Kumis.*] What I'm asking for is a concession. I don't care if our hut has to go, as long as the field is left untouched.

KUMIS — Fine, no problem, as long as there's a kickback. Come here, I'll tell you what I'd like.

Tibal goes up to Kumis, who whispers something in his ear. Tibal's face suddenly goes red.

There, I knew you wouldn't like it. Well, okay, that's out, but don't think you're going to be able to stay around here any longer.

TIBAL — [*To Kumis.*] You filthy sack of maggots. [*To Tuminah.*] Come on, Tum, we're going. [*Drags Tuminah out of the guardhouse.*]

KUMIS — You got three days! After that, don't expect my door to be open. And you can clear out, the whole lot of you.

Tuminah and Tibal exit. The lights in the guardhouse dim.

Scene Seventeen

The same night. A light shines on Tuminah and Tibal as they make their way home.

TUMINAH — What did he say to you?

TIBAL — Shut up.

TUMINAH — I want to know. What did Kumis ask for in return for letting us stay?

TIBAL — Shut up, I said.

TUMINAH — I'll shut up if you tell me what Kumis wants. We can work harder if we have to. I don't want to see that field cleared either. We've put too much work into it to let it be ripped up. I'll do whatever I can to prevent that.

TIBAL — [*Exploding.*] He wants you, your virginity—that's what he wants! How could I accept that? How could I not get angry? If I'd been alone, I would have taken him on.

TUMINAH — [*Reflecting.*] He gave us three days to think about it. I heard him say that.

TIBAL — Let the field go. He's not going to have you. We can try our luck somewhere else. There's more to the world than this place. You go on home. I'm going to see a friend. Maybe he can give us work.

TUMINAH — But—

TIBAL — Go home and get some sleep!

Scene Eighteen

Night, a few hours later. At Tuminah's hut. Tuminah is making herself up to look as pretty as possible. Holding a little mirror in her hand, she puts on lipstick and then, looking into the mirror, begins to sing.

TUMINAH — For a worm like me
Is there another choice?

Though what is offered is poison,
Is there any other choice?

All over the world
Arrows are taut in their bows,
Knives and daggers are ready,
Always ready to wound.

Here and there, poison
Is there another choice?
Oh, is there any choice?

Tuminah goes off in the direction of Kumis's place. Bilun and Sawil enter, quarreling.

BILUN — I'm tired of counting. Counting and counting—all the time. What for? I've just begun to realize it's all for nothing.

SAWIL — If we didn't count, what would we do? What can we do besides count?

BILUN — We can stop.

SAWIL — How? When we die, that's when we can stop. Come on, let's count again. How much did you say for a bunch of onions? Three thousand rupiah? Think of it! If we bought them directly from the farmer for only six hundred, think of the profit we'd make on a truckload.

BILUN — Where's the money, the onions, the truck? Where?

SAWIL — They'll come later. Let's count the profits first. Money can be found. Think of it: a two-thousand-rupiah profit just on one bunch. If a truck holds two thousand bunches, that's two thousand times two thousand.

Sawil leaves, and Bilun is forced to follow. The lights change. Tuminah walks slowly back to her hut. The sound of a cane being struck against a metal pole is heard: it is the sound of the night watch. Kumis and Bleki are making their rounds.

BLEKI [*Loudly.*] Remember: one month after the announcement, these shacks must be demolished. If they aren't gone, they'll be burnt down. [*Softly while walking past Tuminah's hut.*] Tum ... are you asleep, Tum?

KUMIS Shut up, big mouth. If Tibal gets his hands on you, then you'll know.

BLEKI She's quite a girl, isn't she, sir?

KUMIS Shut your mouth.

BLEKI It's too bad I didn't get a share. Hmmm, quite a girl. [*Loudly.*] Remember: you got one month!

Bleki and Kumis exit. Tibal appears and wearily approaches his hut. He looks troubled and sits down in front of the hut. A moment later, Tuminah comes out.

TIBAL [*To Tuminah.*] Aren't you asleep yet?

TUMINAH Any luck?

TIBAL [*Shaking his head.*] I didn't go anywhere in the end. Where was there to go? We don't have any friends. What with the field already planted, I'm out quite a lot. I don't want to see it cleared.

TUMINAH It won't be cleared.

TIBAL What? [*Suddenly noticing her appearance.*] What's going on? You've got your good clothes on, and you're wearing lipstick ... Where did you go? Tell me: where have you been?

TUMINAH I went to see Kumis.

TIBAL You mean you ...

TUMINAH Yes, I did, and now we won't have to move. After the Governor's inspection, we can stay here, build a hut and farm.

TIBAL You, you ... [*Screaming.*] Goddamnit! What has all my work been for? For what? For who?

TUMINAH Don't worry, it didn't hurt. The important thing is that you can work in peace.

TIBAL [*Wearily.*] Ours is a rotten lot.

The lights dim.

Scene Nineteen

The same place. A few days later.

ROIMA — Yeah, ours is a rotten lot.

JUMINI — Never have it easy. Always up against it.

JULINI — We try hard, but it never seems to get any better.

KASIJAH — A good life . . . It always seems far from our grasp. Well, at least Tarsih got out. She won't be coming back.

JUMINI — What do you mean?

KASIJAH — The Subdistrict Head asked her to be his second wife. No need for her to work anymore. She has a house and money every month. She can have a decent life while we kill ourselves just to make a cent. And then we have those bastards, always breathing down our necks.

JUMINI — So what about it, Jul? Roima? Have you made up your minds? Gosh, this might be the last time we meet.

Turkana, who is seated off to the side, looks on but says nothing.

JULINI — If . . . we don't go, what will we do? Yeah, Roima and I are leaving together, but to different destinations.

JUMINI — Where are you going, Roima? And what about you, Julini?

ROIMA — I don't know yet.

JUMINI — We'll miss you.

TURKANA — We'll be scattered everywhere. Where will we all end up?

ROIMA — Are you ready?

JULINI — With steeled heart!

ROIMA — Let's go.

Julini nods. As Roima and Julini shake hands with their friends, the song "Auld Lang Syne" plays on percussion and gamelan. Roima and Julini's friends wave their hands in unison as the couple leaves. Sawil appears, counting his steps as he walks. Bilun, following close behind, drags along a sack.

SAWIL — One, two, three, four, five, seven, nine . . .

With Bilun still dragging his sack behind him, the pair exits. With the exception of Jumini and Turkana, the others leave. The Diners up above relax around the dinner table. Abung is reading a book. The Singer appears at the window of the hotel and begins to sing.

SINGER
In the sky, so many stars
And a sliver of moon, peeking
Like a young girl's breasts
On her wedding night

Bleki and Kumis, who are still on their rounds, walk past.

BLEKI
Remember: you had one month. Now there's one week left. This area must be cleaned up. Remember: one month. In one week, time is up.

Bleki and Kumis exit. A darkened figure—Tibal—follows them silently, keeping out of sight. For a moment the stage is silent. Abung then begins to read aloud from his book.

ABUNG
Everyone knows that we have the right to ask. And the right to get a reply. Everyone knows that if we ask questions, it's not because we're trying to light the fires of rebellion. If we ask questions, it's not because we're disloyal. If we ask what our real role is, it's not because we're distrustful. [*Closing the book.*] But now, almost no one knows to whom they must address their questions.

TURKANA
It's lonely now, what with Tarsih and all the others gone away.

JUMINI
There's still Abung and that singer. And Sawil and Bilun pass by now and then.

TURKANA
Another week, Bleki says. What about us?

JUMINI
Does anything have to change? We'll stay here. When the Governor comes, we'll tell him what we're doing. If he brings in troops to drive us out, we'll tell them the truth: that we're here to look at the moon. There's no regulation against looking at the moon.

TURKANA
Looking at the moon all the time . . . Aren't you tired of it? Deceiving yourself . . . Haven't you had enough? This game consumes our time, our strength, our thoughts. It has to stop.

JUMINI
Tibal and Tuminah are still here.

TURKANA
That's their business.

JUMINI
Well, we have our own business, too.

TURKANA
Looking at the moon? I've had it!

JUMINI [*Emotionally.*] Whatever you want to say, say it. Tell me that Sueb will never come back. That he didn't go to Lampung to raise cloves. That he ran off with another woman and took my baby with him.

TURKANA Jum...

JUMINI [*More emotionally.*] Do you want to tell me that I'll never be able to forget Sueb? Or that your patience is exhausted? That you're going to leave me just as Sueb left me?

TURKANA Jum...

JUMINI Tell me that I have no self-respect, waiting for a man who's taken another woman for a wife. Say it if you want to. It's not that I'm not tired. I'm tired, too. I don't care about Sueb, but my baby—he's my boy. Why did Sueb take him from me? I don't want him raised by another woman. I want them to come back... [*Crying.*] I know it's not possible. Of course I know. I don't even know where they are. But the moon knows. She always smiles whenever she appears in the sky. She knows everything that happens on the face of the earth, and I ask her. I ask her...

TURKANA [*Softly.*] It's hard for a man not to lose his patience when he keeps coming up against a brick wall. I promised that I would follow you wherever you went. Forgive me. Go on doing whatever you want to do. I won't pester you again.

Jumini goes into the hut.

Jum, Jum...

Turkana goes into Jumini's hut. The lights slowly dim.

Scene Twenty

Night. Bleki, Kumis, and Tuminah are inside the guardhouse. Outside, Tibal lurks in the shadows. Kumis begins to sing.

KUMIS A sad face, a heart full of woe
Whatever for?

A perfumed body, satisfying one's needs
What else could one ask for?

What's the meaning of purity
If, when the lights go out,
All one knows is pleasure?

Tuminah, Tuminah... your virginity was so precious to

you. But when you were with me, in my bed, you were panting just as hard as I was. What took place between us cannot be called rape. You wanted it, too.

[*Singing again.*]
For the first three minutes you rejected me
For the next three your tongue assaulted me
I felt myself caught between two hills

[*Chuckling.*] Turn out the lights, Bleki, and wait outside.

BLEKI — [*Appears drunk.*] Yes, sir. I'm ready for my prize.

KUMIS — The only prize for a dog like you is my drool. [*Spitting.*] Now get out.

Bleki leaves the guardhouse to slump outside the door. Kumis slams the door shut. As the lights fade, Bleki can be heard muttering under his breath.

BLEKI — [*In sing-song fashion.*] The first three minutes, it was "Oh, stop, don't!" But for the next three minutes, "Oh, don't stop!" [*Chuckles.*]

The lights fade to black.

Scene Twenty-One

Night. The prostitution complex. Deserted, except for Kasijah, who sits, smoking. Tarsih enters, looking tired and unsteady on her feet.

KASIJAH — [*Surprised.*] Tarsih! What happened?

TARSIH — There's no rest for people like us. For a while there I thought I could be happy. I had a house and monthly support. But now it's all gone.

KASIJAH — What happened?

TARSIH — The Subdistrict Head's first wife came to my place with two soldiers and kicked me out. She took everything her husband had ever given me and treated me no better than a beggar.

[*Half singing, half screaming.*]
Hurt, what can I do?
Hurt, that's our lot
Hurt, hurt, hurt

KASIJAH — I thought it was only me who had a hard time, every day having to drink the piss of layabouts. But it looks like you've been through it, too. [*Laughing.*] I can just imagine the look on her face. And she brought soldiers?! [*Laughing.*] Why not an armored tank?

TARSIH [*Unemotionally.*] Life's never going to change.

KASIJAH [*Laughing harder.*] She pulled out your hair, scratched your face, and screamed that her twat's still clean and her moves still hot.

TARSIH [*Laughing, too.*] Gawd, she looked like a spook. And the way she dressed... like Minnie Mouse with a stomach the size of a hippopotamus.

KASIJAH And she had no teeth. She smelled, and her thighs hung in folds...

TARSIH / KASIJAH [*Singing together.*]
Butterflies of the night
Shining in the light of the moon
When the sun comes up
They turn to filth

KASIJAH That's us all right!

The two women sit down, wearily. Jumini enters, carrying her bundle of belongings. She looks wistfully up at the moon.

JUMINI A night talking to you slips by like a passing car. Without my realizing it, it's dawn already. We have to leave today. I see; you're not sad. You keep on smiling as if you don't care that one of your friends is going away. The eastern star is beside you, and in a moment the sun will come up and outshine your light. I must say good-bye. Turkana says that this little game of ours is useless. And maybe it's true. I'll think about it as he and I travel along.

I know that after I've gone it will be hard to find again what we enjoyed this year. Maybe you won't be able to see anymore your face mirrored on the surface of the river. Maybe no one will pester you with questions. No one will care about the beauty of your light. No one, only me... [*Begins to cry. Turkana comes up quietly behind her, carrying a suitcase.*] In a different place I may not be able to—may not want to—look at you again. Because, I know, it's only here that you can smile. In another place you might cry. I've never seen your tears.

TURKANA [*Softly.*] Don't start again.

JUMINI — Oh, it's time. You're not yellow anymore but white. By day you're nothing but a corpse, unwilling to reveal the beauty of your face. Yes, now I'm ready.

TURKANA — That's enough. Dreaming can be sweet, but working is surely sweeter. We'll go back to our village and work. And not because we're defeated . . . Because this is not our place.

JUMINI — All right, I'm ready.

The day progresses. From a distance comes the sound of Bleki shouting.

Scene Twenty-Two

Morning. Outside Jumini and Turkana's hut. Kumis and Bleki are supervising the demolition of the remaining shacks. Tuminah remains silent in her hut.

BLEKI — We gave you one month, remember. Today, time is up.

KUMIS — There's no need for talk. Just get to work.

BLEKI — You mean clear everyone out?

Abung peers down.

KUMIS — Yes, everyone.

TURKANA — [*To Jumini.*] Are you ready?

JUMINI — [*Adjusting her bundle.*] Yes.

TURKANA — You knock these places down, Kumis, and I hope you're struck by lightning. Even without you driving us away, we would have left, one by one. How are we supposed to resist our rotten destiny? Jumini and I will go somewhere or other. And someday, who knows, we might come back.

KUMIS — [*To Bleki.*] Don't just stare. Demolish these shacks.

BLEKI — Yes, sir. [*Starts tearing down the shacks.*]

KUMIS — [*To Turkana.*] You hate me, don't you?

TURKANA — Hate you? What for? There will always be people like you. And people like those up there who can only eat, drink, shit, and pee. And people like us who are ready to be buried, to become the foundation on which things are built—we, too, will always exist. Why should we hate? We're shadow puppets. What we do is up to the puppeteer.

ABUNG — [*Shouting.*] Like puppets! And I'm a puppet who remains forever in his box and never appears on the screen. What am I?

TURKANA — Let's go, Jum. If we talk too long, they'll think we're making a speech. Speeches are given by officials, not by nobodies like us. Our duty is to listen.

Turkana and Jumini exit. Bleki approaches Tuminah's hut.

TUMINAH — You're going to tear down my place, too?

BLEKI — [*To Kumis.*] Sir?

KUMIS — Tear it down.

TUMINAH — What about your promise? I gave you what you wanted, and you're still going to drive us out?

KUMIS — I didn't promise you anything. [*To Bleki.*] Tear it down.

TIBAL — [*Dragged in by guards.*] They've torn up our field, Tum.

TUMINAH — And they're tearing down our house.

GUARD — Shut up, idiot, shut up!

KUMIS — Don't stop, Bleki. One down, all down. We can't play favorites.

TUMINAH — But you promised.

KUMIS — I never promised anything.

TIBAL — [*Exploding.*] My field is gone. What was Tuminah sleeping with you for? Son of a bitch!

The Subdistrict Head, his Secretary, and several Guards enter. Tibal's outburst is quickly quashed.

SUBDISTRICT HEAD — Is that man resisting? Arrest him. Put that madman in jail.

With his hands tied behind him, Tibal looks at them with vengeance in his eyes. Tuminah cries. The Singer at the hotel window belts out his song.

SINGER — In the sky, so many stars
And a sliver of moon, peeking
Like a young girl's breasts
On her wedding night

KUMIS — Jesus, that singer is still here. Tear down that hotel, Bleki. And throw that singer into the river. I'm going to go deaf from his screeching.

A black cloth falls over the Singer, silencing him.

TIBAL — Maybe we can't do anything now, Tum. But later, when the time comes for people like us, then they'll be sorry. I swear they'll regret it.

KUMIS — Regret it? In what way? There will always be the army, police, and civil guards. Power can move from one hand to another, but police, soldiers, and civil guards will always be needed. We will always be here. If I weren't here, someone else would be. And in the name of order, guards have a right to act tough. You come here, set up house, and say that all this is yours, that we're not to interfere. What grounds are there to prevent us from driving you out? Take this man away. And the woman, too. Hand her over to the police.

Tibal and Tuminah are taken off. Sawil is counting. Bilun drags a sack.

SAWIL — One, two, three, five, seven, nine, ten . . .

BILUN — Sawil, wait for me, Sawil.

The pair exit. Julini enters. She dances and sings for a moment, then begins to cry and laugh.

BLEKI — There sure are lots of loonies around here.

ABUNG — [*Exploding.*] And now is the moment when I shall find the answers! Who am I? Why am I here? What am I doing here? Why is everyone else given problems and worn away by them while I remain a puppet in the box? Who am I? What am I . . . ? [*Appears to go berserk. Climbs downs and begins to run after the Subdistrict Head.*]

KUMIS — He's going off again.

BLEKI — This is bad, sir. Should we shoot him?

SUBDISTRICT HEAD — [*Screams to his Secretary and Guards as Abung pursues him.*] Help! [*To Abung.*] What are you asking me questions for? I don't have the answers. Ask the Governor when he comes.

ABUNG — The Governor? One of those people up there who do nothing but eat?

SUBDISTRICT HEAD — The Governor hasn't come yet. What people? I don't see any people up there.

ABUNG — That's right—I must ask the people up there. People who eat a lot are sure to have the answers. You're stuffed—all of you—and all you can do is eat. You're hopeless. You've got no guts. Your brains are in your stomach. Stuff it. You won't even answer.

BLEKI — This is getting bad, boss. Do we shoot him or not?

KUMIS — Here's the pistol.

BLEKI I don't know if I can do this. [*Takes the pistol and aims. Just as Abung is about to reach him, the gun goes off. Abung is hit. He starts for a moment, then cries out.*]

ABUNG What am I? Is this me? Jakarta, Jakarta. Indonesia, Indonesia . . . It's always like that, always like that, but why does it *have* to be like that?

The others say nothing as Abung dies. One of the Diners turns on a radio. A radio announcer's voice can be heard faintly.

ANNOUNCER [*Offstage.*] Our deepest thanks to those who have made possible the holding of these general elections. With the completion of the elections, which have run almost a month in an atmosphere of order, calm, peace, and mutual respect, the outside world will know that we are a country that has successfully carried out our festival of democracy, that we are a country with respect for the rule of law. [*Gradually fades and is replaced by a pop song.*]

Why do you forget, darling
Do you want to remember, darling

The lyrics are repeated over and over. The record appears to be stuck. Final blackout. Curtain.

Translation by Barbara Hatley

PUTU WIJAYA

Ought

Translator's Note: Pronouns are not gender specific in Indonesian. In fact, the playwright purposefully employs this characteristic as a source of humor and ambiguity. Therefore, the use of he/she or his/her in this English translation is arbitrary.

Cast of Characters

Sick One
Sympathetic One / Possessed One
Propositioner
Balsam Owner
Brave One
Envious One
Leader
Pathfinder
Angry One
Spokesperson
The One
The Other
Cucumber Eater
Investigator

Act One

A large group of people is engaged in activity, which stops suddenly when a siren goes off. The siren begins quietly, then gets louder and louder until it is deafening. The group waits for something to happen. And waits. Gradually the siren fades away. Emptiness. The people look around. One person laughs. Others join in. They resume their activity but are interrupted by the arrival of the Sick One wrapped in a blanket. This new arrival appears to be both mentally and physically ill, and advances as if wanting to complain to the group.

SOMEONE What's wrong?

Untitled,
Yogyakarta, 2011.
Kurniadi Widodo

Through gestures, the Sick One indicates his condition is worsening. A different Someone then addresses him.

SOMEONE What is it? Are you sick?

SOMEONE [*Together or individually.*] What's wrong? What hurts?

Because the Sick One doesn't answer, the crowd carefully and sympathetically examines him. Then they launch again into a series of questions.

SOMEONE Are you sick?

SOMEONE Do you have a cold?

SOMEONE A fever? Dizziness?

SOMEONE It's probably epilepsy.

The Sick One moans.

SOMEONE What's wrong? Out with it. Don't be shy, we want to help you.

SOMEONE Poor thing. See how old his face looks. Could be from overwork. Have you eaten yet?

SOMEONE It's windy here, and what with this weather, you'll likely pass out if you don't eat. You really shouldn't be here!

SOMEONE You'd better go home or to the hospital. There's a hospital if you walk due north of here for about one kilometer. Straight that way.

SOMEONE It's probably a better idea to rent a buggy or use public transport. What's a little money out of pocket if you're less than well? And alone too.

SOMEONE Are you alone?

The Sick One groans pathetically.

SOMEONE What hurts? What is it? What?

SOMEONE What did he say?

SOMEONE He doesn't look like he's from around here.

SOMEONE Where are you from? The mountains? The islands?

SOMEONE Maybe he's Javanese.

SOMEONE Try speaking to him in Javanese!

Someone asks a question in Javanese.

SOMEONE — No, he's not!

SOMEONE — Don't be afraid. No one is trying to trick you. Don't be afraid, we want to help.

Someone asks another question in Javanese.

SOMEONE — No, he's not Javanese.

The Sick One tries to speak.

SOMEONE — That's right! Don't be scared. Is it your stomach? Your chest? Your feet?

SOMEONE — He's probably deaf. [*Yells.*] What hurts? Hey! What hurts?

SOMEONE — See! He heard that!

SOMEONE — Maybe he's mute!

Someone asks a question using sign language.

SOMEONE — Again! Do it again! That wasn't clear enough!

Someone repeats the sign language. Still no response.

SOMEONE — Hey, guys, maybe he just doesn't want to talk.

SOMEONE — Enough already. Quit bugging him.

SOMEONE — But he needs help, and right away.

SOMEONE — Definitely. He looks like shit.

SOMEONE — Well, I think that if he really needed help, he would have asked for it already. The fact is, he's just been silent no matter how many questions we ask.

SOMEONE — So, why did he come here if it wasn't to ask for help? What for, if not for help?

SOMEONE — He was just passing through.

SOMEONE — No way!

SOMEONE — Why not? His not talking proves it.

SOMEONE — No way, believe me.

SOMEONE — Maybe it is true. Come on, is everyone who passes by here supposed to ask for help?

SOMEONE — Maybe not, but this wasn't by chance. He came here on purpose.

SOMEONE — Let's hope he's not faking it like the other one!

SOMEONE — Hush! Don't be that way!

SOMEONE Yeah, yeah. Why indulge him?

SOMEONE This guy's sick. How's that indulging him?

SOMEONE He could be faking it like that other one!

SOMEONE Which other one? . . . Could be, but not this time.

SOMEONE How could he be faking it? Maybe he got out of a car . . . You know, just wanted to piss . . . And then, I don't know, the car just sped away . . . The others forgot him and now, you know, he's all confused because no one knows him here. It would be better if we took him to the hospital. Look!

The Sick One's condition deteriorates.

SOMEONE Damn, he looks like he's getting worse!

SOMEONE Looks fit to me. Just look at his body.

SOMEONE Yeah, yeah. If he's so fit, how come he's sick?

SOMEONE Hold on! He's not pale, not like someone who's sick. Look closely. Ha! See? Ha! He's faking it! This is that same guy again!

SOMEONE How could it be? He died.

SOMEONE Well, the same kind of guy then. Learn from experience, man!

The Sick One gets even worse.

SOMEONE Well, I'd say it's all in his head. He doesn't look sick, but he feels sick. Yeah, sure, sick my ass.

SOMEONE Quit fussing over this guy. He doesn't need help.

SOMEONE Exactly! Don't pay any attention to him. Come on! He's acting like that to get our attention. It's not our fault we're not sick. Is it our fault?

SOMEONE He's so over the top with that sick act of his . . . Please, give me a break!

SOMEONE He's wasting our time!

SOMEONE That's why we have to act quickly!

SOMEONE Yeah, right away!

SOMEONE Don't think about it too much, just do it. It'll be too late if you keep holding out. Should we call a taxi, the police, or just take him to the hospital?

SOMEONE No! We have other things to take care of.

SOMEONE — So, what's supposed to happen then? Should we just ignore him until he stops behaving like this? It's fucking annoying!

SOMEONE — Do that and people will say we didn't want to help.

SOMEONE — So what?

SOMEONE — Because people spout shit.

SOMEONE — You shouldn't care what other people say. That's the educated way of looking at things.

SOMEONE — Hey, hold on. Educated or not, that's another matter. This person needs our help, fast. Don't be a jerk. Another time, okay?

SOMEONE — Sure. So, what's the best thing to do? It all sounds well and good, but we don't want what happened before to happen again, right?

SOMEONE — Of course not. We have to be careful. We need to make sure it's not him. We don't want that happening again. Whether he's seriously ill or not, what's clear is that he needs help, and fast. We have to help quickly, right?

SOMEONE — Yes, the point is to be careful. The thing is, we have to show that we would feel obligated to help any creature that requests help—man or beast.

SOMEONE — I got it. Probably this is just some kind of misunderstanding . . . This guy didn't tell the driver when he wanted to get out. It's not our fault!

SOMEONE — What happened is not our fault, but we'll be blamed for it.

SOMEONE — Right, so listen to me: now it's our problem too.

SOMEONE — Our fault?

SOMEONE — Because we're going to help!

SOMEONE — Wait a minute!

SOMEONE — Huh?

SOMEONE — What did I just say? What I meant was that we could be blamed.

SOMEONE — Hey, that's what I meant.

SOMEONE — Look at it this way: don't think about who's wrong or who's right . . .

SOMEONE — Right, it's better to say that everyone's wrong and everyone's right!

SOMEONE That's fucked.

SOMEONE Look!

The Sick One gets worse.

SOMEONE [*Suspiciously.*] Oh yeah, yeah. Sure, sure!

SOMEONE Hey, look!

To everyone's amazement, the Sick One begins to moan.

SOMEONE Whoa!

SOMEONE Hey, he can talk!

The Sick One falls over.

SOMEONE Hey!

SOMEONE Enough already, maybe he really is sick. Could be malaria or even kidney stones. It's not nice to stare like that!

The Sick One tries to stand up.

SOMEONE He must be wondering why no one's helping him.

SOMEONE Or maybe he's embarrassed because his scam is up?

SOMEONE Or maybe he's really sick?

SOMEONE Wait. Maybe he has a trick up his sleeve.

The Sick One's attempt to stand fails.

SOMEONE Hey!

The Sick One tries to stand again and fails.

SOMEONE Hey!

SOMEONE Okay, enough! What is this? We're just going to stand around and watch?

SOMEONE So, do what?

SOMEONE Do something. Quickly!

SOMEONE Isn't this doing something?

SOMEONE Watching a sick guy?

SOMEONE Someone pretending to be sick!

SOMEONE So if he's faking it, just leave him alone. Why are you still watching him? Don't you have any feelings?

SOMEONE We're observers. Just observing if he's sick or faking being sick.

The Sick One begins crawling.

SOMEONE Poor thing . . .

SOMEONE Poor thing . . .

SOMEONE Poor thing! I'm not going to be scammed again!

The Sick One manages to stand up, but totters precariously. The group steps back.

SOMEONE Hey!

SOMEONE There, see: he got up all by himself. Just like that!

SOMEONE Little by little his true colors come out.

SOMEONE We almost fell into the same trap again. Hey, look!

SOMEONE Determined little motherfucker. The problem is we know where he's coming from. Didn't take us long to unmask him, did it? Maybe once we could have been shot like fish in a bucket, but not now.

SOMEONE But I think he's really sick! Look!

SOMEONE Well, he's certainly got the moves down pat. I'll give him that.

SOMEONE Which proves that he's the same guy as before. Amazing, he comes back again and again, and again and again we don't recognize this guy. We haven't learned shit. Remember, we were just about to help this guy.

SOMEONE Our memories are crap. What was his name?

They all try to remember, but can't.

SOMEONE It hasn't even been a year, not even two or three months, and we've forgotten it. What was his name?!

SOMEONE It was easy to say but hard to remember.

SOMEONE The problem is we're too busy. We don't pay attention to the details. We forget our friends' names—never mind the name of a stranger like this guy.

The Sick One totters forward.

SOMEONE Well, look at that! He walks.

SOMEONE Look at his feet. Looks like they've been chained. Wonder why.

SOMEONE He's probably an ex-con or some nut on the loose.

SOMEONE It's hard to believe he's sick if you don't look at his face.

SOMEONE Yeah.

SOMEONE Remember when we were scammed the last time? We were eating, and a beggar came by and asked for food? Yeah, we had food and we were eating it too. But we gave him a share anyway. And what did the others say when they saw us do that? Ooh, burns me up thinking about it and all, because we tried to help.

SOMEONE That's right, we shouldn't have even bothered.

SOMEONE Yeah! And now we almost get tricked again. Hey, check to see if there is anyone else around. If there is, you can be sure they'll say something to piss us off.

SOMEONE Hey, look! His hand's really hurt from crawling. And his face is getting paler.

SOMEONE You're right. We have to watch out for him.

SOMEONE Watch out, you say. So why all this talking? Do something. Quick!

SOMEONE I seriously dislike seeing someone sick like this guy. I really can't stand it!

SOMEONE But look. Look at him closely!

SOMEONE Don't pay any attention to him! He can get better all by himself if we just monitor the situation.

Moaning, the Sick One falls down.

SOMEONE Look at that!

SOMEONE His hand is bleeding!

SOMEONE Shit!

SOMEONE What should we do?

SOMEONE So, it's for real?

SOMEONE You see, it gets dangerous when there's an outsider involved.

The Sick One groans and rolls around on the ground.

SOMEONE Don't let him go over there! There's broken glass. [*Holds the Sick One.*]

SOMEONE He's bleeding more.

SOMEONE Hey, don't let go of him.

SOMEONE Hold on!

Someone holds the Sick One, who still tries to roll. The Sick One screams in response.

SOMEONE Shit, it's too late!

SOMEONE Couldn't do anything to stop it.

SOMEONE Do something fast!

SOMEONE We're going to be blamed again. Quickly, this is critical.

The crowd begins to panic.

SOMEONE Even just a little mistake, and we could be ruined. Move quickly; there isn't much time. We have no choice!

SOMEONE Who are you talking to? Me?

SOMEONE No, everyone! We're all responsible. We can't just run around aimlessly. Quick!

SOMEONE What's this? He's bleeding!

The Sick One falls flat on his back.

SOMEONE Calm down! Calm down!

SOMEONE Oh, he seems to be sick for real.

SOMEONE Hey stupid, this isn't the same guy as before. See his blood, it smells like real blood.

SOMEONE Hey, he's not moving anymore. Is he dead? Oh my God, help him. Come on, someone, anyone!

SOMEONE Hold on! This situation is not black and white! Who said the guy was dead? Who said he wasn't the same guy as before? Patience, we haven't studied this situation properly. Settle down, okay?

SOMEONE Come on!

SOMEONE Just calm down a moment so we can do something.

SOMEONE Do what?

SOMEONE Yeah, what should we do? Isn't that what we're trying to figure out?

SOMEONE I thought we decided just to observe the situation, so that what happened last time doesn't happen again.

SOMEONE Okay, so then who's going to help?

The Sick One moans and moves.

SOMEONE Look, he's not dead.

The Sick One appears to be struggling at death's door.

SOMEONE What are we waiting for?

SOMEONE We haven't been waiting for anything.

SOMEONE Okay then, come on!

SOMEONE You're going to help, aren't you?

SOMEONE Don't look at me.

The Sick One begins to weep heavily until the group gets fed up. Actually, there is no blood.

SOMEONE Oh my!

SOMEONE Enough already, this has gone on too long.

SOMEONE We know the game.

SOMEONE We're not going to be fooled again.

SOMEONE You think we can't learn from experience, man?

SOMEONE That our brains aren't sharp?

SOMEONE We have other things to do besides helping sickos. You think we're just having fun here?

SOMEONE Hey, why not? Why can't we enjoy ourselves? Our money's legit; no need to defend ourselves.

SOMEONE Enough already. Stop being a pest.

SOMEONE Rattling off like a coin in a can. Calling attention to yourself like a little kid. Please! We have better things to do. What are we supposed to do: roll over and die? Who wants that!

The Sick One lies motionless.

SOMEONE Go away! Why come here again? Why keep bugging us? Go that way, or that way, or that way. There are lots of people over there. Give them a taste for once instead of us. Why, because we're easy and nice guys to boot? Sick, yeah, sick my foot. Don't you feel even the slightest shame?

SOMEONE How could he feel any shame? He's dead.

Everyone is shocked. The Sick One is stiff.

SOMEONE What the . . . ?

SYMPATHETIC ONE [*Points to the stiffened body.*] Look. I've been trying to warn you guys. Now there's nothing we can do. I can't confirm it, but I think our friend here is dead. [*The rest of the crowd is dumbfounded.*] You see . . . I'm sure of it. There's no way out. We are now accomplices in the murder of a person who just needed help.

SOMEONE How could he have died?

SYMPATHETIC ONE Pay attention. Listen up. This person has died because you didn't help him!

SOMEONE Who, me?

SYMPATHETIC ONE All of you.

SOMEONE We're all responsible if anything happens.

SOMEONE Hey, that's a bum rap. Come on, be fair. And who is it who died?

SYMPATHETIC ONE This one here.

SOMEONE Are you sure?

SYMPATHETIC ONE Positive.

SOMEONE A doctor hasn't confirmed anything!

SYMPATHETIC ONE Look for yourself. Check it out.

The group hesitates. Someone examines the body.

SOMEONE [*Upon examination.*] The body is cold and stiff. Breathing has stopped. Eyes are white, mouth is open. Cheeks are dry and blue. Leg is wounded badly.

SOMEONE [*Examining the body.*] Hmmm!

SOMEONE So, what's the verdict?

SOMEONE It's true, he's no longer moving. There's no air coming from his nose or mouth. He's beyond hope. Rigor mortis has already set in. He's hmmm . . .

SOMEONE [*Comes forward to examine the body, but then withdraws.*] Yeah, no frigging way he's still alive. Look, there's a fly on his nose.

SYMPATHETIC ONE So, are you convinced?

SOMEONE You need me anymore?

SOMEONE No.

SYMPATHETIC ONE It looks like he's faking it, but his soul is definitely gone. Be careful, the body will rot in the next twenty-four hours, or perhaps sooner since his breath was so hot. Look at all those flies. *Ssst!* [*Swats at the flies.*]

SOMEONE A lot of people are actually still alive even though they look dead.

SYMPATHETIC ONE This one's truly dead.

SOMEONE So fast?

SYMPATHETIC ONE Because no one was willing to help.

SOMEONE Help? Why him? Who was supposed to help? You?

SYMPATHETIC ONE All of you.

SOMEONE Or himself! If he died because he didn't help himself, who's to blame? He died. So he's dead. But since when? Since before, when he started crawling? Or after he fell? Or maybe he was dead before he even got here!

SOMEONE Make sure first. Did he die before or after?

SYMPATHETIC ONE After.

SOMEONE Okay, so now what do we do?

A few people examine the scene.

SOMEONE Yeah, he really does look dead, doesn't he?

SOMEONE Yeah, looks dead.

SOMEONE Well, if he's not dead, what is he?

SOMEONE Poor guy . . .

SOMEONE Hey, hey, hey . . . Holy shit!

SOMEONE All right, okay, he really is dead.

SYMPATHETIC ONE So, do we all agree that he's dead?

SOMEONE We all believe that he's dead for sure. But whether he's dead or not makes no difference. We have to do something quickly before someone blames us for what happened.

SOMEONE What do we say if someone asks? Someone is definitely going to look into the cause of this.

SOMEONE If the body's cold, limbs are stiff, breathing's stopped, and rigor mortis has set in, there's no question. He's dead.

SOMEONE But why? Malaria, tuberculosis, cholera, dysentery . . .

SOMEONE Yeah, for sure it was something serious.

SOMEONE I think it was because he was ashamed of himself.

SYMPATHETIC ONE Even so, that's not the point. We need to figure out what to do now.

SOMEONE What about burying him?

SOMEONE Only if we want to.

SYMPATHETIC ONE We must!

No one objects.

But we have to do it quickly. Look, the sun's beginning to set.

Everyone looks at the sky.

SOMEONE Shit, he's starting to smell already!

They all hold their noses and move away.

SYMPATHETIC ONE Don't go anywhere! Let's take care of this. Come on! Your nose will get used to the smell. It's too risky not to do something.

They reluctantly return despite the smell.

Let's move him over there first. Come on, what's the matter?

The Sympathetic One directs the others as they try to lift the body. They make half-hearted attempts to help each other because they are reluctant to touch the body.

SOMEONE Argh!

SOMEONE Shit, this guy's heavy.

SOMEONE Something must be causing it.

SOMEONE Or he's still testing us.

SOMEONE Usually, corpses get contrary when the person sinned a lot.

SOMEONE At least it's windy, so the smell's not bad.

SOMEONE He'd remind me of a friend of mine if his face weren't so ugly.

SOMEONE His right leg is shorter than his left.

SOMEONE He's got a good body for a dead guy. Too bad he was so spineless.

SOMEONE Leave the blanket on for identification in case someone asks.

SOMEONE Shouldn't we check his pockets?

SOMEONE Yeah . . .

SOMEONE [*Checking.*] What the . . . ? [*Finds a cucumber, which gets passed around.*]

SOMEONE Does he have any ID?

SOMEONE Nothing!

SOMEONE So, we'll have to bury him without a name. I guess he wasn't planning on dying. No message, no nothing. Poor thing... Come on, lift him up.

They try to lift the body, but can't.

SOMEONE Come on!

SOMEONE Damn!

SOMEONE Too frigging heavy! Something or someone is holding him down. Hey, you!

SOMEONE Me? You think I'd go messing with his body?

SOMEONE And why not?

SOMEONE Hey, don't all lift in one spot. Go over there, and there. Good. Now come on. Lift!

They still can't lift the body.

SOMEONE Damn!

SOMEONE Maybe he wants to be buried here!

SOMEONE Here? This isn't a cemetery.

SYMPATHETIC ONE Come on, hurry. It'll be dark soon. Look, the sun is setting already. Come on!

SOMEONE Wait.

SYMPATHETIC ONE Why? Is there anybody here who is unable?

SOMEONE No.

SYMPATHETIC ONE Unwilling?

SOMEONE No.

SYMPATHETIC ONE Afraid?

SOMEONE No!

SYMPATHETIC ONE So, everything is set! Whoever objects to burying this body is putting himself in jeopardy, because as long as you simply witnessed... So, if we are all in agreement, let's do it!

They try again, but fail.

SOMEONE Shouldn't we just call the police?

SOMEONE No way! They'll suspect us of torturing him.

SYMPATHETIC ONE Come, try again. Slowly, arrgghh . . .

Failure once again. Someone steps back and holds his nose.

SOMEONE God, how can he be dead and still fart?

SOMEONE [*Also stepping away from the corpse.*] What is going on here? We've already been taken for fools. When he was alive, he was a pest. Now that he's dead, he's a burden. Damn!

SYMPATHETIC ONE Come on! It's getting dark. Some on the left and some on the right.

No one helps. The Sympathetic One tries to pick up the body on his own. The others watch.

SOMEONE Before, we watched him. Now, his spirit is watching us.

SYMPATHETIC ONE *Shhh!* [*Opens the blanket.*] Look at him laughing!

They all gather around.

SOMEONE Was he laughing when he died? Grinning, right? Now he can laugh?

SYMPATHETIC ONE His spirit hasn't traveled far.

SOMEONE Now it looks like he's smiling. Imagine what he feels like having his soul stuck there in his body.

SOMEONE Probably feels like himself, asshole.

SYMPATHETIC ONE Hey! Focus! Humanity dictates we bury this guy.

PROPOSITIONER Might I suggest something first?

SYMPATHETIC ONE What?

PROPOSITIONER I'm a bit embarrassed to say.

SYMPATHETIC ONE Whatever. What? Maybe it's important.

PROPOSITIONER This is what I'm thinking. Before we bury the corpse, I think we need to make sure that it's a man that we're burying. That's what we've been assuming. I mean, if he is a guy, why do his eyes look like they belong to a girl? Look at it this way. If he's a girl, well . . . Check it out!

They all take a look.

SOMEONE Yeah, yeah. Wow, man, what if we hadn't checked?

PROPOSITIONER Go on, what do you think?

SOMEONE Yeah, the eyes are watery like a woman's.

SOMEONE Oh, do you think there are any kids or a family left behind?

SOMEONE How the hell should I know?

SOMEONE Just look at that face. If you look at it for a while, you start feeling all sad inside.

PROPOSITIONER Why's that?

SOMEONE I might look the same when I die.

SYMPATHETIC ONE The way to determine this person's gender is with proof. Who decided that what's-his-name here is male?

SOMEONE Don't go digging for trouble. It is what it is!

PROPOSITIONER Look at the genitals. Look under the blanket!

SYMPATHETIC ONE It's clear enough from the outside. Are you interested in seeing or proving?

PROPOSITIONER Both, if possible. How can we prove anything without seeing for ourselves?

SYMPATHETIC ONE That's obscene. Why don't you just do a little groping?

PROPOSITIONER Who's a skilled groper? Even a good grope can be deceptive.

SYMPATHETIC ONE I can. But there's no need to feel, no need to look. Enough. I am convinced he's male. His smell!

SOMEONE [*Copping a feel.*] Let me try . . . Man, I can't tell.

SOMEONE Let me. [*Gropes for a long time.*] Damn!

PROPOSITIONER So?

SOMEONE It's hard. It's hard to tell if this is a woman or a man. Maybe both, like Tintiya, that Balinese deity.

PROPOSITIONER Well, if it is Tintiya, there's no way you're going to be able to tell. Try for yourself.

Someone examines the corpse's crotch while the others watch. Suddenly, as he's doing this, the Sympathetic One becomes possessed and begins shrieking and bouncing up and down. The others start to panic. They try to subdue the Sympathetic One, but he struggles and breaks free from their grasp. He continues to bounce around and begins a strange dance. Then he moves and groans in the same manner as the Sick One. The group watches him dispassionately. Darkness falls.

SOMEONE Look, it's getting dark!

Everyone panics.

SOMEONE Quickly!

SOMEONE Quickly!

SOMEONE Come on!

SOMEONE Quickly!

SOMEONE Come on!

SOMEONE Come on!

SOMEONE Come on!

The group grabs the corpse to lift it. But they can't. The lights fade. Even in the dark they continue their attempts to lift the body while encouraging each other.

Act Two

The body of the Sick One lies in the same place as before. The group waits faithfully yet appears unable to do anything. The darkness is gradually broken up by starlight. Sprawled out next to the body is the Sympathetic One, now the Possessed One. He mumbles and cries in the dark. The group squats quietly on the far side.

SOMEONE I can't stand the smell anymore. I'm going to throw up.

SOMEONE Anybody have a little balsam?

SOMEONE Anyone bring balsam?

SOMEONE Hey, he usually has balsam.

SOMEONE None left. Just ask her for some.

SOMEONE Hey, there's no reason to get stingy over a little jar of balsam. I'll buy you a dozen tomorrow.

BALSAM OWNER Do you want Tiger Balm?

SOMEONE Got some? Give it here!

BALSAM OWNER Just don't use it all!

SOMEONE My God! It's only balsam; you'd think I'd asked for your soul. Don't be so stingy; if you die, who's going to come and carry your body?

They pass the bottle of balm around and rub it on different parts of their bodies.

SOMEONE That's better. Covers the smell anyway.

They use up all the balm. Someone tosses the empty container. It makes a dinging noise.

BALSAM OWNER Don't throw it away!

SOMEONE It's all gone.

BALSAM OWNER — But I use the container for storing needles. [*Looks for the container in the dark.*]

SOMEONE — Stinginess has no cure.

ENVIOUS ONE — She wouldn't be herself if she weren't stingy.

SOMEONE — We'll see if she can find any pallbearers when she dies. Not me!

SOMEONE — Her own kids would want to be paid before they lifted her casket.

ENVIOUS ONE — Just because she owns a store, she thinks she can do whatever she likes—acting like a Westerner.

Suddenly from the darkness, the Balsam Owner screams with fear and runs back to the group.

SOMEONE — What?

BALSAM OWNER — [*Panicked.*] There's an evil spirit over there!

SOMEONE — What kind of evil spirit?

BALSAM OWNER — An evil spirit! It's hanging over there with a white face. Its arms are covered in black hair. When I was bending over there, it blew air on my bottom! Oh my! Please, God, why me?

SOMEONE — Over there?

BALSAM OWNER — Yes!

SOMEONE — That probably means his soul hasn't gone far. That's why we can't lift the body.

SOMEONE — Near the stream that runs to the left of those bamboo next to the fountain?

BALSAM OWNER — Yes.

SOMEONE — Oh, there. Well, of course!

SOMEONE — Yeah, that's the place where that satay seller's nephew committed suicide, isn't it? Of course. That place is haunted.

SOMEONE — It's not just haunted; it's the spirit hub for the whole southern district. Be careful.

The Brave One gets up and walks in that direction.

SOMEONE — Hey, where you going?!

The Brave One doesn't answer and proceeds into the darkness. The group begins taunting him.

SOMEONE — Oh, so brave!

SOMEONE — So determined!

SOMEONE — Typical—thinks he's so great! And he's always like that, showing off just because he's a championship boxer. Even if no one else had one, that's still no reason to show off—not if he really is brave or powerful. [*Points to the corpse.*] Take care of that!

The Brave One laughs in the darkness, making the group nervous.

SOMEONE — He really is brave.

ENVIOUS ONE — What a show-off! What's the point of acting like that!

The Brave One whistles in the dark. Still whistling, he reappears carrying the dead man's blanket. Some in the group look at him with amazement.

BALSAM OWNER — Well?

BRAVE ONE — Well what?

BALSAM OWNER — Was he there, that white guy?

SOMEONE — What's that you're holding?

SOMEONE — Oh, that must be what you saw!

SOMEONE — Oh yeah? This? Where did you get this?

BRAVE ONE — It was hanging on the bamboo.

ENVIOUS ONE — Oh, no wonder. What a 'fraidy cat—thinking the blanket was an evil spirit!

BALSAM OWNER — No, it wasn't that. I know that's a blanket. I saw it over there. But there was a white guy next to it. Really! A big, tall, white guy with red eyes, super long fingernails, and a mark on his neck like he'd hanged himself. He blew on my ass, then . . .

BRAVE ONE — Hey, there's nothing over there. Got it? There's nothing! Nothing at all!

SOMEONE — So how come the blanket was there?

BRAVE ONE — Huh?

SOMEONE — The blanket was hanging on the bamboo, right?

BRAVE ONE — Yeah!

SOMEONE — Well, who hung it there?

BRAVE ONE — Yeah, who?

SOMEONE — Who had this blanket earlier? Come on, fess up.

SOMEONE — Yeah, confess! Who?

SOMEONE — It's yours, isn't it?

ENVIOUS ONE — Yes, it was me. I put it down on the ground when we were trying to lift that corpse!

SOMEONE — Yeah, I saw it there on the ground.

SOMEONE — Are you sure?

BALSAM OWNER — If what you're saying is true, then this blanket, I suppose, just picked itself up and moved over there when we were distracted. [*No one says anything.*] Watch what you say around here. We're next to a haunted area. It could be we are being watched even though we can't see anything. No wonder all of us together can't lift a single corpse. That's proof. Disaster strikes any outsider who shows his face here with bad intentions. Instead of being afraid, we should respect that there are others living among us. We have to be careful not to step on other people's toes. So, someone saw the blanket there and decided to have it for his own . . .

POSSESSED ONE — [*Screams, shattering the quiet. Looks angrily at the group and suddenly speaks.*] Don't be so lazy! Bury me now! Quickly! I'll be late crossing the river!

The group is stunned. The Possessed One resumes his pitiful crying. One person emerges from the group as the Leader.

LEADER — Okay, my friends, let's not be lazy. Step lively! Responsibility is in our hands. From now on, I am the leader and commander. I'll be in the middle. Step lively now! [*Passion begins to replace the group's lethargy.*] On the right. On the left. I'm in the middle. Let's go, let's go, let's go! [*They begin to make progress in lifting the corpse.*] It's getting heavier.

SOMEONE — How many fucking times has he fucked with us . . .

SOMEONE — And how many times have we tried to help? Maybe after this, we'll finally be free.

LEADER — Lift!

SOMEONE — Aarrgghh!

They lift the corpse knee high.

SOMEONE — Damn! [*Gasping for breath.*] This dead guy—whoever he is—is too much, and only because we didn't do anything! Dying's normal, right? Lots of people go through it, not just him. So what makes him so special?

LEADER Stop. Don't badmouth him. It'll just make things more difficult. It's too late for that.

SOMEONE Why are we always so indecisive?

SOMEONE Stop fretting over the details. The point is to work out this problem. Now. If we don't take care of this quickly, he's going to be eaten by maggots. And we'll be blamed. We'll be criticized as useless.

SOMEONE He's only one guy, yet he overpowers us wimps like a herd of bulls.

LEADER If that's the case, then let us use our brains.

PATHFINDER [*Runs ahead to prepare the way.*] Hold on! [*Offstage.*] I'll prepare the way.

LEADER Hurry. His body's getting wet.

SOMEONE Uh-oh! What is this wet stuff? Yuck! It's piss! The guy can still piss!

SOMEONE He can still be wicked too.

LEADER Steady! Let's put our minds together as one! Together!

SOMEONE Come on!

LEADER As one!

SOMEONE Slowly, altogether now, lift!

LEADER Come on, together, as one . . . Watch where you're going. Hey! What's on the path ahead?

PATHFINDER [*Offstage.*] A lot of rocks, holes. It's really dark!

LEADER Let's get this over with. We're almost there . . . Whoa!

Half off the ground, the body suddenly gets heavy again.

Hold on . . . Keep lifting! Work as one. Keep clearing the way!

PATHFINDER [*Offstage.*] Ah! The further along, the darker it gets!

LEADER Keep going, keep going! Together now . . . Together . . . [*They drop the body again.*] Damn! [*Everyone seems to want to give up.*] Okay, let's catch our breath, then we'll try again. [*Yells.*] Take your time! We haven't succeeded yet. [*Reclines.*] But at least we tried . . .

Everyone lies down to rest.

SOMEONE I have never encountered a corpse like this one.

SOMEONE — [*Taking off his shirt.*] This is what I call work!

BALSAM OWNER — Why is it that whatever we do is futile? Believe it now. This place is truly haunted. Just who took the blanket over to the bamboo?

SOMEONE — It's getting hard to breathe. The smell is getting worse. I'm going to barf! Where's the balsam?

SOMEONE — Yes, the smell! The corpse has shit on itself. It's making my head spin.

SOMEONE — I feel so weak, like I've just had the runs. Can anyone give me a massage?

They all stretch out on the ground. The Possessed One begins to bounce again. He moans. Doubting that the man really is possessed, the Leader rises in annoyance.

LEADER — Hey, hey, hey!

SOMEONE — Leave him alone. It's not nice to harass him.

LEADER — Hey, hey! Hey! Heeey!

SOMEONE — Don't yell like that.

The Possessed One begins to cry. Disturbed, the Leader slaps the Possessed One, who falls silent.

LEADER — Hey, wake up, wake up! Don't add to it!

POSSESSED ONE — [*Begins to snap out of his trance.*] It hurts . . .

LEADER — Because I slapped you.

POSSESSED ONE — Ouch.

LEADER — It was hard, I know. But things had gone too far.

POSSESSED ONE — It's as if my head is split in half . . .

LEADER — Life's unfair. Does it still hurt?

POSSESSED ONE — Yes.

LEADER — So enough already. You have it easy.

POSSESSED ONE — Huh?

LEADER — Look at the dead man over there. You know, seeing him like that makes me think of myself. That could be me one day.

POSSESSED ONE — Yeah?

LEADER — Or you too! I hate him for that . . . But thinking about how it would be to be like him—and not as we are now—with no one knowing who we are, and set free, like a chicken on the highway, sick and alone, and then having to fend for yourself, but dying just like him. Well, we could end up just like him, and what happened before could happen again, just like it is now.

POSSESSED ONE — You think I'm like him?

LEADER — Who knows?!

POSSESSED ONE — I'm not like him.

LEADER — Hopefully not.

POSSESSED ONE — I know who I am.

LEADER — But what if this was forced on you, and you had no other choice?

POSSESSED ONE — There's always you to give advice! You're good at that.

LEADER — All those things you said when you were possessed. I can't tell you what might happen if others overheard you.

POSSESSED ONE — And if they did, so what?

LEADER — They could get very upset. We could be arrested. Calumny! Good thing there's no one else around. Good thing too that we here are all the same. Bastard! Help him out, and he still causes problems! I don't like it that you put the rest of us at risk. You're weak and defenseless, like a woman. You should have resisted. But forget it. There's nothing you can do now; it's past.

POSSESSED ONE — I don't know what got hold of me.

LEADER — Everyone makes mistakes.

POSSESSED ONE — What will the others think about me?

LEADER — Nothing special.

POSSESSED ONE — I'm sorry...

LEADER — Sorry? [*Laughs.*] Sure, whatever. As long as you don't bother the others. They're resting, gathering their strength.

POSSESSED ONE — I'm sorry... [*Cries.*]

The Leader walks away from the Possessed One, who's feeling sorry for himself. The group drifts off to sleep. The Leader assumes watch, investigates the perimeter, and then approaches the corpse. He looks carefully at the ring the corpse has on its finger. He looks around, and when he feels it's safe, he removes the ring and other valuables. He then moves toward the others, intending to rob them of their belongings too. The Pathfinder, who's been trying to find a path to the graveyard, calls from afar.

PATHFINDER [*Offstage.*] I finally found it! You won't find anything if you're not patient. Wait until it's finished first. Here is the path. It's a bit narrow. Lots of scrap metal here. It looks like no one's been buried there in a while. There's an empty hole. It's not very big, but real deep, like a well. Damn, it's cold. It's past midnight. The smell of morning's in the air. The sky's getting lighter, the morning star's gonna make its appearance, and if we don't get a move on there's gonna be trouble. A little more, a little more, yah, ahh, almost there. Almost there, almost, almost, almost, ack! I've got it! Enough, enough! Finnnisssshhed!

[*Starts to sing.*]
We are all different
They are all different
Because our nature is different
Because our form is different
But because our stomachs are all the same
We are all the same
They are all the same
Because our names are the same
Because our brains are the same
But because our mouths are different . . .

The Leader, who has finished robbing the corpse, takes the blanket and goes to the dark, haunted spot while the Pathfinder continues singing offstage.

We are all hmm!
You are all hmm!
Because our customs are hmm
Because our nature is hmm
And because our whatsies are hmm.

[*Enters and is shocked by the silence. Not only is everyone asleep, but it's also apparent that the corpse has been robbed. Furious, he begins to shake.*] Wake up! Wake up! Waaake uuuppp! [*The Possessed One stops wallowing in self-pity and looks at him.*] Over here! Look here!

The Possessed One comes closer and looks at the violated body. He displays his hatred toward the dead man. The Pathfinder becomes angry.

POSSESSED ONE — Serves him right!

PATHFINDER — What? [*The Possessed One steps back.*] Tired of the responsibility, huh? What do you want to do? Leave the body here to be eaten by dogs? Its smell has already spread to the town, and the dogs are howling like crazy because of it. We have to act quickly. It won't take much to put the body in the hole that's already there. No need for any monetary contributions either. Come on! Why don't you want to help?

The Possessed One holds his nose. The Pathfinder goes over to the sleeping people and wakes them.

Get up! Everyone get up! We need everyone to pitch in to bury him. We need helpers! Let's go! Let's go! Why are you guys so out of it, like it's not your problem? Geeettt uuuppp! [*Storms around, making a fuss. Finally, the group begins to wake up.*] Come on! Let's go! Look here! The body was robbed! Look, look, there are maggots in his eyes already. Ah, we'll be too late if we don't get a move on. Come on!

The group watches the Pathfinder from a distance and starts to grumble.

ONE MEMBER — It's not right. First his blanket was lost; now everything is stolen.

ONE MEMBER — The smell is getting worse. I can't stand it! Where's the balsam? [*Vomits.*]

ONE MEMBER — I have a headache. I feel woozy.

ONE MEMBER — Let's go home.

PATHFINDER — Hey. When I left earlier, you were full of pep, and now you're all lame? Come on!

[*Tries to rein in everyone, but they avoid him.*] What is it? Something making you afraid? The maggots? The smell? The maggots are only maggots. The smell is only a smell. Come on, it's already past three. We'll be caught by the watchman. Do you want to go to jail? Aren't we the ones who killed him? The road has been staked out, the grave is ready. All we need to do is carry him there. Come on, let's go! [*Pulls their arms, but everyone avoids him as if they are afraid.*] What is it? Enough already. Look at his head, his hair, nose, stomach, his whole body—all of it will suffer if you don't do something soon. Why are you afraid? What are you scared of? The maggots and the smell? [*Touches the body.*] See? There is absolutely no danger.

ONE MEMBER Ahh, don't do that!

PATHFINDER Enough?

ONE MEMBER Why us?

ONE MEMBER Why not the others?

PATHFINDER Who?

ONE MEMBER The point is, we shouldn't have to do it alone.

PATHFINDER Well then, who?

ONE MEMBER Other people!

PATHFINDER What other people? This is our responsibility!

ONE MEMBER But why ours alone?

ONE MEMBER There are lots of other people!

PATHFINDER Ugh, what a pain! There are no other people here besides us.

ONE MEMBER Look for them! You're sure to find someone if you look. Get with it!

ONE MEMBER Don't just throw around orders. Everyone needs to share responsibility here.

PATHFINDER With who? Who? Who? If not us, then who? For heaven's sake!

ONE MEMBER We're just a bunch of idiots, don't ask us.

ONE MEMBER Besides, we're tired of taking care of him.

PATHFINDER So you feel no obligation toward this corpse anymore, right? Right?

ONE MEMBER *Shhh!* Don't answer. Whatever you say will be wrong.

ONE MEMBER Yeah, don't.

ONE MEMBER We shouldn't have to deal with this alone. We still don't actually know who he is.

PATHFINDER But we have been taking care of the victim up until now. Why stop all of a sudden?

ONE MEMBER It was fine during the afternoon. But now it's nighttime. We tried our best. And furthermore, who is this guy? We didn't cause this to happen. He did it all by himself!

PATHFINDER True! But he can't help himself to his grave right now. Are you daring me to drag him there by myself? [*Tries to drag the corpse, but is unable to.*] Damn, is this a dare? The smell's here to stay; we're never gonna forget it. Trust me, it's not going to hurt you to touch the body a little bit more. So that the dogs don't eat it!

ONE MEMBER We've sacrificed enough.

ONE MEMBER And we have our own dependents and responsibilities.

ONE MEMBER Please, please, don't bother us. Please, just leave us alone. We are simple folk. Morning's on its way, and we have to return to work. Our families are already worried that we've gone missing for a day. Please! It's not that we don't want to help, but there are limits. We implore you! You're a smart guy!

PATHFINDER Implore? Me? Nooo. Ask the victim.

ONE MEMBER Okay, fine, him. We implore you!

ONE MEMBER Stop! Implore him? I don't want to ask for anything from him. He needs to beg for our forgiveness. Man, this is not our fault!

PATHFINDER He has asked for our forgiveness. Look at the maggots and smell him decomposing. That's his way of asking since he can't talk anymore. We are the ones who have to do the talking!

ANGRY ONE [*Steps forward in anger and speaks slowly.*] You know, it's not that we don't understand what's happening here. We don't like being shouted at and treated like little children, even though we might appear childlike to other people. It only seems as if we haven't helped him. You weren't even here when we were working on it earlier. It's easy for you to talk that way. We know what needs to be done, don't forget. It's a timing problem, and our capabilities are limited. You should get this through your head. Bastard! Bastard! Motherfucker!

The Angry One hits the Pathfinder. They fight. The group neither breaks up the fight nor takes sides. The Leader enters the stage from the dark, haunted spot. He breaks up the fight by shoving the two men apart.

LEADER What's going on here?

ANGRY ONE He's a bastard! He insulted us! He slandered us! He said we weren't living up to our obligations. Coming from him, ha!

PATHFINDER I never said you weren't living up to your obligations.

ANGRY ONE You deny it now!

PATHFINDER I said the body's gonna be eaten by dogs if we just leave it there!

ANGRY ONE But you blamed us! Bastard!

PATHFINDER Well, only because a dog can't be blamed; it's an animal. Are we the same as dogs?

ANGRY ONE Bastard! The body was just fine before we fell asleep. Then, when you came and woke us, the body had been robbed. And you won't admit it's your fault! Instead, you blame others!

LEADER Hold on! What's the problem here?

PATHFINDER [*Approaches the body.*] This!

LEADER What? Go on! Let him explain what he means.

PATHFINDER The victim is going to be eaten by dogs.

LEADER So?

PATHFINDER We have to bury the victim before that!

LEADER Yes, correct.

PATHFINDER But quickly! Smell that! Look at the maggots! If we don't move fast, this victim is gonna be eaten.

LEADER Where are the dogs?

PATHFINDER What?

LEADER Dogs!

PATHFINDER What about the dogs?

ANGRY ONE Where are the dogs that are going to eat the corpse?

PATHFINDER Oh, they'll be here.

ANGRY ONE Liar! All of the dogs are in the next village over. There was a cremation there. All the dogs are there, partying.

LEADER Let him answer. You believe that those dogs want to eat this corpse?

PATHFINDER Yes.

LEADER And from where did you get this notion?

ANGRY ONE He made it up. He was trying to kiss ass, but we refused to play that game. And now dogs!

LEADER Where did you get this notion? Ah?

The Pathfinder can't answer.

SPOKESPERSON [*After some thought, steps forward.*] May I intervene here?

LEADER How so?

SPOKESPERSON Even though I'm not their spokesperson and they'd rather be silent, I feel it is necessary to explain what is going on in their hearts. May I?

LEADER You may.

SPOKESPERSON [*Pointing to the Pathfinder.*] This man, after being absent for quite some time, doing who knows what over there, suddenly shows up while we are sleeping. Self-importantly and of his own accord, he declares the body of this stranger, a person none of us had ever seen before, a victim. Let me repeat: v-i-c-t-i-m . . . [*Stops and gazes at the Leader.*]

LEADER And then? Go on!

SPOKESPERSON There's no need to say anything more. What was the meaning of "victim"?

LEADER [*To the Pathfinder.*] Is this true?

PATHFINDER The reason I called him a victim is because he was a dead man surrounded by a bunch of living, dressed, and sleeping people who didn't even want to help this poor victim to his burial.

SPOKESPERSON Hear that?! He said "victim"!

LEADER And that's why you called him a victim?

PATHFINDER Yes.

SPOKESPERSON If he's a victim, who victimized him? Must have been the person who wasn't sleeping, right? So actually, the truth is the other way around!

LEADER Yeah, is that what you meant?

SPOKESPERSON And why does he insist that he's not implicated in this matter? Here we have the deceased, a corpse; those who were sleeping, us; and one person awake, him. Now, if we abide by his line of reasoning, we, who were sleeping, made the deceased a victim. But we have also been victimized by the one who was not sleeping or deceased. What about that?

LEADER What about that? No answer?

PATHFINDER You are free to express your opinion and your defense. But I also have a question. If—

SPOKESPERSON Stop! Tone it down a bit! We're overdoing it with the questions. Want to bury us with questions, or what? [*Approaches the corpse.*] Come over here, over here! It's not enough to have the nerve to ask us questions from over there. Come on, over here! [*Stamps his foot impatiently.*]

PATHFINDER [*Without moving.*] What's he going to answer?

SPOKESPERSON [*Stamping his foot harder.*] Come here!

PATHFINDER [*Approaching.*] What's he gonna answer?

SPOKESPERSON Ask him, go on! [*Points to the body.*]

PATHFINDER Ask him what?

SPOKESPERSON Ask away—whatever you want.

PATHFINDER Isn't he gonna rot if we just stand around here, asking questions?

SPOKESPERSON Sheesh! Ask him that. Him! Not us! Come on! Why the silence?

PATHFINDER I can't.

SPOKESPERSON Why is it you're all talk with us, but not with him? What's the difference?

ANGRY ONE Little by little his mask is coming off.

LEADER Shhh!

SPOKESPERSON Go on! Go on!

PATHFINDER [*Walks up to the corpse to ask a question.*] Why, why, why . . .

SPOKESPERSON There you go.

PATHFINDER What can you ask a dead man?

SPOKESPERSON Exactly! Ask him that. What, why are you coming back over here?

The Pathfinder becomes confused. The Angry One steps forward and speaks to the corpse in a local dialect.

ANGRY ONE Why don't you get up? Why don't you answer? Why don't you want to help? Have we been let off the hook? Should we just leave things to the dogs?

The group becomes cheerful, the Pathfinder still doesn't know what to do, and the Angry One asks more questions, determined to make a fool of the Pathfinder.

Wassup? When we left you alone, you were full of yourself.

And now, why the change? Scared? Scared of what? [*The group applauds.*] What is making you scared? The maggots? The smell? The maggots are just maggots? The smell is just a smell? [*More applause.*] The road has been staked out, the grave is ready, right? Why the laziness?

LEADER — Enough!

ANGRY ONE — [*Happy with his progress, ignores the Leader and continues his interrogation in his local dialect.*] Who's motivating you, who's helping you? Who's telling you what to do, how much are you being paid, when, where are they now, where are they hiding, with whom, why are you silent, why are you silent, why are you silent—

The group immediately grabs the Angry One and pulls him away as he continues questioning in his local dialect. He's dragged to the dark place, where, annoyed, he continues his questioning.

LEADER — Hold him there until he comes to his senses! Only then can he come back here. The rest of you, please curb your emotions. Your head may be hot, but your heart must remain prudent. Otherwise, we'll all just keep asking questions and get no answers.

PATHFINDER — Yeah, what purpose is that serving?

SPOKESPERSON — That's been the case all along. Look, it's almost morning. We were resting because we were exhausted. But now that it's almost morning, we have to get back to work. Roll up your sleeves, my friends. Let's go!

THE GROUP — Let's go!

SPOKESPERSON — Go ahead. You too!

PATHFINDER — Yes!

SPOKESPERSON — Let's learn from experience. The elderly will never lose a cane twice. Patience, and our cause will be successful. Patience is a virtue. Take up the necessary tasks; don't just seek the easy way out. Just like our ancestors, who could overcome anything if they only worked together. Attention! [*Everyone assumes position.*] One, two, three! Go!

They easily lift the body.

ONE OF THEM — Damn, nothing like a good sleep to make things easy.

ONE OF THEM — Really, it's not a big deal.

LEADER — Let's quickly take what's-his-name here to the graveyard.

ONE OF THEM — His right leg is decomposing.

ONE OF THEM — Which graveyard?

ONE OF THEM — The closest.

PATHFINDER — [*Walks ahead of the group.*] Follow me. [*Exits toward the graveyard.*]

ONE OF THEM — But I've heard there are a lot of empty graves over there.

ONE OF THEM — It's too dark, and it's too far. Aren't we going to be too rushed?

PATHFINDER — Come on, quickly, the grave's been dug already.

A rooster crows.

ONE OF THEM — Listen to that. It's almost morning. Come on!

ONE OF THEM — That path is too rough over there. Go left!

ONE OF THEM — What's going on with the grave?

ONE OF THEM — Ugh, what is it with the grave? Quickly, clear a path to the left!

ONE OF THEM — To the left? Next to the stream that runs along the bamboo grove near that fountain, right?

ONE OF THEM — To the left? No, that's not the graveyard!

ONE OF THEM — Hurry! Daylight's coming!

ONE OF THEM — That's sacred ground!

ONE OF THEM — Get a move on!

While carrying the body, they argue over where to take it.

ONE OF THEM — The spirits won't like it if we bury him over there.

ONE OF THEM — He could be ejected from his grave. What would happen if someone else saw the body? It's too dangerous!

ONE OF THEM — Okay. Over there, quickly!

ONE OF THEM — I don't have a good feeling about this.

ONE OF THEM — We're going to be late. Maybe the village dogs have come home from their party.

ONE OF THEM — Shut your trap! Get moving!

ONE OF THEM — Where to?

ONE OF THEM — To the right. There's an empty grave there already.

ONE OF THEM — No, left. Quickly, clear the way!

ONE OF THEM — Always thinking of what you want. Quickly, just go over there.

ONE OF THEM — Just clear the way, shithead! Snap out of it!

PATHFINDER — Where to?

ONE OF THEM — [*Picking up a rock.*] Quickly, snap out of it!

The Pathfinder is confused. He becomes disoriented when One of Them throws a rock at him. He runs toward the haunted spot.

ONE OF THEM — Go right! Not left!

ONE OF THEM — Quit yakking. Just walk!

ONE OF THEM — Hey, quit pulling!

ONE OF THEM — But we haven't decided anything yet.

ONE OF THEM — Enough already. Go that way, quickly!

ONE OF THEM — Come on, get going!

ONE OF THEM — Go where? Don't pull!

ONE OF THEM — That guy's the one . . . there!

ONE OF THEM — Damn it, what are you doing to my foot?

ONE OF THEM — Don't crush my head like that!

ONE OF THEM — Who's dragging us down?

ONE OF THEM — Damn! [*Falls down.*] Idiot, don't do that! You!

ONE OF THEM — Shit, my hand!

ONE OF THEM — Pull, pull, to the left, not over there!

ONE OF THEM — Right! Hold on! We'll be late!

ONE OF THEM — Hold on!

ONE OF THEM — Bastard. All we'll find if we turn left is ghosts!

ONE OF THEM — Asshole! You're a liability! Hear that? The dogs are barking.

ONE OF THEM — Serves you right!

ONE OF THEM — It's not fair!

They struggle with one another.

ONE OF THEM Don't argue!

ONE OF THEM Careful, I'm going to stab you in the stomach!

ONE OF THEM To the leeefffttt! Ghost!

ONE OF THEM To the right! You're looking for trouble!

ONE OF THEM Shit! Ghost! Forget it!

ONE OF THEM Motherfucker!

ONE OF THEM Ghost! Right!

ONE OF THEM Hold on! Hold on!

They all pull.

ONE OF THEM Motherfucker. Instead of this, better to . . . [*Exits.*]

ONE OF THEM Keep going, keep going right!

ONE OF THEM Ghost! Ghost! [*Exits.*]

ONE OF THEM Pull left!

ONE OF THEM Damn! [*Exits.*]

The dogs approach. Startled, the group freezes. Then they run in a panic, each trying to save himself as the barking becomes louder. Two people—The One and The Other—are left holding the body. They are bewildered and unable to act. The barking becomes wilder. Soon after, the dogs pass by, barking viciously. The One and The Other shut their eyes.

THE ONE Don't move.

THE OTHER [*Praying.*] They're sniffing my feet.

THE ONE Hold still.

THE OTHER Damn, they're licking my calf.

THE ONE Hold still.

THE OTHER They're biting my toes.

THE ONE Hold still.

THE OTHER Damn, damn, damn . . .

THE ONE What is it, you being bitten?

THE OTHER Motherfucker . . .

THE ONE Hold still!

THE OTHER It's pissing on my leg!

THE ONE Hold still!

THE OTHER Damn, I'm getting pins and needles in my feet . . .

THE ONE Hold still! [*The dogs exit. The One opens his eyes.*] Thank God! [*Slaps his friend on the shoulder.*] Hey!

THE OTHER [*Opening his eyes.*] Goddamnit, motherfucker! [*Stamping his feet.*] My leg's mistaken for a bitch.

THE ONE Forget it. Let's move on. We have a lot of work to do. Where to? Left? Right?

THE OTHER Too many thorns over there. A ton of mud, holes, and it's dark on top of it all. Let's just go over there.

THE ONE It's getting late.

THE OTHER What can we do?

They slowly carry the body in the darkness.

THE ONE It's a bit dark, but this is it. This is the marker. I think the fence is over there. We can enter here. Go right a little, okay?

THE OTHER I don't have a good feeling about this. The hairs on the back of my neck are standing up.

THE ONE Quiet, hold on. Watch out!

THE OTHER *Ow!* I stepped in something. Ugh!

THE ONE Be careful. Not over here, it's safer over that way a bit.

THE OTHER I don't feel right, I feel crowded.

THE ONE Oh yeah, I remember now. This cemetery has been sealed off. The plans are to build—

THE OTHER The smell! I can't stand it anymore. I'm going to barf again. Damn it, let's just leave it here, okay?

THE ONE It's like a grave.

THE OTHER Yes, right there.

THE ONE Oh no, it's actually a well.

THE OTHER Whatever, just leave it there. I can't stand it anymore.

THE ONE Be careful. [*They reach the hole.*] Okay? Now, let go. Just let go! [*They drop the body into the hole.*] Ah, finally free. How about it—still feel like barfing? Why is your face like that?

THE OTHER I feel like I'm also going to fall into the hole.

THE ONE It's always something. Come on, let's go home.

THE OTHER Lucky the dogs didn't bite.

THE ONE They were full, and who'd want rotting flesh anyway? Look, the sky's turning pink. Dawn is here. It's going to be morning soon. Let's talk at home, come on!

THE OTHER It's so quiet here. I can't move my leg. I think I stepped on something.

THE ONE Let me take a look.

THE OTHER *Ow!*

THE ONE Maybe it's a thorn.

THE OTHER *Ow!*

THE ONE Let me look. [*After checking.*] There's nothing wrong; it'll get better on its own. Just give it a massage with balsam. Come on.

The One supports The Other as he tries to walk. Suddenly, they hear the siren again, faintly. They are both taken aback.

THE OTHER Hear that?

THE ONE Yes.

THE OTHER Like yesterday morning! [*A louder siren answers the first, then becomes faint.*] This is just like yesterday. I don't feel good. They're coming again! What if they're coming to find the dead guy?

THE ONE Patience.

THE OTHER I have a bad feeling.

THE ONE Pull yourself together. You're getting feverish, probably from your leg. Look. Damn, it's swollen. Your face is really pale.

THE OTHER I have a bad feeling. Don't leave me alone.

THE ONE Who's leaving? Don't worry. Stay still. Try to bandage it first. [*Looks for a bandage. Finds something and wraps his leg.*]

THE OTHER *Ow!*

THE ONE Hang on a bit longer. Maybe you were bitten by the dog but didn't feel it. Bad news if that dog was sick; you could get rabies if you don't get a shot right away.

THE OTHER What?

THE ONE — Nothing, just wrap it so it doesn't come undone. You just stepped on a thorn. Wow, you're burning up. Come on, time to go.

THE OTHER — I don't feel good.

THE ONE — What doesn't feel good?

THE OTHER — I can't move, *ow*...

THE ONE — Jeez, hardly hurt at all and you can't handle it. Let's go, it's almost morning. The sky's getting redder. The homing pigeons have been released.

They hear pigeons flying overhead with bells around their necks.

THE OTHER — *Ow,* I can't.

THE ONE — Quit fussing. We'll do it together. Come on!

THE OTHER — *Ow*...

THE ONE — Yeah, it must really hurt. But try. I know it hurts, I feel it too. I've been hurt before too. But it's almost morning. We'll be found out if we stay here any longer. We're in for it if we're caught. Caught in the act. Let's go. [*Ignoring the moans and complaints, he forces his friend to walk, supporting him.*] Move that foot a bit; the path is tricky here. Argh, quit whining. Quiet. Be quiet. Damn it!

They both slip and fall. The Other groans in pain. The One tries to help The Other up.

Fuck, we almost fell into the well. Idiot. You poor thing, it must be painful. No matter, try again.

Ignoring The Other's moaning and complaining, The One tries to keep him erect. The One almost succeeds, but falls again. He ends up carrying The Other.

Come on and try! There ya go! Ahh, you are heavy. Like a hundred-kilogram sack of rice. I can't do this for long. There are so many holes! [*Exhausted, puts his friend down, then inspects the sky.*] It's already morning over there. Shut up! Want to go home or not?

The One tries to sling The Other across his shoulder and then tries to cradle him, but can't because The Other seems to be getting heavier. The Other shuts his eyes in pain. The siren sounds again. Finally, The One drags The Other even though it's excruciatingly painful.

For goodness' sake! Hang on.

The siren gets louder. The One stops dead in his tracks. The louder the siren gets, the more he panics. He finds the strength to carry The Other over his shoulder. The One runs, but doesn't get far before he tumbles forward and they both fall down and roll. Frightened, The Other struggles against The One. They wrestle. The One tries to calm The Other, but he's terrified. The One is forced to hit The Other.

I had to!

The Other lets go of his grip. The siren is nearby. The One hesitates, wondering whether to help The Other or just leave him there. He moves as if to leave, but returns because he feels pity for The Other. Suddenly, the siren stops, creating an eerie silence. Morning breaks, and light creeps over the area. The One flees. The Other moans. He rolls around, and then tries to stand up. He succeeds even though it is extremely difficult. He walks, not unlike the sick person who first appeared before the group.

Act Three

Morning. The group has reassembled in the original place. The Pathfinder, The One, and The Other are not there. Dogs, barking as if tempted by something, can be heard in the distance. After listening attentively to the barking, members of the group start to speak.

ONE OF THEM — What's with the dogs? Are they hungry?

ONE OF THEM — No. The smell of rot is getting to them. [*Sniffs the air. The others do the same.*]

ONE OF THEM — Still there, isn't it?

ONE OF THEM — Yeah. [*Sniffs himself. The others do the same.*]

ONE OF THEM — I washed myself with gasoline, with kerosene, with carbolic acid, and with Helping Hands soap. [*Smells his fingers.*] Ugh, it's still there. Smell! [*His neighbor pulls away.*]

ONE OF THEM — Mine too. [*Points to one of his hands.*]

ONE OF THEM — For me, it's here. [*Points to his neck.*]

ONE OF THEM — My left ear stinks.

ONE OF THEM — It's in my hair. I've washed it I don't know how many times and it still stinks.

ONE OF THEM Not me. I have something else. Every time I try to sleep, the smell comes from somewhere, really foul. Smells like a carcass. You too?

ONE OF THEM When I eat, everything stinks.

ONE OF THEM Different for me. When I open my mouth, out comes the stench. I'm getting scared to open my mouth.

ONE OF THEM Hey, not too close, man.

ONE OF THEM Hey, what's with you? Like you don't stink too?

ONE OF THEM I have something else. I haven't been able to smell a thing for days because of a stuffy nose. But every dog I run into barks like it can smell dead meat.

ONE OF THEM Damn. Looks like we all got it.

ONE OF THEM Pain in the ass 'cause it won't go away.

ONE OF THEM Yeah, why do we all stink over here if the guy's over there?

ONE OF THEM *Shhh!* Careful!

They lower their voices for fear of being overheard. However, their voices are still quite loud.

ONE OF THEM Yeah, why?

ONE OF THEM Where?

ONE OF THEM Yeah, where is what's-his-name? Where is he?

ONE OF THEM Maybe that car found him.

ONE OF THEM Wonder what's with them. Must be pissed. Was he really dead? Or just faking it?

ONE OF THEM If he didn't die, where's that stench coming from?

ONE OF THEM *Shhh!*

ONE OF THEM Was it that car that dropped him off? Maybe another one.

ONE OF THEM Either way, his corpse is definitely still there. That's it. I'm sure that's why it stinks.

ONE OF THEM Why don't we go look?

ONE OF THEM And then?

ONE OF THEM Yeah, we bury it to get rid of the smell.

ONE OF THEM Why look? Yeah, if we're really going to bury him. And what a hassle if we get caught. Enough already—forget it. We should thank God for our blessings.

ONE OF THEM — But the smell will only get worse if we don't do anything. Those dogs are suspicious. Be prepared for a huge fuss if they find the corpse. Look, let's say those dogs drag it into the street. People as far as over there will see. They'll ask whose dogs are those. It'll get back to us in the end. What then?

ONE OF THEM — Yeah, that's the problem. Why were we duped again—like we asked for it?

ONE OF THEM — We should have split—zip, zip, zip—as soon as we saw him coming.

ONE OF THEM — Yeah, but who knew it would turn out like this?

ONE OF THEM — Waddya mean who knew? This has now happened how many times?

ONE OF THEM — Go on, how many times?

ONE OF THEM — Well, more than once, right?

ONE OF THEM — Indeed.

ONE OF THEM — So heed my words: it doesn't have to be like this. Damn, it's getting worse! [*Sniffs parts of his body.*] It's definitely stronger!

The others sniff parts of their bodies.

ONE OF THEM — Yeah.

ONE OF THEM — Yeah.

ONE OF THEM — Now it's coming from both of my ears.

ONE OF THEM — Now my leg smells too!

ONE OF THEM — Both of my elbows!

ONE OF THEM — My stomach too.

ONE OF THEM — Balsam! Who brought balsam?

ONE OF THEM — My whole body's going to be contaminated soon. My back even.

ONE OF THEM — We're in trouble now!

ONE OF THEM — Balsam, the balsam! Quick!

BALSAM OWNER — [*Brings out some balsam.*] Take it easy, there's only a little left. Let everyone have some.

They divide up the balsam.

ONE OF THEM — [*While smearing it on.*] Luckily there was some. Imagine if there wasn't.

ONE OF THEM Good enough for now.

ONE OF THEM That's better, isn't it?

ONE OF THEM All fresh again.

ONE OF THEM Give me a bit more. I haven't done my left ear yet.

ONE OF THEM What about me? The smell's getting in my mouth.

ONE OF THEM Yeah, well then just keep your mouth shut.

ONE OF THEM Damn, what if—

ONE OF THEM [*Snappily.*] Forget it!

ONE OF THEM Well, I'm getting hungry. [*Pulls out a cucumber and offers it to the others.*] Want some? [*Nobody wants any. He peels the cucumber.*]

ONE OF THEM Can the others smell this stench?

ONE OF THEM What others?

ONE OF THEM Yeah, whoever. Because if they smell that stench, what are we going to do? And what if they connect us to that lost person and then find out he's dead?

ONE OF THEM It's possible.

ONE OF THEM I, however, will not bring misfortune upon my friends. They can go ahead and arrest me and implicate me; maybe they will even torture me. But believe you me, from my point of view, it's not going to happen. And I hope that you others are with me on this. Agreed?

ONE OF THEM I believe that's impossible, sir!

ONE OF THEM Why?

ONE OF THEM Well, because we're in this together, right? We're not going to make you, sir, take sole responsibility for this. You shouldn't feel that way.

ONE OF THEM That's not what I meant.

ONE OF THEM What then?

ONE OF THEM That smell!

ONE OF THEM Yes.

ONE OF THEM It will be discovered, correct?

ONE OF THEM Yeah, so?

ONE OF THEM Okay, so it could be, it could be, correct?

ONE OF THEM Yes, yes!

ONE OF THEM Okay then, so what?

ONE OF THEM Yeah, they'll think we murdered him! Get it?

Everyone is startled.

ONE OF THEM Murdered? We murdered?

ONE OF THEM Yes.

ONE OF THEM Murdered that corpse?

ONE OF THEM Murdered him before he became a corpse.

ONE OF THEM Wait, why would we murder him? We didn't even touch him. We helped him. Actively even, right?

ONE OF THEM Yeah.

ONE OF THEM So who murdered? Didn't happen.

ONE OF THEM Yeah, we even asked him nicely how he was. We also recommended he take a taxi to the hospital right away.

ONE OF THEM I remember saying, "Don't be scared, we'll help." Right? Remember?

ONE OF THEM That's ridiculous. Murdered. How?

ONE OF THEM Any person who says we murdered him didn't see what happened. Or just someone who wants to give all of us a bad name as murderers! We helped out, we didn't murder nobody. What the fuck?

ONE OF THEM *Shhh!* [*Lowers voice.*] That's what often happens.

ONE OF THEM Murderers get harsh sentences. Don't mess around.

ONE OF THEM I don't want to go on trial.

ONE OF THEM Obviously!

ONE OF THEM Imagine if we have to go on trial . . . Fuck, that'll be messed up.

ONE OF THEM The main problem is that we . . . [*smells his body*] stink!

The others also sniff their body parts.

ONE OF THEM Still smell?

ONE OF THEM Here?

ONE OF THEM [*Smells his body and calms down.*] No, not anymore.

ONE OF THEM Me too.

ONE OF THEM — All gone!

ONE OF THEM — *[Laughing.]* Hey, yes!

ONE OF THEM — Maybe it stunk because we were thinking about it.

ONE OF THEM — It happened at the moment I grabbed his rotting leg.

ONE OF THEM — Well, check this out! When I was carrying him, the maggots from his eyes fell into my ears—that's when they began to stink.

ONE OF THEM — Motherfucker. I got stuck carrying his you-know-what!

The others laugh.

ONE OF THEM — Me too. I got stuck with his ass. Then some jerk stepped on my foot, *clomp, clomp*, then I fell like this . . . *[Falls.]* Then I was trampled. I was so pissed, I just bit butt. Huh! Whose butt was that?

ONE OF THEM — You stupid shit, that was me! *[Kicks One of Them. The others laugh.]* And when I was being bit, someone elbowed me from the left. Hey, it was you, wasn't it? *[Pushes One of Them.]*

The One who was pushed remains silent. The others laugh.

ONE OF THEM — When I got elbowed, I *zzt, zzt, zzt,* left and right, *zzt* behind *zzt,* and got everyone. Got you, right?

ONE OF THEM — Figures. *[The others laugh.]* I was getting it from all sides. Attacked from the left, from the right, bitten from below. Couldn't fight back. My hands were being crushed by the body. They're all blistered. *[Sniffs his fingers.]*

ONE OF THEM — They smell?

ONE OF THEM — No!

The others burst out laughing. In the midst of the laughter, the Cucumber Eater shrieks. The cucumber shoots straight ahead. Everyone is surprised.

ONE OF THEM — What the . . . ?

The Cucumber Eater points to the cucumber.

ONE OF THEM — Huh?

The Cucumber Eater tries to speak, but can't.

ONE OF THEM — What's up with you?

The Cucumber Eater excitedly points to the cucumber. One of Them moves to pick up the cucumber.

CUCUMBER EATER Don't!

The One who jumped up to grab the cucumber stops.

ONE OF THEM What? What?

CUCUMBER EATER Don't . . . don't.

ONE OF THEM Why not?

CUCUMBER EATER His spirit is still here.

ONE OF THEM Whose spirit?

CUCUMBER EATER While I was eating the cucumber, it jumped like someone was pulling it!

ONE OF THEM Jumped out of your hand?

CUCUMBER EATER Yes, *whoosh,* just like that. I was here, like this, just like this. I was getting ready to eat it, like this, when suddenly *whoosh,* like that! Then *whoosh,* like that. Like someone grabbed it.

They all think.

ONE OF THEM *Whoosh,* like that?

CUCUMBER EATER Yes, *whoosh,* like that. And I was here. I was hungry, ready to eat. Just wanted to pick it up like this, then *whoosh,* suddenly, like that. Like someone grabbed it!

All are astonished. One of Them wants to investigate.

INVESTIGATOR Maybe his spirit is still here.

No one objects to giving the Investigator the floor. The cucumber becomes the focus of the investigation.

Is this the cucumber in question?

CUCUMBER EATER Yes.

INVESTIGATOR An ordinary cucumber?

CUCUMBER EATER Ordinary.

INVESTIGATOR Are you sure?

CUCUMBER EATER [*Hesitant.*] I dunno if an ordinary cucumber can go *whoosh,* like that.

ONE OF THEM Waddya mean his spirit is here? Where?

INVESTIGATOR It's possible! From where did you get that object?

CUCUMBER EATER [*Thinking.*] The market.

INVESTIGATOR When?

CUCUMBER EATER [*Thinking hard.*] Yesterday.

INVESTIGATOR Do you normally eat cucumbers . . . uh, objects such as those?

CUCUMBER EATER [*Thinking hard.*] Yes.

INVESTIGATOR Oh?

CUCUMBER EATER Just "oh"?

INVESTIGATOR Just a moment. [*Walks around deep in thought.*]

The group members talk quietly among themselves, analyzing the evidence. Suddenly, the answer comes to the Investigator. He stops near the cucumber. Everyone is silent.

Yup. Now it's clear. Indeed, it's customary for the soul not to wander far from its murderer.

ONE OF THEM Ah, what?

INVESTIGATOR [*Shocked.*] What? What did I just say?

ONE OF THEM The soul doesn't wander far from its murderer—isn't that what you said?

INVESTIGATOR I said that?

ONE OF THEM Yes, that's what you said! Yes, that, yes!

INVESTIGATOR [*Panics.*] But I didn't mean to say that. We killed someone?

ONE OF THEM But that's what you said!

INVESTIGATOR I said that? Impossible. Not a chance!

ONE OF THEM Oh my God, oh my God, it's starting.

INVESTIGATOR Calm down, calm down. There must be a reason.

CUCUMBER EATER It's true, I'm not lying: that cucumber jumped, *whoosh*, right out of my hand.

ONE OF THEM Yeah, yeah.

INVESTIGATOR I really said that?

ONE OF THEM Absolutely.

INVESTIGATOR His soul's not going anywhere if we're the ones who killed him.

ONE OF THEM Get out!

INVESTIGATOR What? Come on, are you telling me the soul doesn't know who killed it? What kind of soul would that be?!

ONE OF THEM Everyone's different, right? There are those who just like to bug people. Who knows, maybe he's one of those!

ONE OF THEM Get a hold of yourself.

INVESTIGATOR What if he's accusing us?! [*Changes his mind.*]

ONE OF THEM Maybe he's made a mistake.

INVESTIGATOR He made a mistake accusing us—*us!* That's terrible. [*Changing his mind again.*] You know, that "he" is someone's soul.

CUCUMBER EATER But whatever . . .

INVESTIGATOR Okay, let me explain. Try to keep in mind that he came here—came here, I repeat—came here to us, without us knowing him beforehand. It wasn't us who went to him. We asked him what was wrong. Then he died because we didn't help him quickly enough, meaning before we had the chance to help him. Then we did nothing, nothing at first, and then we buried him, well, yeah, even though we weren't actually able to, there's a reason for that, those dogs ambushed us. We were irresponsible—um, we all are responsible, 'cause we didn't report everything, because we still don't know what happened for sure. Just that, did we murder him if we really killed him, ah, or we wanted to help him until, until it went only so far. And now it's a lost cause. And, and, and *kkk* . . . [*Tries to speak but has difficulty and punches himself in the mouth.*] Damn, what's up with my mouth? And *kkk* . . . ah! *Kkk* . . . damn!

Furious, the Investigator leaps over to the cucumber and crushes it underfoot. Once it's flattened, he kicks it away. He tries to speak again, but continues to have a very difficult time. Astonished and dazed, the others regard their friend who is unable to speak. They wait. Suddenly, One of Them smells the stench again.

ONE OF THEM The smell's back!

The others sniff.

ONE OF THEM Right!

ONE OF THEM It's worse!

ONE OF THEM Balsam, balsam, quick!

ONE OF THEM Where's that balsam? You were the last with it!

ONE OF THEM Empty!

ONE OF THEM — We're screwed!

ONE OF THEM — Mercy, it stinks! [*Holds his nose.*]

They all hold their noses.

ONE OF THEM — It's getting worse.

ONE OF THEM — It's creeping over my body. You too?

ONE OF THEM — We stink like rotting corpses.

ONE OF THEM — We'd be fucked if there was anyone else here.

ONE OF THEM — Good thing no cops have been by here.

One of Them lets go of his nose a bit to smell the air, then shrieks.

ONE OF THEM — Damn!

ONE OF THEM — Careful, don't let go!

ONE OF THEM — Let's go over there. Those dogs are com—ugh! [*Quickly covers his mouth.*]

The others also cover their mouths and noses. No one takes any initiative in the moments that follow. They hover close to speaking, but it's not clear what they want to say.

ONE OF THEM — Mmm . . .

ONE OF THEM — Mmm . . .

The others repeat until a cry is heard in the distance: "Owww, owww, owww . . ." They speak while covering their noses and mouths.

ONE OF THEM — What's that?

ONE OF THEM — Take a look!

ONE OF THEM — Come on!

The moaning continues.

ONE OF THEM — You think it's his soul?

ONE OF THEM — Impossible.

ONE OF THEM — It's like what's-his-name's voice . . . Who was that?

ONE OF THEM — Careful, it's coming closer.

ONE OF THEM — What if it's . . . ya know?

ONE OF THEM — Maybe the body's not dead?

ONE OF THEM Everyone can hear that, right?

ONE OF THEM It's like I'm its target.

ONE OF THEM Me too!

ONE OF THEM We're doomed!

One of Them takes on the role of the Leader.

LEADER Quiet, quiet. It's still not clear what that is.

The voice becomes more distinct.

ONE OF THEM There!

ONE OF THEM Poor thing!

ONE OF THEM Waddya mean "poor thing"?

ONE OF THEM Can they hear it too?

ONE OF THEM It's getting closer, so prepare yourselves!

ONE OF THEM Let's run!

ONE OF THEM Why—where to?

ONE OF THEM Come on, run!

LEADER Don't!

ONE OF THEM We're doomed!

ONE OF THEM Come on!

LEADER Don't! Hold on! [*Grabs the person preparing to run.*]

ONE OF THEM Hold on?

LEADER Stop it!

ONE OF THEM Hey!

LEADER Enough!

ONE OF THEM But . . .

ONE OF THEM Yeah, yeah! Go!

LEADER Go where?

ONE OF THEM First go! The where comes later.

The voice is gone.

ONE OF THEM Huh?

ONE OF THEM What?

ONE OF THEM Well!

LEADER Yeah, yeah.

ONE OF THEM [*Seriously.*] Weird, wasn't it?

ONE OF THEM Just like that.

ONE OF THEM *Tsk, tsk, tsk!* Strange!

ONE OF THEM Huh! What's that?

They all wait stiffly. One of Them screams in response to something.

ONE OF THEM *Ooowww!*

The others are taken aback. They grow angry once they figure out who yelled. They yell at him, and some even begin kicking him.

ONE OF THEM Asshole!

ONE OF THEM Fooling around, eh?

ONE OF THEM What were you thinking?

ONE OF THEM Monkey!

ONE OF THEM Take that!

ONE OF THEM [*Kicked to the ground.*] *Ow! Ow!*

ONE OF THEM Shut up, you stiff.

ONE OF THEM Damn it!

LEADER Enough, enough! I can't tell what's going on. Quiet!

All of a sudden, the dogs begin barking wildly. The barking is no longer distant. It sounds like the dogs are out on the chase.

ONE OF THEM Listen!

ONE OF THEM Come on, quickly, quickly!

The group scatters, each looking out for himself or herself.

LEADER Don't go over there. To the right! Quickly, quickly!

Those who impulsively ran to the left quickly change direction and run to the right. They all exit. Offstage, the group members are heard yelling, trying to save themselves as the dogs pass them by, barking. Pell-mell, they enter, returning to their original positions.

Go left, quickly! Quickly! Be careful!

They run left. The dogs thunder by again. The group members chase each other offstage, then back and forth. Finally they enter, returning to their original positions.

To the right! Quickly! Quickly! Stop! Wait!

They skid to a halt. Some fall, others slam into each other. The Leader raises his hand. The barking fades in the distance. The group is relieved. Their breathing is labored. Suddenly, the Pathfinder appears. He is surprised to see his comrades. He chuckles with amusement when he sees them. The Leader takes offense and whacks him. The Pathfinder tries to fight back in protest, but The One shows up and strikes him. They both fall down. Eyes closed, The One quickly rises and tries to run. Another One of Them catches The One, but The One is very strong. The others help. It turns into a struggle. Nevertheless, The One manages to break free and run. He runs but collides into a wall. Only then does he open his eyes. It gladdens him to see his friends. He tries to speak, but cannot. He uses sign language to explain something that happened in the direction from where he came. The group doesn't understand him, but looks in the direction he has indicated. They wait for whatever is supposed to come from that direction. Moments later, Someone screams as if being tortured. The screams affect everyone. The voice wails, moans, calls for help, and so forth. The cries culminate in a piercing scream, which suddenly stops when something heavy hits the ground.

The group breathes a sigh of relief. One or two people offer a silent prayer as if Someone has just died. A dog howls in the distance. The light fades. Night arrives. At first, no one notices the darkness falling. But as it becomes pitch black, chaos ensues. Everyone mills about until One of Them falls and screams loudly and clearly.

Everyone runs in circles, pushing and colliding with one another. Only when the morning light appears do they all begin to calm down. Short of breath and happy, they bathe themselves in the light. It is as if they have been liberated. Soon, however, a moaning is heard once again. The group focuses its attention on The Other, entering with bandaged feet.

THE OTHER *Owww, owww, owww...*

The group regards The Other with great interest. Several people point their fingers. One of Them is pushed forward to ask questions. After a moment of observation, he begins his questions.

ONE OF THEM — Are you ill? Are you ill? What hurts? What is it? In pain? You poor thing, what's wrong?

The Other moans pitifully. The members of the group come forward with questions.

ONE OF THEM — Are you sick?

ONE OF THEM — Do you have a cold?

ONE OF THEM — A fever? Dizziness?

ONE OF THEM — It's probably epilepsy.

The Other moans.

ONE OF THEM — What hurts? Out with it. Don't be shy. We want to help you.

ONE OF THEM — Poor thing. His face looks so old. Maybe he's overworked and underfed. Have you eaten yet?

ONE OF THEM — It's windy here...

They speak and act as they did when the play began. Everyone speaks over one another as the curtain falls.

Translation by Cobina Gillitt

Dwi & Ucok,
Yogyakarta, 2008.
Kurniadi Widodo

Langgeng Art Foundation,
Yogyakarta, 2013.
Kurniadi Widodo

LUNA VIDYA

The Kitchen

Translator's Note: In this dramatic monologue adapted from the short story of the same title by Lily Yulianti Farid, one actress plays all the roles. The story originally appeared in the January 2009 issue, Tropical Currents: Writing by Indonesian Women, *of the Chicago-based journal* Words without Borders.

Cast of Characters

Older Kalyla
Young Kalyla
Ruth
Kalyla's Mother

Act One

The stage is dark. A static light shines on the actress who plays the roles of Older Kalyla, Young Kalyla, Ruth, and Kalyla's Mother.

OLDER KALYLA Take this blank receipt with you! I can wait for your payment, but I'm not going to sign a blank receipt. I will not be part of your scam. Never!

What? You'd better watch what you say! This isn't a question of me getting a share or not!

Excuse me? You really don't get it, do you? This is a catering business. What I sell here is food, not my self-respect!

And don't you ever, ever again send someone to my home like you did last night to arrange a meeting!

Maybe you think I am my mother. Well, you're wrong! You're wrong to think you can trap me because of my background—because of who I am.

But let me be clear: I am a different person from my mother.

What? Do you think because of who I am I should have no self-respect? Is that what you think?

Well, my name is Kalyla. And I am not my mother!

The lights fade.

Act Two

Onstage is a flour-spattered kitchen table on which are heaped baking pans, a rolling pin, and other cooking implements. Also on the table are a mound of rising dough; a pan of flour; different kinds of pastry fillings; and jars of spices, chocolate, and red and green cherries. Parenthetical text in the dialogue is a translation of the Maluku dialect spoken by Ruth.

OLDER KALYLA — I was raised in this kitchen. I grew up amid the hustle and bustle around this kitchen table.

I learned to walk while holding on to the hem of Mother's dress as she diced onions, boiled potatoes, and minced meat.

At first I watched and then I began to help Ruth—Mother's helper and my nanny—sift flour and stir different kinds of dough.

I rested on Mother's lap, napped on the slickly ironed expanse of her long skirt.

On Ruth's lap, on her oil-stained sarong that always smelled of spices, I was coddled.

I used to wet my pants—often and almost anywhere: in my bed, on the sofa, on Mother's lap, on Ruth's sarong.

Little Miss Wet-Her-Pants! That's what Ruth called me when I was a girl.

RUTH — *Dolo-dolo nona pung bakas kancing di bolsak persis map pulau Jawa . . .*

(When you were a girl, those puddles of piddle you made looked just like a map of Java!)

OLDER KALYLA — Ruth *did* love flour, but she was obsessed with the island of Java. Anything beyond her imagination was always connected with Java.

YOUNG KALYLA — Look at this, Ruth . . . The flour is just like snow.

RUTH — *Barang apa lae tu salju kah? Beta seng tau, nona . . .*

(What is snow? I don't know what that is, Little Miss.)

YOUNG KALYLA You know, Ruth—that soft and fluffy white stuff in foreign countries that looks like shaved ice... Like the stuff you see in comic books and on television.

RUTH On television? *Sio di Jawa sana ada salju lae ka?*

(So, is there snow in Java?)

YOUNG KALYLA [*Laughing.*] Snow in Java? You're stupid! There's no snow in Java. Mama! Ruth thinks there's snow in Java!

MOTHER Kalyla! You must not be that way. It's not nice. You must never call an older person stupid.

Don't laugh at Ruth because she doesn't know there is no snow in Java.

You have to be more sensitive of other people's feelings.

What if you hurt Ruth's feelings by calling her stupid? What if Ruth were to get angry with you?

How would you like it if Ruth were to leave us?

If she were to go, who would help me with my cooking and baking? And who would take care of you when I had to go out on business?

That's right! No one. We'd be here all alone.

You're a smart and pretty girl, Lyla, but if you laugh at people like you just laughed at Ruth, people will say that you're bad mannered. Stuck up!

You must never be stuck up. God forbid that when you're older you show no regard for other people's feelings!

No matter how pretty or smart you might be, people will still think you're bad mannered.

YOUNG KALYLA Ruth, what does bad mannered mean?

RUTH You know, like that woman...

YOUNG KALYLA What woman?

RUTH That woman who took your father away.

YOUNG KALYLA Are you mad at me, Ruth? Don't be mad. If you don't want your feelings hurt, I can say that there is snow in Java. I can do that... even though there is no snow there.

RUTH [*Laughing.*] *Nonae, seng apa-apa. Tapi nona, nona seng boleh parlente par bikin orang pu hati sanang.*

(I'm not mad, Little Miss. You don't have to pretend something just to make people feel happy.)

YOUNG KALYLA But Mama said I'm supposed to watch your feelings.

RUTH *Tapi su seng banar kalau tagal mo jaga orang pung hati, nona seng stori banar. Itu lai seng banar.*

(That's fine, but it's not right to lie to people just to make them happy. No, not right at all!)

OLDER KALYLA For our faithful Ambonese caregiver, the world was simple: there was right and there was wrong. There was no gray area for Ruth. Java was the farthest place that Ruth could ever imagine going. And outside of Java, there was nowhere at all.

Even as a girl, she said, Ruth had dreamt of taking a train across Java, traveling from one end to the other . . . Just like her grandmother—the wife of a colonial army soldier stationed in Java—had once done.

Ruth's life was a journey, one that would not end until she set foot in the Javalands—which is what she used to call the island.

I don't know why, but Ruth was always so sure that one day she would go to Java.

For all the years she lived with us, she never gave up hope of seeing Java through the window of a train.

In our kitchen, Ruth often recalled the stages in her life's journey—one that had brought her here, to this kitchen and into our lives, but one that would, one day, begin again.

RUTH *Bet ni, harus sampai di Jawa nona. Karena kalo bet seng dapa injak itu Tana Jawa, lalu par apa bet barangkat?*

(I have to go to Java, Little Miss. Because if I never make it there, then why did I ever leave my own island of Ambon?)

YOUNG KALYLA Well, why didn't you go straight there at the time?

RUTH *Ooo bet ni mo pi Jawa nona. Waktu itu katong naik kapal barang. Kapal akang singga di mana-mana. Di Ternate, Tidore, Buton, Kabaena, Salayar. Mar bet salalu mabo lau. Bet sakit seng bae di kapal nona.*

Trus waktu su balayar mo pi Jawa baru bet rasa, balayar ni akang paling lamae.

Seng lai . . . Beta pi bet pung Om sa di Makassar, lebe dakat . . . kalau su kuat, bet barangkat lae pi Jawa.

(Oh, I was fully intending to do that, Little Miss. But the cargo ship on which I traveled stopped all over the place—in Ternate, Tidore, Buton, Kabaena, Salayar—and I was always getting seasick. Really bad!

You see, I didn't know how long the trip would take until I was actually on the ship.

After a while, I just couldn't take it anymore. So I got off the ship here, in Makassar, where I had an uncle living.

Besides, I thought, Makassar isn't that far from Java. Once I got my legs and stomach back, I'd continue my trip.)

OLDER KALYLA Our home was thus a transit point, and Ruth would never let herself forget that her journey had not yet ended.

Ruth's life was a journey under an open sky. She felt the blazing heat of the afternoon sun. She witnessed the change of seasons. She watched dark clouds as they covered the sky. She basked in the light of a full moon.

Everything was in the open. Nothing was hidden from Ruth.

[*Music plays and is followed by the sound of voices coming from a radio or television. Newscasters' voices tell of the violence—the bloody riots and mass destruction—that has befallen the island of Ambon.*]

RUTH [*Smacks a slab of dough on the kitchen table as hard as possible, then wields her rolling pin as if it were a weapon.*] *Kanapa musti baku prangka? Sio katong basudara tu kio.*

(Why is there all this fighting? We're family, aren't we?)

[*Again smacks the slab of dough as hard as possible on the table. Once again, rolls out the dough.*] *Kenapa ka . . . ? Jang lai jua kappa. Sio gandong. Gandong e.*

[*Music plays.*]

Kantong ni basudara. Kampung Salam deng kampung Kristen angka pella. Tagal apa tu? Perkara basar apa yang su biking dara akan cair? Cair lawange, sampe musti baku binci bagini? Kanapa? Kanapa katong musti baku bunu? Orang basudara su seng dapa tidur lai. Hidop su deng takotang. Seng tahu, eso ni masih bisa bernapas ka seng.

YOUNG KALYLA — Mama and I don't hate you, Ruth. We would never fight with you. Even if we don't pray the same way, you can stay with us here. There's no reason to be afraid.

RUTH — *Sio Nonae. Sakarang su seng mungkin orang macam katong dua ni... nona Acang beta Obet dudu satu meja.*

Disini bet tidur sanang. Di sana, bet pung basudara baku bunu. Bet pung hati badara nona.

(It's not like it is here, Little Miss. It wouldn't be possible for the two of us to sit at the same table.

Here, I can sleep in peace, but there, my family is killing one another. My heart bleeds...

Why? Why is there war? We're family. We're one family, aren't we? Oh, my loved ones...

We've always been family. It doesn't matter if we're Muslim or Christian; we all share the same blood, down through the generations.

So why, why does it have to be like this? What problem could be so great that it could weaken the bonds of blood?

Blood is thicker than water... How much hatred would it take to make it so thin?

Why do they hate one another, as if they are not family?

Why? Why do they have to kill one another like they're doing now?

They're all related, all one family, but now cannot sleep in peace.

They live in fear, not knowing if they'll still be breathing the next day.

Now it wouldn't be possible for two different people like us to sit at the same table.

Here, I can sleep in peace, but there, my family is killing one another.

My heart bleeds...)

OLDER KALYLA — In her sadness and her anger at that time of bloody conflict in Ambon, Ruth's breads became more evenly textured and soft.

The breads and rolls that she produced while watching the

violence on television turned out to be the best she ever made.

But for me, the strawberry jelly–filled rolls seemed to contain large clots of blood.

My stomach turned whenever I saw them come out of the oven.

At that time, Ruth's open sky was heavily overcast. But, beneath that cloudy sky, she made her way . . . Just as Mother did, too.

But Mother was not like Ruth. She was no open sky.

My beautiful mother, who liked to sing in the kitchen, was in fact a dark cave full of secret tunnels.

Mother's eyes were the opening of the cave, but the sadness in them was an obstacle not to be passed.

Although I shared all my tears and fears with Mother and Ruth, Mother never once opened herself to me.

In much the same way that she would never disclose the secrets of her favorite recipes, she never spoke of her past.

Mother was a secret gate with lock upon lock securing the story of her life.

I knew of the cave and the secret door because Mother cried whenever she watered the flowers in the garden.

Sadness never broke Mother, however. She loved the kitchen. Ruth loved flour. I loved Mother and Ruth.

I grew—just as our activities in the kitchen did: more and more all the time.

In the end, I came to love the kitchen and flour too.

Mother's catering business grew rapidly.

So beautiful and carefree, Mother always smiled patiently when dealing with her customers' demands.

Every day there was flour to be sifted, butter to be melted, bars of chocolate to be shaved, chicken meat to be shredded, red chilies to be ground.

Every day, the kitchen filled our lives. Every day brought with it a new culinary creation.

Ruth, Mother, and I immersed ourselves in our work in our beloved kitchen.

As our work increased, so too did the number of people in uniforms who came to our house.

The telephone rang almost nonstop with orders for meal packages for meetings. Every day, there was one meeting or another.

RUTH *Orang-orang kantor ini, dong makang gaji par rapat ka par karja?*

(Are those government guys paid for meetings or for work?)

OLDER KALYLA . . . So said Ruth at the time.

The people in uniforms were government civil servants whose job it was to negotiate catering services. Scam artists, one and all!

They came with blank receipts, asked for a special discount, submitted their next order, gave Mother another blank receipt, put in another order, and so on and so forth, like a never-stopping windmill.

They'd bow superciliously, narrow their eyes, and cough. Some would pretend to be busy with their calculators, punching in numbers like a grade-school student preparing for a mathematics examination.

. . . Before they say, "Oh, I'm sorry, Mrs. Andis, the budget for the meeting is only five million rupiah. Is a discount possible?"

Or "Excuse me, Mrs. Andis, could we pay for the next three months at the same time, combined with the food budget for meetings for the next two months? There will be a little percentage in it for you . . ."

Or even "Could you leave the receipt blank? That's possible, isn't it? For the following meeting, we'll be sure to use your catering service again . . ."

RUTH *Eh, itu orang-orang kantor, selalu saja mo minta potong harga, dorang ni nona, kasta makang pancuri.*

Jang bagitu kalo nona besar trus karja kantor, nona seng boleh jadi orang macam bagini.

Jang sampe tagal mo kepeng nona makang pancuri.

(Those kinds of people—they're always asking for discounts. The little thieves!

When you grow up, Little Miss, if you work in an office, you are not to be like them.

My Little Miss, you must never be a thief!)

OLDER KALYLA Until the day came . . .

The two windows in the kitchen, which usually revealed an expanse of blue sky, now showed rolling dark clouds.

The air was filled with the mad clanking of pots and pans.

From the corners of the kitchen, cockroaches emerged, bringing with them bad news.

Broccoli, carrots, cabbages, tomatoes, and green beans rotted and began to smell.

My beautiful mother, who loved our kitchen so much, who sang as she created dishes with an equal measure of love and skill, was now mincing meat with her jaws locked shut.

The more onions she diced, the more she cried.

Every once in a while, between hisses of oil in the fryer, you could hear her growl.

Ruth, meanwhile, chose to bury her head in the flour bucket.

MOTHER Take care of those food orders!

OLDER KALYLA Only once before in my life had I heard Mother speak in such a tone. That was the time she kicked my father out of the house for having secretly taken another wife.

The sound of them fighting in the bedroom was audible in the kitchen.

. . . Which is where Ruth had sat me down—here, at this table—to calm me with a whole jar of chocolate candy.

The chocolate melted in my hands.

Ruth didn't lift a finger to prevent me from eating as much chocolate as I wanted.

Then, after the screaming voices had finally died, Father came to the kitchen and hugged me. Very hard. Then left.

He never set foot in our house again. I never liked chocolate after that either.

YOUNG KALYLA — What's wrong, Mama?

OLDER KALYLA — She didn't reply.

YOUNG KALYLA — What is it, Ma?

OLDER KALYLA — Mother was indeed a dark cave—a claustrophobic place that provided no illumination for my questions at all.

My questions bounced off the cave walls, coming back to me in the same form: as questions.

Only with Mother and Ruth could I share my every pain or pleasure. But Mother never shared those same feelings with me.

YOUNG KALYLA — What's happening, Ruth?

OLDER KALYLA — She said nothing either.

A rumor had begun to spread, causing our large refrigerator to heave a sigh of sadness.

The atmosphere in the kitchen was like oil boiling in a pan—sizzling and hot.

The rumor that Mother was the mistress of a high government official—that being the reason she had been able to secure catering orders from numerous government offices—crept across the kitchen ceiling, turning into soot and char, black and disgusting.

One evening I came home crying. I huddled beneath the kitchen table.

YOUNG KALYLA — I heard the owner of the food stall say bad things about Mama.

RUTH — Just what did he say?

YOUNG KALYLA — That Mama is some big shot's mistress.

OLDER KALYLA — Ruth said nothing, but her face darkened.

Half running, she left the house and went to the end of the road, where the food stall was located.

From where I was standing beside the fence of our yard, I could see her put one hand on her hip and point her finger in the face of the food-stall owner.

Then she strutted, head high, back to the house.

In the end, I gave up and stopped my wheedling, stopped trying to figure out a way into Mother's secret cave, stopped trying to think about the dark forbodings that seemed to hover in her eyes.

I decided not to try to uncover Mother's secrets. By doing so, I might find myself trapped in the secret tunnels of her dark cave.

I said, Enough! To hell with rumors.

I have orders to fill!

The lights fade.

Translation by John H. McGlynn

Women watching guests dance in the Kraton Sasana Handrawina banquet hall, Surakarta, Java, 1949. Henri Cartier-Bresson/ Magnum

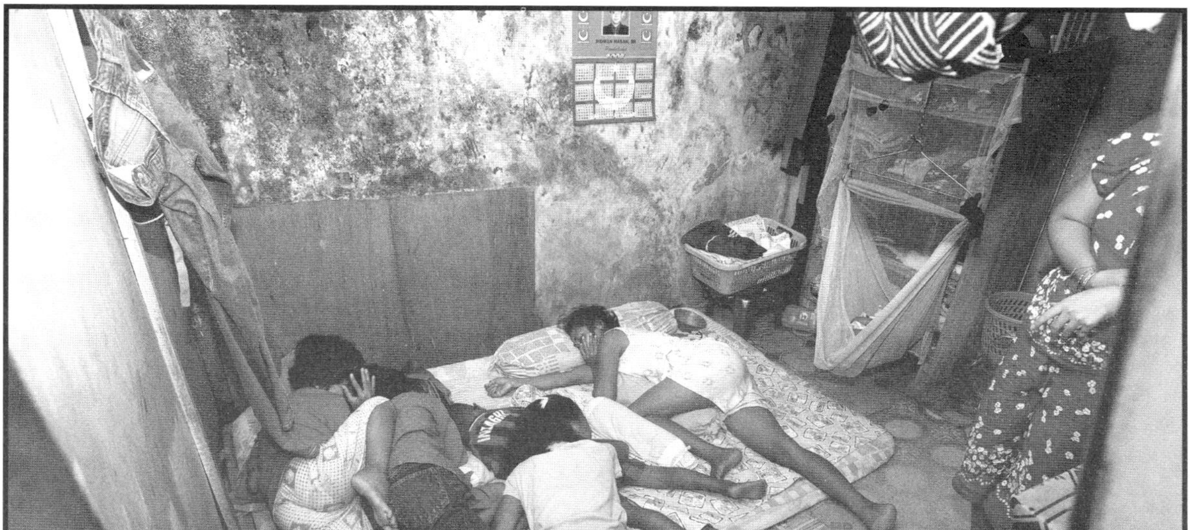

Muslim building for internally displaced people, Ambon, 2004. Carl De Keyzer/Magnum

The day before Indonesian independence, 300 portraits of former Dutch governor-generals are removed from the governor-general's mansion, now known as the Palace of Freedom, Jakarta, 1949.
Henri Cartier-Bresson/ Magnum

The Prostitute and the President

Cast of Characters

Jamila 1
Jamila 2
Mrs. Wardiman
Zaelani, servant to Mrs. Wardiman
Ria, prison warden
Mrs. Darno, prostitutes' manager
The President
Prison Guards
Lawyer
Cleric
Government Official's Wife 1
Government Official's Wife 2
Prostitutes
Police Officers
Little Children

Opening Scene

The stage is empty and dark. As if dawn approaches, rays of light appear on the backdrop. The voice of a young woman singing a sawalat*—a song of praise to the Prophet Mohammad—can be heard. After a few seconds, a group of pre-adolescent girls pass by in silhouette. Mrs. Darno and several thugs herd the children forward, sometimes slapping their butts, sometimes pulling their hair.*

After the adults and children exit, spotlights explode from various directions. The sound of a siren is heard blaring in the distance, followed by the siren of a police car. There follows the voices of television newscasters reading reports about the death of a government minister. Their voices overlap with one another. While they read, a funeral cortège crosses the stage with lights shining on it from the side.

NEWSCASTER 1 Nurdin Hidayat, cabinet minister, was found dead this morning in the room of a five-star hotel. Having sustained a number of stab wounds to the chest and stomach, his body was covered in blood.

NEWSCASTER 2 A young woman by the name of Jamila reported the death of Minister Nurdin to the police. She confessed to having killed him with premeditation.

NEWSCASTER 3 Today's cabinet meeting was conducted under the cloud of this news. Both the manner and the location of Nurdin's death were cited by various parties as signs of failure on the part of the President to select cabinet members of high moral caliber.

NEWSCASTER 4 Numerous political observers have called on the nation's political parties and the nation's politicians, in particular, to take a lesson from Nurdin's death. His murder has given the President an opportunity to cleanse the minister's office from political interests.

[*The voices of the newscasters fade as the funeral cortège exits the stage and the spotlights dim. The sound of the siren grows more distant.*

A light fades in on Jamila 2, who is seated on a cot in her prison cell. Her eyes, burning with anger and hate, are fixed on a single point. Meanwhile, on the backdrop, the blurred silhouette of Jamila 1 can be seen as she recites sections of the Quran.]

JAMILA 1 *Bismillahhirohmah nir rohim. Allahumagh firli maqaddamtu mawa akhartu wama asrartuwama a'lantu wama asraftu wama anta a'alamu bihi minni antalmuqaddimu wa antal muakhkhiru laaillaaha illa anta. Allahuma inni a'udzubika min adzabilqabri wamin 'adzabin nari wamin fitnatilmahya walmamati wamin fitnatil masihid dajjal. Allahuma inni dhalamtu nafsi dhulman katsira wala yaghfirudz dzunuba illa anta faghfirli maghfiratan katsiratan min 'indika warhamni innaka antal ghafururrahim.*

[*The light fades out on Jamila 2 and fades in on Mrs. Wardiman, who is paralyzed and in a wheelchair. She comes to the front of the stage. Her harsh and angry voice shatters the pensive atmosphere. She calls out for Zaelani, a male servant with markedly effeminate mannerisms.*]

MRS. WARDIMAN [*Screaming.*] Zaelani! Zaelani!

ZAELANI [*Offstage.*] Yes, Madam. [*Runs from the back of the stage to Mrs. Wardiman.*]

Here I am, Madam.

MRS. WARDIMAN Order that woman to stop! Her praying makes my ears burn.

ZAELANI I don't understand, Madam.

MRS. WARDIMAN [*Repeating her order with a yell.*] Order her to stop praying!

[*Jamila 1 stops praying.*]

ZAELANI I'm confused, Madam.

MRS. WARDIMAN Don't play games with me, Zaelani.

ZAELANI I wouldn't do that, Madam.

MRS. WARDIMAN Don't pretend you don't know what happened in this house.

ZAELANI I'm sorry, ma'am, but I really don't understand.

MRS. WARDIMAN Fool! Call Jamila for me.

ZAELANI Yes, ma'am. [*Stands and runs to the back, exiting. At that moment, Jamila 1 enters. She moves with precise steps toward Mrs. Wardiman, stopping directly in front of her.*]

JAMILA 1 Excuse me. You called me, ma'am.

[*The sudden appearance of Jamila 1 incenses Mrs. Wardiman, and she yanks the wheel of her chair to turn in a different direction.*]

MRS. WARDIMAN What's that *jilbab* you're wearing? [*Grumbling.*] Seeing you in that thing, I feel like I am in a conspiracy with the devils, insulting your mother.

[*With trembling hands, Jamila 1 pulls the scarf from her head. She bows her head, looking at the* jilbab *in her hands with a combination of sorrow and anger.*]

Your father sells you off as a child, and then your mother, poor off as she was, steals you from the *mucikari* who bought you and brings you here, hoping to see you raised in the home of a respectable family. She hopes that you'll grow up strong and healthy. But what do you go off and do . . . ? You were destined to be a whore.

[*The woman's words hurt Jamila 1. She stands stiffly, her head cocked, trying hard not to react.*]

All I asked was for you to give me one name, Jamila: that of my husband, Mr. Wardiman, or my son, Hendra. That's the only way that I could have done something to protect you. But, instead, you sealed your lips.

[*Jamila 1 slowly, but resolutely, withdraws.*]

That's it, always the same: saying nothing and going your own way!

[*Jamila 1 stops mid-step. Sound effects indicate her anger.*]

Where do you think you're going? To parade that big belly of yours in the streets?

[*Jamila 1 turns her back on Mrs. Wardiman and quickly leaves the stage. Mrs. Wardiman angrily watches Jamila exit. As if seeking to discharge her anger, she pushes on the wheels of her chair while screaming for Zaelani.*]

Zaelani! Zaelani!

[*Mrs. Wardiman speeds off the stage. From two opposing directions, several night guards appear with flashlights in their hands. A few seconds later, screams are heard.*]

ZAELANI [*Offstage.*] Murder! Murder!

MRS. WARDIMAN [*Offstage.*] Help! Murder!

[*The night guards stop, each one focusing the light of his flashlight in the same direction. They run offstage in that direction. Jamila 1 rushes in from a different direction. In her trembling hand she clutches a knife. The night guards reenter in pursuit of Jamila 1, who falls down in the very center of the stage. The night guards form a semi-circle around her and point their lights at her as she remains motionless.*

In the background, a choir of men and women sing a salawat.

One set of lights illuminates Jamila 1, who remains motionless on the floor. A brighter set of lights is on Jamila 2, who, inside her prison cell, is bowing her head in prayers. Her position is the same as that of Jamila 1. Slowly, Jamila 2 raises her body. Suddenly her arms shoot up, and she screams with all her might.

Ria, a female warden of around thirty years of age, enters with a cigarette dangling from her mouth. She takes a drag on the cigarette and looks coldly at Jamila 2. Though she tries to keep her volume down when speaking, her tone is abrasive.]

RIA What's all this screaming?

[*Jamila 2 suddenly freezes in response to the harsh tone.*]

Hey, you're not the only one here, you know. A nightmare? Big deal! You kill a bigwig government official in cold blood and that doesn't faze you, but you get all upset about a bad dream. Give me a break!

[Jamila 2 doesn't respond. She appears to be very tired. She lies down and curls into herself.

The light on Jamila 2 dims as the light on Jamila 1 brightens. Encircled by the night guards, Jamila 1 starts to rise while using her scarf to clean the blood from the knife that she clutches in her hand. She doesn't seem to be able to remove the blood from the knife. She stares at the blood and her scarf with horror.]

JAMILA 1 [*Trembling with emotion.*] What is this . . . ? Dear God, what is this . . . ? Mother said my birth was a blessing. There was a ceremony . . . Prayers and songs to the Prophet . . . Mother taught me about virtue and self-worth . . . But look at me now! Here I am, alone, in the midst of a darkness that has no end.

[*As the night guards drag her away.*] What kind of virtue do you see here, Mother? What kind of self-worth?

[The light on Jamila 1 fades as the light on Jamila 2 brightens. Jamila 2 remains curled up. Ria approaches her, then sits down with her back to her. A plume of smoke rises from Ria's cigarette.]

JAMILA 2 And that, Ria, was the worst experience in my entire life. I was entrusted to that family, placed in a respectable home so that I could grow up in a safe and healthy environment. And yet the two men in that most respectable family had their way with me every night.

[Ria stands and looks at Jamila 2. She takes a long drag on her cigarette and exhales the smoke.]

RIA [*Cynically.*] Yeah, right, a prostitute talking about virtue . . . [*Raising her voice and speaking as if completely out of patience.*] Hey, you listen to me, Mila! I've been warden here for three years, and I've had my fill of stories of defense like yours. [*Shaking her finger at Jamila 2.*] Raped, tortured, sold off, whatever! No matter what happened, nothing gives you the right to murder someone and then expect to receive sympathy.

[Jamila 2 slaps aside Ria's pointing finger. At that moment, her attitude suddenly changes. She pulls herself up. Now seated erect, she stares straight ahead. She appears strong. The choir voices singing the song of praise to the Prophet fade.]

JAMILA 2 I killed the two of them, at the same time. I killed them with my own hands.

RIA [*Sneering angrily.*] Oh, really! And you're proud of it? What are you proud of, Mila? For becoming famous? For making the headlines in the newspapers? [*Unable to control herself, Ria suddenly approaches Jamila 2 and shakes Jamila's head with her hands.*]

Listen to me, you little whore, you should be ashamed!

[*Jamila 2 doesn't respond. She continues staring, as if seeking a path to the past. Ria leaves the cell in disgust. In choreographed movements, a group of Prostitutes proceeds across the stage. As Jamila 2 finds herself drifting into the dark world that fate chose for her, a song of praise in a solo voice is heard. The stage lights fade out.*]

Scene One

The lights on Jamila 2's cell come up. A Prison Guard, carrying a newspaper, enters from the back of the stage. Jamila 2 suddenly lies down and raises one of her legs, causing her prison frock to fall to the base of her thigh. The Guard's mouth falls open. He tries not to stare at Jamila 2's thigh but momentarily finds himself unable to. Finally, he forces himself to turn away.

PRISON GUARD 1 Put down your leg, Jamila.

[*Jamila 2 ignores the order and spitefully raises her other leg.*]

[*Turning back toward her and speaking angrily.*] I told you to put your leg down!

JAMILA 2 [*Laughing, as if pleased with herself.*] Why should I? Turns you on, huh? Well then, don't look!

PRISON GUARD 1 [*Grumbling.*] Damn whore!

JAMILA 2 I'm not in this prison for prostitution, Mr. Policeman, but for murder—which means I'm a killer, not a whore.

[*Not wanting to continue the debate, the Guard moves away.*]

You got a family?

PRISON GUARD 1 Yes.

JAMILA 2 Any girls?

PRISON GUARD 1 Yes, two.

JAMILA 2 [*In one move, shifts to a sitting position.*] Then take good care of them. We all know that no child is born evil, but I am a witness that this world, which is full of hypocrisy and greed, easily soils innocent souls and ensnares them . . . [*Seems suddenly anxious. Pulls her legs up and puts her arms around her calves. Staring straight ahead, sharply, she then speaks in a deep voice.*]

And I am one of them! I was a murderer from the time I hardly knew right from wrong. And *that* is very frightening.

[*The Guard moves away as she laughs at him cynically. He stops moving when hearing her speak.*]

What's wrong? Knowing that I really am a murderer, you now despise me?

PRISON GUARD 1 [*Doesn't respond. Opens the newspaper in his hands and starts to read aloud.*] "The special committee of Parliament, established to regulate against pornography and indecency, has deceived both those who support the bill and those who oppose it . . ."

[*Suddenly angry, Jamila 2 approaches the Guard and takes the newspaper from him. She roughly turns the pages until, finding what she's looking for, she folds the paper and returns it to him, pointing out the article that he should be reading.*]

JAMILA 2 Today the Court will decide my verdict. [*Again pulls the newspaper from the hands of the Guard, opens it to another article, and hands the paper back.*]

I bet you all the papers are full of the news today . . .

PRISON GUARD 1 [*Reading aloud the article that Jamila 2 found.*] "The National Forum for Defense of Religion has called on its members to gather outside the Justice Department tomorrow to show their support for the death sentence expected to be meted out to Jamila—"

JAMILA 2 "The National Forum for Defense of Religion" . . . Morality police! Those hypocrites! [*Sashays around the Guard in streetwalker style while clarifying her cynical view of the news report.*]

If they actually knew the meaning of "morality" they would know what kind made my life this way! And they would have selected me to be an honorary member!

[*Ria appears with a Lawyer. She doesn't like the way Jamila 2 is acting, and she coughs loudly. Seeing Ria, the Guard distances himself from Jamila 2. Jamila 2 returns to her cot in silence.*]

RIA — [*Calling to the Guard.*] Where are you going? [*Approaching him.*] Your job is to guard the inmates, not fool around with them.

[*The Guard doesn't like the way Ria has spoken to him, but he chooses to bite his tongue and leave the cell. Ria takes a deep breath, then approaches Jamila 2. Ria's manner and tone of voice are unsympathetic. She sits down with her back to Jamila 2.*]

Jamila! Here, I brought you a lawyer. I, myself, don't believe in them. But, who knows, maybe your luck will be better.

[*When Jamila 2 doesn't respond, Ria stands and moves toward the Lawyer.*]

This is Mister Malik. He has volunteered to defend you at your trial. If he's offering to defend you, that means it's *pro bono*, for free. [*To the Lawyer.*] That's right, isn't it?

[*The Lawyer answers with a smile and moves toward Jamila 2, who suddenly jumps up from her cot.*]

JAMILA 2 — [*Defiantly.*] I don't need a defense.

[*The Lawyer thinks for a few seconds, deciding which approach is best to reach her. Again, he moves toward Jamila 2.*]

LAWYER — [*In a "lawyerly" voice.*] Jamila, you killed a high government official. But, in this instance, there are many people who have doubts about the judicial process. It's all going too fast, it doesn't make sense . . .

[*The tone of the Lawyer's voice makes Jamila 2 even less willing to talk to him, and she pulls farther away. Even so, the Lawyer does not desist and continues his approach.*]

Millions of people out there feel sympathy for you, Jamila—

RIA — [*Interjecting.*] You see? What did I tell you? If I killed my old man because he came home drunk every day and beat me up, no one would show sympathy . . .

JAMILA 2 — [*Standing quickly. Growling.*] "Sympathy"? I just read how they want me dead.

LAWYER — Not those ones, Jamila, the other millions out there.

JAMILA 2 — Enough said, sir! [*Returns to her cot.*]

LAWYER — [*Follows her.*] What about the hundreds of millions of voiceless people out there? They are the ones who understand your situation.

JAMILA 2 I said, enough!

LAWYER They don't want your case to ride on political expediency.

JAMILA 2 Enough! Enough already! I already said I don't need a defense.

[Jamila 2's emotion startles the Lawyer. A few seconds of silence.]

LAWYER Jamila . . .

JAMILA [*With a quavering voice.*] Out! Or I will scream.

RIA Enough, Mister Malik. She's determined to play the martyr. [*Gives a signal to the Lawyer to leave. The Prison Guard then escorts the Lawyer out.*]

[*Immediately faces Jamila 2. Emotionally and with ridicule in her voice.*] Whore, murderer, and now "martyr"! You're a whore, Mila. A murderer, too! Don't even dream of being a hero. [*Grumbling.*] Politics . . . Politics . . .

JAMILA 2 [*Pauses. In explanation, with dignity in her voice.*] Prostitution is politics, Ria. I'm no different from a politician.

RIA Watch what you say, Mila.

JAMILA 2 They scream about morality. Men are so passionate when speaking about morals.

RIA [*Loudly.*] Mila!

JAMILA 2 What is it? You take me to them, and I show a little leg—all of a sudden, morals don't count anymore. [*Laughs.*]

RIA [*Pulling Jamila 2 by the hand.*] Sit down.

JAMILA 2 [*With increasing force.*] I despise people who place such importance on political positions—both the ones wearing ties and the ones wearing turbans. We're the same, Ria. We're all whores.

RIA But you're a whore who's going to be put to death!

JAMILA 2 So? I killed that government official with my own hands, Ria, and in cold blood. [*As if to herself.*] People like that deserve to die.

RIA [*Standing, angrily.*] Enough, Mila!

JAMILA 2 [*Increasingly irritated.*] Why?

RIA [*With greater authority in her voice.*] Because whatever you say might only make your sentence worse.

JAMILA 2 — [*Draws back and sits on the edge of the cot angrily.*] Hah! After all this time condemning me, ridiculing me, and despising me, now you're pretending to care?

RIA — [*Tense but firm.*] But I do care, Jamila, I do. That's why I don't want what you say to be heard by others; it might only make matters worse.

JAMILA 2 — [*Roughly frees herself from Ria's grasp and stands up with a cynical grin on her face. Melodramatically.*] Oh, and is that so? But what if I want everyone to hear it? [*Leaping onto the cot and making Ria feel more panicked.*] Hey, all you out there whose suffering is the same as mine—

RIA — Stop that, Jamila!

JAMILA 2 — Yes, honorable officials and your wives—

RIA — [*Screaming.*] *Stop!*

JAMILA 2 — All you judges and Moslem scholars—

RIA — *Stop!*

JAMILA 2 — Do you know what those clerics see in people like me? Fire and brimstone! [*Laughs.*]

RIA — [*Panicking and calling out.*] Guards!

[*Two Prison Guards enter, but their presence makes Jamila 2 act even wilder and more wanton.*]

JAMILA 2 — What's wrong? I'm going to be sentenced to death! Doesn't that give me the right to do what I want before meeting my end? [*Aggravated by the sight of the two Guards suddenly standing at the edge of her cot. Swings her legs high in the air.*]

And as for my last request, Ria . . . How about if I ask for the president to fuck me?

[*Unable to control herself, Ria slaps Jamila 2. For a moment, there is silence as the two women stare at each other. Ria looks surprised at what she has done; Jamila is wary and moves away.*]

I would rather ask the president to sleep with me, Madam, than ask him to consider giving me a pardon. A pardon would only lengthen my misery.

RIA — [*To the Guards.*] Put her in solitary!

[*The Guards try to grab Jamila 2, but she resists them and manages to stand by Ria.*]

JAMILA 2	No child born on this planet has ever wanted to be a whore. You got to know that, Ria . . .
RIA	Guards! [*The Guards begin to drag away Jamila 2.*]
JAMILA 2	[*Screaming and crying.*] Who wanted me to be a whore? Who first planted hate in my chest? Tell me! Who planted hate in my chest?
	[*Pause. Ria sits at the edge of Jamila's cot, troubled by her thoughts. Prison Guard 1, who has remained onstage, looks at Ria with annoyance.*]
PRISON GUARD 1	Playing hardball with new inmates is good for their mental discipline, I grant you that. But inciting Jamila like that, ridiculing her and harassing her—
RIA	Enough.
PRISON GUARD 1	You can count the days she has to live. What kind of satisfaction do you get from hurting her? Tell me . . . Are you jealous of her?
RIA	[*Standing angrily and approaching the Guard.*] Look in the mirror! There's not a man in the world good enough for me, and that includes you. So don't act so very sure of yourself.
PRISON GUARD 1	But, ma'am, she shouldn't be put in solitary confinement.
RIA	I told you—enough.
PRISON GUARD 1	She hasn't done anything threatening.
RIA	Get out.
PRISON GUARD 1	All right, but if you don't want to have a problem, I suggest you bring Jamila back in here now.
RIA	[*Screaming.*] *Out!*
	[*Prison Guard 1 leaves. Deeply frustrated, Ria sits down on the edge of the cot. She presses her hands to her head as if it hurts.*]
	Dear God, what kind of hate is this? Dear God, what kind of hate . . .

Scene Two

The light fades out in the cell and fades in on centerstage. Mrs. Darno, a middle-aged madam, is roughly pulling a group of underage girls across the stage. Tati, a prostitute, comes running after Mrs. Darno.

TATI — Mrs. Darno! Just a second, Mrs. Darno!

MRS. DARNO — [*Stops walking. Perturbed.*] Now what, Tati?

TATI — Jamila wants to be a migrant worker, Mrs. Darno.

[*Mrs. Darno starts walking again. Jamila 1 enters, musters courage to speak, and turns to Mrs. Darno. Mrs. Darno looks at her, upset. Tired and irritated, she sits down on a bench nearby.*]

JAMILA 1 — Please help me, Mrs. Darno. I want to get a job abroad.

MRS. DARNO — Then find yourself a migrant-worker agent! You know what? You give me a headache. I don't know you, I don't know where you come from, but there you are, all of a sudden, in my house, washing in my bathroom and eating in my kitchen, and still you won't listen to my advice about what's best for you.

JAMILA 1 — I won't always be a burden, ma'am, but I have to work. That's why I want to get a job abroad.

MRS. DARNO — As a migrant worker? [*Pause.*] Have you ever read the newspaper, Jamila, or watched television?

[*Jamila 1 nods her head.*]

Then you've seen what becomes of lowly female migrant workers, how they are terrorized and treated like garbage.

JAMILA 1 — [*Nervous, answering almost inaudibly.*] I know, ma'am, but . . .

MRS. DARNO — Have you heard of Bonet? Or Ningsih, who has the death sentence hanging over her?

[*Hopelessly, Jamila 1 sits beside Mrs. Darno.*]

What if your crazy boss over there decides to take an iron to your nice, smooth skin? Are you prepared for that? Or to be raped every night after you've almost killed yourself scrubbing the floors all day?

TATI — [*To Mrs. Darno.*] Jamila's only asking for an introduction to Mami, the migrant agent.

MRS. DARNO — Shut your mouth when I am speaking, Tati. [*Tati immediately shrinks back.*] Since when have you become the go-between?

JAMILA 1 — [*Pleading.*] I don't have the papers I need. I've heard that Mami could help with that.

MRS. DARNO — Can't you see what I'm saying? Without papers, the only kind of job you're going to get abroad is as a servant. [*Sneering.*] And that woman you all call "Mami"—the only thing she's going to do is try to extort from you every last cent you earn. Becoming a migrant worker is like gambling. If you're lucky, you might get a decent boss, but if not, and you get a devil instead, you're going to end up victimized and penniless.

JAMILA 1 — But I need the money, ma'am, and don't have any papers.

MRS. DARNO — Aren't you listening? Without papers, the best you can hope to become abroad is a house servant. But here, you could be your own boss, open a food stall or something. Don't let yourself be dazzled by tales of workers who have found their fortune abroad. Listen to me, Jamila: it's far better to be a queen in one's own town than a slave in someone else's country.

JAMILA 1 — [*Insistent.*] But I need the money, ma'am. I want to be able to send my younger sister to school. I don't want her to be like me.

MRS. DARNO — I can show you, teach you how to earn lots of money, both quickly and easily.

TATI — But Jamila wants to work abroad!

MRS. DARNO — [*Out of patience.*] Shut up, Tati! Don't interfere! Get out of here! [*Tati immediately exits. Mrs. Darno looks again at Jamila 1, examining her closely.*]

[*In a cordial tone of voice.*] You do want to learn, don't you?

JAMILA 1 — I do, ma'am.

MRS. DARNO — That's good. [*Looks at Jamila 1 and inspects her body, feeling her from head to toe, as she asks questions.*]

How old are you now?

JAMILA 1 — Fourteen.

MRS. DARNO — That's good, but from now on you're eighteen.

JAMILA 1 — But I'm fourteen, ma'am.

MRS. DARNO — [*Shrilly.*] I know, but starting now your age is eighteen.

JAMILA 1 — [*Confused.*] But why?

MRS. DARNO — [*Steps closer to Jamila 1 and grabs her blouse, causing Jamila 1 to rise onto her toes.*] Because I want it that way and because you want to get a lot of money! You do want lots of money, don't you?

JAMILA 1 — Yes, ma'am.

MRS. DARNO — Then you will do what I say! Do you agree to that? [*Jamila 1 nods.*] Good, then we have an agreement. Don't ever forget that.

JAMILA 1 — I won't, ma'am.

[*Suddenly, a police siren starts to blare in the distance. Mrs. Darno grabs hold of Jamila 1 and starts to pull her offstage.*]

MRS. DARNO — Hurry up, would you?! Do you want to get caught?

[*Mrs. Darno and Jamila 1 exit. A group of Prostitutes run onto the stage from different directions, panicked. Spotlights illuminate them, one by one. Police Officers appear and chase after them, finally cornering them, but before the Officers can begin their raid, the Prostitutes start to heckle them, pointing their butts in the air.*]

OFFICER 1 — Bitches. [*Kicks the butt of one Prostitute, and all the Prostitutes fall to the floor, like a row of dominoes. Just then the Chief Officer enters.*]

CHIEF OFFICER — Stand up! Come on, stand up!

[*The Prostitutes try, with difficulty, to stand. The Officers pull them to their feet, one by one.*]

OFFICER 1 — Stand over there! Line up! Hey! Did you hear me? Line up!

[*A Plump Prostitute, who is entangled with another prostitute, is having a difficult time getting to her feet.*]

[*Muttering in wonder as he pulls the Plump Prostitute to her feet.*] Jeez, a chunky one like this . . . Who'd ever want her?

PLUMP PROSTITUTE — [*Makes a fist and shakes it at Officer 1. In a shrill, mocking voice.*] What? You want to try?

The other Prostitutes start heckling in unison.

CHIEF OFFICER — Enough! Come on, line up.

OFFICER 1 — Back up! Don't you know what a line is? Hey, fatso, get over there.

CHIEF OFFICER — [*To the Plump Prostitute.*] Fatso, you come forward.

PLUMP PROSTITUTE — [*Flips off Officer 1 and advances with her hips swaying.*] You see, I am in demand!

The other Prostitutes roar with laughter.

CHIEF OFFICER ID.

OFFICER 1 Hand over your ID.

[*The Plump Prostitute gives her ID card to the Chief Officer. The Chief Officer turns it back and forth, at the same time eyeing the Plump Prostitute.*]

CHIEF OFFICER Are you really nineteen years old?

PLUMP PROSTITUTE Yes, I'm nineteen years old.

CHIEF OFFICER Now, help me by collecting the ID cards of all your friends here. [*The Prostitutes move forward all together to protest.*] What? What's going on?

PROSTITUTE 2 [*Interjecting.*] We can settle this peacefully, sir . . .

CHIEF OFFICER [*Looks around to see which Prostitute made the comment. Angrily.*] Who said that?

[*The other Prostitutes shield Prostitute 2.*]

Hey, which one of you said that? Come here! If you're going to talk, at least have the guts to show your face!

[*When no one steps forward, the Chief Officer calls to the other Officers.*] Men!

[*Finally, an Officer pulls Prostitute 2 from the group and shoves her toward the Chief Officer.*]

What did you say? "Settle this peacefully"? You're not trying to bribe an officer of the law, are you?

[*The other Prostitutes immediately start heckling the Officers. Tati, one of the women, spits at the ground at the Chief Officer's feet.*]

You, the one who just spat, come here!

[*Tati defiantly approaches the Chief Officer.*]

Open up your friends' bags and get their ID cards!

TATI No way! I'm not police.

OFFICER 2 [*Growling.*] Uppity bitch! [*Pushes Tati toward the Chief Officer.*]

CHIEF OFFICER I told you to check your friends' bags!

TATI And I told you I wasn't going to do it!

CHIEF OFFICER — [*As if having no other choice.*] Okay! [*To the Officers.*] Men!

OFFICERS — Yes, sir!

CHIEF OFFICER — Carry out your orders!

OFFICERS — Yes, sir!

[*The Officers prepare to check the Prostitutes' bags, but a struggle immediately ensues. The Prostitutes attack the Officers—kicking, biting, spraying them with hairspray, and so on.*]

[*In unison.*] Help . . . Help . . . Stop, stop! Damn whores!

[*The Officers retreat, nursing their eyes and genitals. The Prostitutes run offstage, laughing loudly.*]

Scene Three

The Prostitutes return to the stage, performing a choreographed dance that symbolizes their moment of victory. A few moments later, Mrs. Darno enters from another side, with a wide, angry stride.

MRS. DARNO — Where is Jamila? [*The Prostitutes suddenly freeze and look at her disdainfully.*]

Well, has anyone seen Jamila or not? [*No one answers.*] So, what is this? Some kind of solidarity? [*Understanding.*] Oh, I see . . . I'm the one who's cruel and sadistic, who boxed the ears of the sweet and gentle Jamila . . . Who "exploited" her. [*Barking.*] Well, we have rules here! Protest all you want, do whatever you like, but there's always going to be a payoff. Jamila got twenty times more than any of the rest of you. Count for yourself the cost of her schooling, the language lessons, the expensive books . . . [*Pause.*] And it wasn't me who asked her to leave. The only thing I did was tell her to stop getting pregnant. How are you going to make any money if you're always pregnant?

[*Tati suddenly turns and runs in the direction from which Jamila 1 appears.*]

[*Snaps at Tati.*] Tati! Where do you think you're going?

[*When Tati stops, Mrs. Darno looks in the direction that she was headed, and sees Jamila 1 coming toward her.*] Oh, so her highness is here. [*To the other Prostitutes.*] You know what your friend's problem is? Arrogant! She thinks that with all the money she brings in, she can bargain with me.

[Jamila 1 walks past Mrs. Darno and toward her friends.]

Where do you think you're going?

JAMILA 1 I'm here to say good-bye.

MRS. DARNO *[To the other Prostitutes, mockingly.]* Did you hear that? *[To Jamila 1.]* You listen to me, girl. You're not going to find another runner as good as me, anywhere.

JAMILA 1 I'm not looking for another runner. I just want to go.

MRS. DARNO Where to? To start a clean life? You were born to be a whore, Jamila, and nothing is going to change that.

JAMILA 1 *[Both angry and dignified.]* You're wrong, Mrs. Darno. I never wanted to be a whore; I was not *born* to be a whore. It was you who made me one, you who cheated and exploited me, just as you have exploited all of these other women here.

MRS. DARNO Bitch! *[Raises her hand as if to strike Jamila 1, but Jamila 1 and the other Prostitutes immediately advance toward her.]*

JAMILA 1 Get back! Don't dare lay a finger on me!

MRS. DARNO *[Retreats.]* Oh, so now that you've got some money—which you got because of all I did for you—you turn against me. *[Sneering.]* So what are you going to do now? Teach college? Give instruction in how to read the Quran? *[Muttering.]* You don't know when you've got it good.

JAMILA 1 *[Takes out a bundle of bills from her handbag, then approaches Mrs. Darno and hands the wad to her.]* Here. This is to repay you for all your kindness.

[Mrs. Darno accepts the money grudgingly. She appears to want to speak, but Jamila 1 has already turned away, followed by the other Prostitutes. Jamila 1 looks back at Mrs. Darno.]

I'm still going to whore, Mrs. Darno, but now I will do it on my own terms.

[Jamila 1 and the other Prostitutes perform a choreographed dance that expresses their desire for freedom from exploitation.]

PROSTITUTES *[Dancing and singing as they exit.]* We're still going to whore, but on our own terms... We're still going to whore, but on our own terms... *[Repeat and fade.]*

Scene Four

As the stage lights fade, the light in Jamila 2's cell grows brighter. Jamila 2 is now curled up on her cot. Mrs. Darno enters, followed by a Prison Guard. Ria stands nearby, puffing on a cigarette. Mrs. Darno leans toward Jamila 2 and strokes her back.

MRS. DARNO [*Softly.*] Mila . . . Mila . . .

[*The sound of Mrs. Darno's voice—gentle, but clearly that of the devil for Jamila 2—startles Jamila 2. She jumps to her feet and casts an accusing look at Ria and the Prison Guard.*]

JAMILA 2 Who gave this woman permission to come in here?

MRS. DARNO Jamila . . . [*Tries to coax Jamila 2 for a moment. Ria and the Prison Guard are silent.*]

JAMILA 2 [*Screaming.*] *Who?!*

[*Ria approaches Jamila 2, embracing her, but Jamila 2 pulls away forcefully. Ria withdraws. Jamila 2 sits on the edge of the cot, speaking angrily to Mrs. Darno.*]

Why did you go to the trouble of coming here? To defend me? To serve as a character witness—that I am a prostitute with a heart of gold who could not possibly have committed murder?

MRS. DARNO Jamila—

JAMILA 2 [*Screaming.*] *Answer me!* [*Pause.*] Or maybe you'd like to appease your conscience for dooming the children I carried in my womb.

[*Jamila 2 rises and stands facing Mrs. Darno, rubbing her stomach as if rubbing a wound that is still raw. Her words spill out.*] Yes, those innocent babies who were never born, Mrs. Darno. I was so afraid that they would end up falling into the hands of people like you, I decided to kill them! Make note of that, Ria! Tell the prosecutor "a-bor-tion." Make sure the reasons they have for sentencing me to death are really complete!

[*Laughs wildly. The look on her face is one of anger, loathing, and pain.*] Wasn't it you, Mrs. Darno, who said that a man's desire is ready to overflow at any time and in any place? Which made it right for your girls to be raped; to be shackled and lose all love for life; to become objects of hypocrisy, pointed at as the cause for the moral degradation of the nation while, at the very same time, you were serving them up as meat for sale in order to fulfill your own greedy needs. They were sold and cheated and ridiculed and legislated against . . .

[*Laughs again.*] And what about the proposed anti-pornography and indecency legislation, Mrs. Darno. Happy? To have legislation replacing Holy Scripture? To have laws that deprive *ulema* and spiritual advisors of their jobs?

And the children, Mrs. Darno, what will happen to them? Ignorant of the very concept of spirituality, they'll become the objects of your immoral trade!

[*Now approaching Ria.*] And the prisons, Ria . . . The prisons will be packed full, and you'll be at wits' end figuring out how to demean so many of them.

[*Angrily walks away, distancing herself from the two other women. After a brief pause, she loudly addresses Mrs. Darno.*] Get out of my sight, Mrs. Darno!

MRS. DARNO Jamila . . .

JAMILA 2 [*Screaming.*] *Out!*

[*Jamila 2 pushes Mrs. Darno, causing her to bump into Ria, who then gives a sign to the Guards to escort Mrs. Darno out. After they have exited, Jamila 2 returns to her cot and sits, brooding. Ria approaches Jamila 2 and takes a seat beside her. She appears to want to say something, but Jamila 2 speaks first.*]

[*In a deep, troubled voice.*] Leave me, Ria . . . Please go. [*Pause.*] Thank you for bringing that woman here and restoring my anger.

[*Ria finally stands and leaves the cell. A solo song of praise is heard. Jamila 2 seems very sad. She picks up her scarf and holds it to her chest, then lowers her body to her cot. There, she writhes, turns over, looks up at the ceiling, attempting to sleep, but after a few moments is suddenly startled by a nightmare: she finds herself surrounded by all the pimps and clients that she has ever known.*]

What's this? All you pimps, madams, and tricks—aren't you satisfied with having sucked all the blood from my life? Aren't you pleased that I'm now to be taken to the gallows? Get out of here! You laugh when the world condemns us, spits on us, goes after us. But you can't fool God. He knows there would be no prostitutes without corrupt people like you. I know I am going to die soon and go to hell, but I also know that I will be in a different ring of hell from you!

[*She kneels on the floor at the foot of the cot as if to pray. Staring forward, she seems to see a thousand Mrs. Darnos standing at the other end of the cot. She falls to the floor, writhing as if being tortured.*]

No, no, don't! Don't! Please help . . . Help . . .

RIA [*Runs into the cell.*] Jamila! Mila . . . What's wrong?

[*She tries to help Jamila 2 stand, but Jamila 2 resists and rises to her feet unaided. She paces the cell, as if confused. Finally, she sits on the edge of the bed with her back to Ria.*]

What's wrong, Mila?

JAMILA 2 [*Both angry and traumatized.*] Do you believe me that I never wanted to be a whore?

RIA I believe you, Mila, I really do. [*Reaches out, but Jamila 2 turns away.*]

JAMILA 2 Tomorrow morning the Court will sentence me to death.

RIA [*Upset. Stands, trying to correct Jamila's thinking.*] That's not certain, Mila. You can't be pessimistic.

JAMILA 2 I killed two men: Mrs. Wardiman's husband and son.

RIA Don't say that!

JAMILA 2 After leaving Mrs. Darno, I ended up in the middle of a jungle in Kalimantan. There, I killed again.

RIA Stop, Mila!

JAMILA 2 [*Screaming.*] *I killed them, Ria!* And then I killed Mrs. Diah—not in self-defense but with premeditation!

RIA [*Firmly, harshly.*] Fine. But that never happened, Jamila. The Court must not learn of this.

JAMILA 2 [*Gets up on the cot and cradles her knees as she sits. Softly.*] Thank you, Ria, for finally wanting to be my friend, but I must die. That's the only way to stop me.

RIA Come here, Jamila . . . [*Tries to hold Jamila 2, but Jamila 2 rejects her embrace.*]

JAMILA 2 [*Moaning.*] I can't erase the memory of their condemnation and scorn, which has turned into hate that keeps building inside me, forever ready to explode and make me kill again . . . To make me kill again . . .

Lights fade out.

Scene Five-A

The lighst fade in on the stage. Jamila 1 enters, panting with fright and holding a bloody knife in her hand. She stops in the middle of the stage and sits on the floor with her legs to the side. She flings the knife to the ground in disgust and fear.

JAMILA 1 — Oh God, what happened? I did it again. I killed again. Allah, I killed again. Forgive me. Forgive me, Mother, forgive me.

[*The sound of footsteps causes Jamila 1 to panic.*]

CHIEF OFFICER — [*Offstage.*] Check every place!

OFFICERS — [*Offstage, in unison.*] Yes, sir.

CHIEF OFFICER — [*Offstage.*] Call all the prostitutes from their rooms. Order them to gather in the main hall. Do it now!

OFFICERS — [*Offstage, in unison.*] Yes, sir!

[*Jamila 1 exits the stage, hiding herself. The area where she had been now becomes a bordello near a coal mine in the middle of the Kalimantan jungle. There is no music. Everything is silent. The place is gloomy. The bordello's staff—Prostitutes, Security Guards, and Other Personnel—enter from different directions. The Chief Officer enters a bit to the rear. He takes up a position where he can see everyone.*]

CHIEF OFFICER — Tonight someone savagely killed Mrs. Diah. As a representative of the state, I swear that the barbaric killer will be paid back in kind. Jamila's argument with the deceased earlier this evening isn't proof that she is the killer, but because she's disappeared, she is definitely a suspect.

[*The Prostitutes stare at the Chief Officer coldly and defiantly.*]

Now, for the sake of justice—as well as for your own service to the community—we must find the killer. I ask that we look for Jamila together, and also for that other girl, Melani, who disappeared four days ago.

[*Eyes the Prostitutes, one after the other. Threateningly.*] Did any one of you see Jamila before she disappeared?

[Silence prevails. The Prostitutes show worry, confusion, and resentment on their faces. The atmosphere changes quickly when Jamila 1 appears from the front, talking clearly and calmly.]

JAMILA 1 — I haven't disappeared. I'm still here. I confess to having killed Mrs. Diah, and now I'm ready to be arrested.

CHIEF OFFICER — [*To his Officers.*] Officers!

OFFICERS — Yes, sir!

JAMILA 1 — But before I am arrested, I want you to answer my question.

[Some of the Officers hold Jamila 1 by the arms to make sure that she doesn't try to escape. She doesn't resist but, instead, continues to speak.]

I want you to tell me what happened to my friend Dinda.

CHIEF OFFICER — [*Insistent.*] Take her away!

[Two Officers take tighter hold of Jamila 1, but she resists.]

JAMILA 1 — Dinda disappeared two weeks ago, and you never gave it any attention, much less looked for her. [*Yelling.*] *Why?!*

[Anger gives Jamila 1 extraordinary strength. With a single movement, she breaks free from her captors' grasp and stands in the center of the stage, looking straight at the Chief Officer.]

Why didn't you look for Dinda?

[*Throws a blood-soaked dress at the Chief Officer.*] Why? Because of this?

[The Officers fall back, as if afraid and guilt stricken. The Prostitutes are dumbstruck, knowing that the dress belonged to their friend. Jamila 1 pulls one of the Prostitutes over to where the dress is lying.]

Whose dress is this? [*The Prostitute screams in panic; Jamila 1 shakes with anger.*] Whose is it? [*Pause.*] It's Dinda's—that's whose it is—and it's soaked in blood!

PROSTITUTES — [*Panicked. Pointing and screaming at the Officers angrily.*] *Murderers! Murderers!*

OFFICERS — Calm down! Calm down! [*A warning shot is fired. For a moment, there is silence.*]

PROSTITUTES [*In unison.*] Murderers!

Transition music.

Scene Five-B

Nighttime in the middle of the forest. With flashlights in hand, three Security Officers appear.

OFFICER 1 [*Loudly.*] Turn yourself in, Jamila!

OFFICER 2 [*Muttering.*] Damn whore!

OFFICER 3 [*Coaxing.*] We're not going to hurt you, Mila. You have my word.

OFFICER 2 Stop acting crazy! If you don't stop, I'll be forced to shoot.

OFFICER 1 You can't get away, Mila. What's the point in running?

OFFICER 2 Answer, you frigging whore!

JAMILA 1 [*Offstage.*] 'Cause I know you won't take me to the police station.

OFFICER 2 Bitch! Show your face, you witch!

JAMILA 1 If you turn me in, I'll be forced to reveal Mrs. Diah's crimes, which, in turn, will implicate all of you.

OFFICER 2 How dare you!

OFFICER 3 But why here?

JAMILA 1 [*Suddenly appears in front of the Officers, frightening them.*] Because if you're going to kill me, I want you to do it in the same place you murdered Dinda.

[*The Officers grab hold of Jamila 1 and push her head first to the center of the stage.*]

OFFICER 2 Take back what you said or I'll slap you.

OFFICER 1 What you said is slander!

JAMILA 1 [*Speaking quickly as she tries to stand.*] No. It's not slander. Tuti was there behind those trees, dumbstruck and terrified, when she saw the three officers rape Dinda and then snub out her life like a cigarette.

[*Frightened, the Officers shrink back. As they lose their composure, Jamila 1 takes increasing charge of the situation. She corners Officer 2, who appears to be the most afraid.*]

Every night the girls were forced to buy and use crystal meth. [*Heckling the Officers by imitating Mrs. Diah.*] "So that you can move your hips till morning. So that you can do ten men in a night. So that you can get rich fast and get out of this godforsaken jungle with a suitcase full of cash."

[*Addressing the audience.*] But Dinda was smarter than the others. She didn't take the meth she was supposed to. She refused free packets of drugs. And so, afraid that others might follow her lead, she was snuffed out, like an irritating insect.

[*Speaking more freely, as the Officers grow more frightened.*] And because I knew too much, that female con artist, Mrs. Diah, marked me as "dangerous." But because I was attractive, she ignored her own rules. At thirteen I was easily deceived. [*Laughs.*] But now at twenty-two I'm not just a sex worker; I'm a sex researcher. And she gave me all the information I needed for my research. [*Laughs again.*]

OFFICER 2 [*No longer able to contain himself.*] You're a whore, not a researcher!

JAMILA 1 Yes, I am a whore, the same as the other girls here. The difference is that you can no longer fool me. [*Jumps on top of the bench—her cot. Between bursts of laughter, she throws packets of crystal meth at the Officers.*]

OFFICER 2 Stop it, Jamila! Stop it or you'll be sorry. [*Screaming.*] *Ja-mi-la!*

JAMILA 1 [*Regains her composure and kneels on the cot. Appears to gather her strength, then looks sharply at Officer 2.*] Thanks for finally calling me Jamila. It's the name my parents gave me, along with songs of praise and prayers to God that I would become a pious child . . . Yet here I am, a prostitute and murderer, surrounded by officer-murderers. [*Laughs. Officer 2 is angry and approaches her, but she snaps at him.*]

Don't come closer! [*The Officers suddenly seem powerless.*] Lily-livered policemen! Gutless wonders only capable of killing defenseless women like Dinda. Well, you know my friend Melani, the one who disappeared four days ago? She should be in the capital by now, delivering my report!

So, I guess you have a choice. You can turn me over to the authorities or finish me off here, just like you did Dinda. For me, it doesn't matter. But if, for once in your life, you want to show yourselves to be responsible men of the law, then you'd better arrest me now. Because if you don't, I will kill again . . . [*Repeats the sentence with mounting frustration, her voice becoming hoarse.*] I will kill again, I will kill again, I will kill again . . .

Transition music is heard, followed by a siren blaring in the distance.

Scene Six

A light illuminates Jamila 2's cell. Ria enters, angry. Newspaper in hand, she approaches Jamila 2, who is seated bent over on her cot.

RIA — [*Sits on the edge of the cot, then reads the newspaper aloud.*] "The death sentence of Jamila, murderer of Minister Nurdin, will be carried out tomorrow. As she had requested, she will be granted a visit with the President and the honored clergyman Kiai Jalaludin before her execution . . ." [*Staring at Jamila 2.*] What is it with you, Mila? I'm surprised at you. Millions of people out there stand behind you. You've given all high officials a lesson. You've put them in shock. It's extraordinary, Mila.

[*Jamila 2 remains silent, cold, and stubborn.*]

[*Frustrated.*] Why didn't you seek a pardon from the President? Why did you ask for him to come here instead? [*In a softer, more soothing tone of voice.*] I can understand why you might want a clergyman, but the President . . . ? Why?

JAMILA 2 — [*Stands up and distances herself from Ria. Without turning, speaks strongly and carefully.*] Because he is the one who is most responsible for all that has happened to me!

RIA — [*Startled.*] What do you mean, Jamila? You shouldn't talk like that—not at this point. The nation will think even more badly of you.

[*Jamila 2 doesn't respond. A clock strikes. From offstage, a crowd of demonstrators can be heard, shouting "Kill Jamila! Whore! Filthy woman!" etc. Two Prison Guards enter and report to Ria.*]

PRISON GUARD 1 — There are hundreds of people demonstrating outside. Some groups have asked to meet with Jamila.

RIA — [*Walks back and forth angrily, as the sound of the demonstration continues. To Jamila 2.*] You don't have to meet with them, but if you want to cool their anger, it might be best . . .

JAMILA 2 — [*Returns to the cot. Bitterly.*] To cool their anger . . . ? What do I have to do with their anger?

RIA — [*Approaches the Guards.*] Select some representatives.

PRISON GUARD 1 — Yes, ma'am. [*The Guards leave.*]

JAMILA 2 — I've experienced just about everything in life, Ria. My life was not completely made of tears. Sometimes, with my friends, we'd find ourselves laughing—laughing away the bitter pain of our existence.

The only thing I never experienced was being loved by, and loving—making love with, being made love to—a man who I loved and who loved me.

RIA — [*Unable to help herself, pulls Jamila 2 into her arms, embracing her tightly. Continues her query.*] But what you said about the President . . .

[*Jamila 2, unhappy with this line of questioning, pulls herself out of Ria's embrace. She straightens up quickly and draws away.*]

What do you mean that he's responsible?

JAMILA 2 — May I not refuse to answer just this single question?

[*Ria still isn't satisfied. But she doesn't have a choice. The cries from outside are more vociferous. "Kill Jamila! Kill Jamila!" The clock strikes. Jamila 2 turns her head in the direction of the voices, but her look is vacant. Prison Guard 1 brings in the first visitor for Jamila 2. The visitor is Zaelani. Ria leaves the cell. Zaelani holds out his arms, beckoning for Jamila to come to him.*]

ZAELANI — Ya, Allah, Jamila . . . Jamila . . . How are you, Jamila? [*Jamila 2 stands up, and the two embrace warmly.*]

I'll do anything for you, Jamila, anything I can. [*Jamila 2 removes herself from Zaelani's embrace and pulls him down to sit on the cot beside her.*]

I'll tell the whole story, Jamila, everything you experienced back then.

JAMILA 2 — How is Mrs. Wardiman?

ZAELANI — She died, Jamila, cursed like you.

JAMILA 2 — What did she die from?

ZAELANI — From being cursed—cursed for what she did to you! Never having the guts to divorce her husband—that's one thing I could never understand. And Mr. Wardiman was such a lecher. Even me, he couldn't keep his hands off. What's more a beautiful thing like you. [*Pinches Jamila 2's cheek. They laugh freely. Zaelani then stands and parodies Mrs. Wardiman.*]

"Order that woman to stop! Her praying makes my ears burn. And what's that *jilbab* you're wearing? No better than the devil himself wearing one; it's an insult to your departed mother."

What a bunch of hypocrites! Supposedly a respectable family, but one with no moral backbone whatsoever! And the same thing goes for that bunch of demonstrators out there. "Youth for Morality" they call themselves! Bullshit! All these Defenders of Law, Defenders of Religion, and so on... [*To the audience.*] Allah gave us religion to protect people... [*To Jamila.*] Yet you, Jamila, are a victim of religion in the hands of politicians. [*Again to the audience.*] Using coercion to get people to repent? What kind of inspiration is that?

[*Returns to Jamila 2's side, calming down and speaking softly.*] Do you still pray, Jamila? [*Jamila 2 avoids the question.*]

I'm sorry, Mila. I just can't hold my tongue... But it's so good to see you. Tell me, tell me what I can do for you. Serve as a witness? As your lawyer? I'd defend you against anyone!

[*Jamila 2 smiles, then stands. She holds out her arms, and they embrace tightly.*]

JAMILA 2 — You were the best person in my life, Zaelani. Your visit has given me such relief, but you'd better go now.

ZAELANI — [*Backs away in protest, and sits on the cot.*] In a little while.

JAMILA 2 — Zaelani...

ZAELANI — I don't want to.

JAMILA 2 — Please, Zaelani...

ZAELANI — No! You still haven't told me what's going on with the President.

[*Jamila 2 motions for the Guard to escort Zaelani from her cell. The Guard approaches Zaelani and signals for him to follow.*]

I'm really impressed, Jamila. If you really do succeed in meeting the President, wow, that would be incredible. You are just the best!

[*The Guard starts to escort Zaelani from the cell, but before exiting, Zaelani stops and speaks again.*]

If they do really end up executing you, I'm sure that Lord Allah himself will sweep you up in His arms and take you straight to heaven.

[*When the rear door opens for Zaelani to exit, the voices of the crowd become distinct. "Kill Jamila! Kill her! That evil woman! Whore!" Ria and Prison Guard 1 enter.*]

PRISON GUARD 1 [*To Ria.*] The wives of two high officials want to see her.

RIA [*To Jamila 2.*] Even if they are high officials' wives, you have the right to refuse to see them.

JAMILA 2 [*Seated upright, takes a deep breath.*] I'll see them.

[*Prison Guard 1 exits. When the rear door is opened for the Officials' Wives to enter, the screams of the crowd are heard again, this time more loudly than before. "Evil woman! Whore! Deceiver! Kill Jamila!" The two Officials' Wives enter and immediately begin to reproach Jamila 2.*]

OFFICIAL'S WIFE 1 You! Are you the whore with the audacity to request a visit from the President?

RIA [*Immediately interjecting.*] Excuse me, ma'am, but I must ask you to show a little respect.

[*Official's Wife 1 turns toward Ria, gives her a haughty sneer, then turns back to Jamila 2.*]

OFFICIAL'S WIFE 1 You shameless hussy! You common whore! What do you want, requesting a visit from the President? What is it? Tell me what you want.

RIA Guard!

OFFICIAL'S WIFE 1 [*To Ria, offended that she would call a Guard.*] Hey, do you know who I am? [*Loudly.*] Do you know who my husband is?

RIA [*While pushing Official's Wife 1 away from her.*] Yes, ma'am, I do. I'm only asking that you be respectful.

OFFICIAL'S WIFE 1 [*To Ria, sarcastically.*] Nothing more than a warden and you already think you're a big shot. I am here as a representative of all the high officials' wives in this country, you understand? [*Grumbling.*] Such airs in a person so small!

[*Official's Wife 2 is busy fanning herself.*]

OFFICIAL'S WIFE 2 [*Approaches Jamila 2.*] Pretty, aren't you? Too bad you have the devil inside! Hey, look at me, you murderer.

RIA [*Afraid that Jamila might do something.*] Be careful, Mila! [*The two Wives shove Ria aside.*]

OFFICIAL'S WIFE 1 Step back!

OFFICIAL'S WIFE 2 [*Grabs Jamila 2 by her hair and pulls her up to a standing position.*] Here you are, a woman who has prostituted herself, who has committed murder, and yet you dare to ask the President to come here.

OFFICIAL'S WIFE 1 Don't even dream of it. Do you understand? Don't even dream of it!

OFFICIAL'S WIFE 2 Here! [*Pulling Jamila 2 toward her, she spits in Jamila's face.*] There, I just spat on you—in the name of all honorable women of this nation.

[*Jamila 2, who has been trying hard to control herself, stares at the Officials' Wives.*]

JAMILA 2 [*In a voice both calm and dignified.*] I, too, am a woman of this nation, ma'am . . .

OFFICIAL'S WIFE 1 [*Muttering.*] Doesn't know when to shut up, does she?

JAMILA 2 . . . Just like the other prostitutes out there are women of this nation.

OFFICIAL'S WIFE 2 You call yourself a woman? You're nothing but a whore, a slut, a devil, a murderer! [*Attempts to slap Jamila 2, but Jamila 2 adroitly grabs her arm.*]

Let me go! [*Screaming.*] Guard!

[*The Prison Guard approaches, but Jamila snaps at him.*]

JAMILA 2 Stay right there, sir! This is the business of this nation's women.

[*The Prison Guard withdraws. Jamila shoves Official's Wife 2 away from her, causing her to stumble backwards.*]

Where is your husband?

OFFICIAL'S WIFE 2 You bitch!

JAMILA 2 You haven't answered my question. Where is your husband?

OFFICIAL'S WIFE 2 You're to be sentenced to death, you whore. I'm going to help make sure of that.

JAMILA 2 — [*Approaches Official's Wife 2. Softly.*] Too late, Madam. I've already been sentenced to death. The court has already decided that.

OFFICIAL'S WIFE 2 — Good!

JAMILA 2 — So now the best thing for you to do is to go home and make sure that your husband is really working, and not making love in the arms of another whore.

OFFICIAL'S WIFE 2 — You bitch! You murderer!

JAMILA 2 — Get out of here!

OFFICIAL'S WIFE 2 — You devil! You whore!

JAMILA 2 — Get out!

[*The Prison Guard escorts the Officials' Wives toward the door.*]

OFFICIAL'S WIFE 2 — You're a disgrace of a woman! A whore!

JAMILA 2 — Out!

OFFICIAL'S WIFE 1 — You're going to die in sin. You are going to die.

JAMILA 2 — Out, I said!

[*Ria approaches Jamila 2 and embraces her warmly.*]

CROWD — [*Offstage.*] Kill Jamila! Kill her! Evil woman! Whore!

[*The sound of a siren approaches from far away. Ria stands up. She appears fearful. Before leaving the cell, she looks at Jamila 2 with sympathy, then hurries out. Jamila 2 stands in the middle of the cell, listening attentively to the sound of the siren and the yells until they stop.*]

Scene Seven

Execution day. The atmosphere is still. The demonstrations calling for Jamila's death have ceased. A song of praise, alternately sung by a choir and a solo voice, heighten expectancy in the three vignettes that follow:

In her cell, Jamila 2 sits in the center of her cot, trying to keep as calm as possible.

In the center, Officers remove a large platform and replace it with a smaller one, along with a carpet and prayer robe.

Ria and two Guards enter Jamila 2's cell. Ria helps Jamila 2 put on her prayer robe, then hands her a copy of the Quran. Jamila 2 appears calm.

Jamila 2, dressed in her spotless white robe, steps out of her cell and into the center of the stage. The salawat badar, *a special song of praise, accompanies her movement toward the prayer rug laid out in the center. In the middle of her procession toward the rug, Jamila 2 stops mid-stride, hearing the sound of a siren. It is the car of the President. The scuffling footsteps of his entourage ensues. On the backdrop, security officers in silhouette can be seen running in rows across the stage.*

Now standing on her prayer rug, Jamila 2 tries to focus on her prayers, but each time she raises her two hands to say "Allahu Akbar"—"Allah is Great"—she halts, as if she is no longer able to bear the pain of the past. As if feeling unclean, unfit, unwell, she dares not continue her prayers. In despair, she collapses in the kneeling position, with her head bowed to the floor. Her forehead rests on the Quran at the edge of the prayer rug. She cries, shaking.

Ria enters with Kiai Jalaudin, a Moslem Cleric, and leads him to Jamila 2.

RIA — Jamila. This is Kiai Jalaudin, your special visitor.

[*Very slowly, Jamila 2 raises her body.*]

Your spiritual advisor is here, Jamila.

CLERIC — [*Greeting her.*] *Assalamualaikum.* Peace be with you, Jamila.

[*Jamila raises her body to an upright position. Instead of acknowledging her visitor's greeting, she stares straight ahead. The Cleric, with a calm demeanor, sits on the bench that is placed not far from Jamila 2. Ria hurriedly leaves the stage.*]

[*Gently.*] Jamila . . . Please sit near me so that we can speak. Or if you would rather, we could begin by praying. Whichever you prefer.

JAMILA 2 — It is I who invited you to be here, sir. As such, it follows that I am the one who will determine what happens here.

CLERIC — [*Appears embarrassed by Jamila 2's words.*] All right, miss, if that's what you want.

JAMILA 2 — Do you know why I chose to see you and not another man—my uncle or my father, for instance?

CLERIC — No, I don't, but I am happy to be here. I see this visit as an opportunity to fulfill my duty as an *ulema*.

JAMILA 2 — Your duty? What would that be? To lecture me until I see the light? To pray for me? To ask God's pardon so I don't go to hell? [*Jamila 2's cynicism makes the Cleric defensive and unable to speak.*]

My father, the person who should have been most responsible for protecting me, was the person who most wanted me to become a prostitute.

CLERIC — [*Automatically.*] *Astagfirullahhallazim.* I pray for God's forgiveness.

JAMILA 2 — With no thought at all, he severed the umbilical cord that bound me to my mother; he took me from my mother's breast and gave me to a procurer.

CLERIC — *Astagfirullahhallazim . . .*

JAMILA 2 — I was two years old.

CLERIC — *Astagfirullahhallazim.*

JAMILA 2 — It was my father's desire that threw me into the darkness, into a life of debasement, where I was condemned, spat upon by people, and forever haunted by fear. For the sake of my father's soul, I pray that he did not know how the procurers and agents I served exploited my sweat and sucked my blood with no measure of sympathy.

CLERIC — *Astagfirullahhallazim.*

JAMILA 2 — [*After pausing momentarily to control her mounting anger.*] Could you stop uttering that prayer of protection for a moment?

CLERIC — [*Surprised, but automatically repeats the prayer again.*] *Astagfirullahhallazim.*

JAMILA 2 — How are you going to hear me if you don't stop praying?

CLERIC — *Astagfirullahhallazim . . .* Oh, all right, miss, uh . . . *Astagfirullahhallazim . . .*

JAMILA 2 — In the place where I was born, selling off girls when they're no more than babies is not a tale—it's reality.

CLERIC — *Astagfirullahhallazim.*

JAMILA 2 — It's a culture of slavery born of poverty, the offspring of ignorance and weakness of faith . . .

CLERIC — *Astagfirullahhallazim.*

JAMILA 2 — . . . A sacral kind of slavery that is honored through ceremonies of flower offerings and mystic mantra, all mixed up with prayers of praise to the Prophet.

CLERIC — *Astagfirullahhallazim.*

JAMILA 2 — You call out for people to distance themselves from sources of evil, to avoid conflict and enmity. I am a human being, sir, God's most perfect creation, no different from you. But I am a whore, sir, and was fated to be one from the time I was in my mother's womb.

CLERIC — Miss Jamila, come and let us pray together.

JAMILA 2 [*Growling.*] No.

CLERIC Allah will hear you, Jamila. He knows all.

JAMILA 2 Excuse me, sir, but I don't need a cleric to ask God's pardon for me, especially not one who knows nothing of my suffering and lacks the power to pull me from the darkness.

CLERIC Miss Jamila.

JAMILA 2 [*Suddenly turns to speak to the Cleric directly. Angrily.*] Why now, sir? Why now? Why weren't you at my side before? Why didn't you seize me from my father's hands before he sold me to a procurer? Why? [*Enraged.*] Answer me!

CLERIC Jamila . . .

JAMILA 2 [*Takes off her white prayer robe and turns, opening her arms wide and displaying herself for the Cleric to see.*] Look at me. Look! See how unclean, how lost I am. But don't dare say that you have no share of responsibility for this.

CLERIC Jamila . . .

JAMILA 2 Get out.

CLERIC Jamila . . .

JAMILA 2 Get out!

[*Silence. The Cleric, embarrassed, begins to leave.*]

If you really want to fulfill your duty as an *ulema*, then go now to my home town and sit there among the elders and wait for the moment of my death while asking God's forgiveness.

[*The Cleric exits. Jamila 2 sinks to the floor, shaking. The scuffling of feet is then heard. On the backdrop, the Officers who will carry out the execution can be seen entering the stage from both directions. Jamila 2 is silent for a moment. Realizing that she must prepare herself for death, she raises her body and looks toward the audience with a calm expression. She speaks softly but distinctly.*]

A million times Your name has passed my lips. Countless times, in tears and pain, I have asked Your pardon.

[*A large man, the President, appears against the backdrop, followed by his guards. He enters and stops beside the execution officers. He looks straight ahead. From another direction, Ria appears. They all look at Jamila 2, who is still speaking.*]

These two hands have been stained with blood since I was a child. It is a stain I cannot cleanse, a birthmark of sin that I cannot make disappear.

RIA Jamila! It's the President!

[Hearing Ria, Jamila 2 stops speaking and is silent for a moment. She bends down, looking for her veil, and picks up from the floor a dull white cloth. She opens the cloth, spreading her arms out wide, showing the cloth to the audience.]

JAMILA 2 *[Speaking as if to the whole world.]* This cloth was once white and pure. It covered my body, protected me, gave radiance to my face... *[Turning toward the President.]* Who wanted me to become a whore? Who defiled me and planted hate in my chest?

[The President leaves the stage. Jamila 2 addresses the same question to the place where he had been standing.]

Who wanted me to become a whore? Who defiled me and planted hate in my chest?

[Stands up and goes to the center of the stage, repeating her questions to the audience and the world.] Who wanted me to become a whore? Who planted hate in my chest? Who wanted me to become a whore? Who planted hate in my chest? Who planted hate in my chest? Who planted hate in my chest? Who...? Who...? Who...?

The lights slowly dim. Music to accompany Jamila 2's execution is heard, followed, a few seconds later, by the sound of rifle fire. Jamila the prostitute is no more. All lights fade. Darkness descends.

Translation by Kathy Foley

RITA MATU MONA

Make Note!

Cast of Characters

Agus
Agus's Father
Agus's Mother
Prof. Djumawa, college director
Dr. Santini, lecturer
Syeni, student
Bonggo, student
Mr. Dar, instructor
Mr. Tedjo, instructor
Mr. Mus, instructor
Mrs. Atika, instructor
Sarman, caretaker
Pleki, student
Ciping, student
Fredrik, student
Bujel, student
Other Instructors and ***Board of Trustees***

Opening Scene

Isolation room in a psychiatric hospital. Agus sits shackled to a chair. Her eyes are vacant, without expression. Everything that has happened passes silently through her mind. There are only the following lyrics:

VOICE-OVER

Nightmares of that dark prison
Whenever roaming in the darkest of night
Without illumination, without a spot of light
There's a bit of air, but no sky
The banished know not when the door will be opened
Feeling stifled
My hands reach out looking for something to hold on to
If I miss my target I will strike and claw at the air
I don't know where I am . . .
I don't know where I am . . .

Jogja Expo Center,
Yogyakarta, 2013.
Kurniadi Widodo

Malioboro Street,
Yogyakarta, 2011.
Kurniadi Widodo

Scene One

Agus reads a psychology book in her room. Suddenly, the figures of Father and Mother move in a portrait hanging on the wall. This portrait exists only in her imagination.

FATHER — So you want to become a psychologist. To take care of others. You think it's easy? We can't even take care of our own problems—and they're getting worse all the time. Never ending. Even statesmen can't take care of their citizens' problems. And we're just small folk.

MOTHER — What's the point of taking care of other people's problems? To be a psychologist, you have to have a strong mental constitution and physical stamina. Does that sound like you?

FATHER — Not at all; you've been sickly since you were small. Not only that, you're a girl. This isn't a gender issue, but reality. There's no way you could succeed at facing other people's problems on your own.

MOTHER — You're still young, and you still have a lot of opportunities for a career. After you've grown up, graduated from a business school chosen by your father, and worked at a multinational company with a decent salary, then you can continue your schooling in psychology, just as you like.

FATHER — What's wrong with becoming an economist? We're the descendants of merchants. Any job we do has to bring in money. There has to be profit and gain. In this era of globalization, the country needs good economists to put our sadly disorganized economy back into shape.

Agus is nervous.

MOTHER — Why don't you comply with your father's wishes? I think it's the best thing to do at this time. We've planned out your future to be this way ever since you were a baby.

FATHER — Don't disregard our good intentions. [*The lights start to fade on the portrait.*]

MOTHER — Think positively. Hey, where are you going? We haven't finished talking, Agus. Don't leave. Agus! Agus! [*The lights on the portrait continue to fade.*]

FATHER — So stubborn. Only thinking of herself!

MOTHER — Like father, like daughter!

The lights on the portrait fade to black. Agus gazes at the empty frame.

Scene Two

Graduation ceremony. Solemn atmosphere. Graduates are receiving their diplomas. Both the dean and the university president are present. Agus is the last graduate to receive her diploma. Once the ceremony is over, Agus and the other graduates throw their hats up into the air and happily strip off their graduation attire. The atmosphere becomes boisterous. Dancing and singing fill the hall.

VOICE-OVER

After graduation that has been so long in coming
From Chandradimuka's cauldron
Young warriors are born
Fighting to realize their hopes
Long Live Academia
Long Live Academia
The world will become ours
The world will become ours

Scene Three

College classroom. Dr. Santini is lecturing to a group of students. Prof. Djumawa and Agus observe from outside the classroom.

DR. SANTINI — Therefore, feeling has a very fluid structure and embraces the entirety of human existence. And it's with this feeling that people hope to find themselves, what in mystical terms is called "Jumbuhing Kawula Gusti." People identify with this feeling, discover . . . [*The Students look at each other. Dr. Santini's lecture makes no sense to them and is boring.*]

SYENI — [*Softly.*] Ma'am . . .

DR. SANTINI — [*Without hearing, continues with her lecture very seriously.*] Its function, role, and position in the life cycle is called "Sangkan Paraning Dumadi." Therefore, souls that . . .

BONGGO — [*Loudly.*] Ma'am!

DR. SANTINI — [*Taken aback.*] Yes, what is it?

SYENI — Could you please repeat the last part? To be honest, you're going too fast. I didn't understand what you meant by "Jumbuhing Kawula Gusti."

DR. SANTINI — [*Annoyed.*] Are you asking or criticizing? Choose one or the other. If it's a question, I'll answer. Wait until later for criticism. Everything has its proper place. As I've stressed again and again, during lectures you may only ask questions relevant to the subject matter at hand. I consider all irrelevant questions to be criticism.

BONGGO But Syeni's question is relevant. She would like you to reread that last part again, louder this time.

DR. SANTINI [*Angry.*] So you think I don't read loudly enough and you want me to read louder, is that it? That's criticism. I deem that irrelevant and not worthy of a reply. The truth is that you're not paying proper attention.

Syeni bows her head in fear.

PROF. DJUMAWA [*To Agus.*] They're diligent, aren't they? See there, Dr. Santini is my most loyal assistant. You're replacing her because she's being promoted to assistant director.

AGUS Is it like this every day?

DR. SANTINI Listen!

PROF. DJUMAWA What do you mean?

AGUS Are the students not allowed to ask questions even if it's something they don't understand?

PROF. DJUMAWA Their questions are usually out of context and not compatible with our disciplinary methods. We consider their questions to be interruptions, and that is forbidden at this educational institution.

DR. SANTINI Make note!

AGUS Attending lectures to write notes?

PROF. DJUMAWA Not exactly. They listen first, then write notes. Then they memorize. Our method is "Listen! Make note! Memorize!"

DR. SANTINI Memorize!

AGUS Has any thought been given to another method?

PROF. DJUMAWA I've been using this method for thirty years.

AGUS Do you think it's been successful?

PROF. DJUMAWA Not yet. I'm not satisfied with it. [*Looks at Dr. Santini and laughs.*] I'm not so easy to please at my advanced age. However, I believe that all efforts have two possible outcomes: a quick success, or success in stages.

AGUS Or it doesn't succeed at all.

PROF. DJUMAWA I've already seen signs of success. Thirty years ago, when this method was first implemented, almost all the students protested. But we knew that they were only uncomfortable with it because it was new and quite innovative. After thirty years of continuous implementation, I've never heard any dissenting voices.

AGUS — Maybe after using this method for a while, they've come to think of questions as something to fear. Or—

PROF. DJUMAWA — [*Quickly.*] Let's go talk in my office. We'll distract them from their studies if we stay here.

AGUS — All right. [*Exits with Prof. Djumawa.*]

DR. SANTINI — Learn this section by heart.

STUDENTS — [*Submissively.*] Yes, ma'am.

Scene Four

Faculty lounge. Morning. The conservative university Instructors have gathered here, including Mr. Dar, Mr. Tedjo, Mr. Mus, and Mrs. Atika.

VOICE-OVER — So-called Intellectuals
Not necessarily true
Often teaching
But still learning
Supervising exams
But still supervised themselves
Take a guess, who are we?
Ooo . . . working until old and feeble
Under the Professor's example
Ooo . . . paid just barely enough
So the work will get done

INSTRUCTORS — [*Yelling as they make their way to Prof. Djumawa's office.*] Suspect! Report! Prevent! Agreed! Okay! Do it!

[*They enter the office. Prof. Djumawa is there meeting with Agus.*]

Good morning, Professor!

PROF. DJUMAWA — [*With only a nod toward the Instructors.*] Meet Agus, your new colleague. Agus, as you know, is joining the faculty here, taking over for Dr. Santini, who's being promoted to assistant director. I hope that you, her seniors, will help her carry out her duties.

INSTRUCTORS — Yes, Professor!

PROF. DJUMAWA — Now, please go about your own duties.

INSTRUCTORS — Yes, Professor! [*Yelling while exiting.*] Suspect! Report! Prevent! Agreed! Okay! Do it!

PROF. DJUMAWA [*To Agus.*] Please sit. Oh . . . you have already.

AGUS [*Stands.*] I beg your pardon.

PROF. DJUMAWA Please sit.

AGUS [*Sits.*] Thank you.

PROF. DJUMAWA I hope you know that in this institution, there is no room for critique or criticism. Especially from lower-downs, such as yourself. I've been director here for over thirty years. Everything follows my rules and methods, which were well received long before you were even born.

AGUS Forgive me, I was just giving my opinion.

PROF. DJUMAWA Giving your opinion as you just did is the same as criticizing. That cannot be condoned, because you were criticizing me as the director here.

AGUS Forgive me, I just wanted to know more about my work.

PROF. DJUMAWA Good. It appears you understand one thing—that you are here to work, not to satisfy your desire for knowledge. Make note! [*Opens and reads Agus's file.*] Graduated summa cum laude with an A+ average, winner of a scientific writing competition, human rights activist, hobby is poetry writing, only child, still single. High recommendation from Professor Sobar, whom I know is a highly qualified dean. Your résumé is very good. You will be a good replacement for Dr. Santini.

AGUS Thank you, Professor.

PROF. DJUMAWA I'm proud to accept a colleague with such high credentials as yours. You also passed the Fit and Proper Test. I hope I have chosen well. Or are you of a different opinion? There's still time to reconsider.

AGUS No. I very much want to work here, and I need this job.

PROF. DJUMAWA Very well then. Under my guidance, you will have the opportunity to carve out your achievements in this educational institution. You must know what you can and cannot do. [*Hands a folder to Agus.*] Please read this and study it well.

AGUS Thank you, sir.

PROF. DJUMAWA Professor!

AGUS I beg your pardon. Professor.

PROF. DJUMAWA Oh yes, one more thing, Agus. You can critique as long as you know the manner in which to do it. In that folder, there's a file listing forty-one ways to deliver criticism properly. You can use that as a reference for delivering criticism. Now, please go move into Dr. Santini's old office. It's now yours.

AGUS — Yes, sir . . . ah, Professor. If you will excuse me. [*Exiting.*]

PROF. DJUMAWA — Please.

Scene Five

Agus's office. Midday. Sarman is tidying the office as Agus enters.

SARMAN — Good afternoon, ma'am.

AGUS — Good afternoon, uh . . .

SARMAN — Pleased to meet you, ma'am. My name is Sarman. I'm the caretaker here—the senior caretaker. More than thirty years on the job. You can just call me Sarman.

AGUS — I'm Agus.

SARMAN — Huh? That is a man's name.

AGUS — [*Smiling.*] My name is Agustina, but you can call me Miss Agus.

SARMAN — Okay, Miss Agus. From now on, if there's anything you need, just give me a holler. Don't hesitate. Everyone who works here is like that, you know. My job is called caretaker because my job is to take care.

AGUS — Thank you. Can I ask you something?

SARMAN — [*Panicking.*] A question?

AGUS — Yes.

SARMAN — Hmm . . . depends on what kind of question.

AGUS — Since you've worked in this place for thirty years, you know a lot about matters here, right?

SARMAN — [*Fearful.*] Don't ask me anything about any sorts of matters or matters of any sort.

AGUS — I'm not asking about all sorts. Just easy questions. For example, does Professor Djumawa wear all black every day, like today?

SARMAN — [*In a fearful whisper.*] I'm just letting you know: never ask anything personal about the Professor. It's a sensitive issue.

AGUS — But my question is easy to answer.

SARMAN — Miss Agus, even though it isn't written anywhere that it's forbidden to question, that question is forbidden.

AGUS — Strange. What Professor Djumawa said about questions not being allowed is true.

SARMAN — Yes, indeed.

AGUS — Okay then, I won't ask any more questions.

SARMAN — Will you please excuse me, if you don't need me anymore. [*Whispering.*] Be careful! [*Sarman exits. With a questioning look on her face, Agus watches him as he goes.*]

Scene Six

Prof. Djumawa's office. Evening. Prof. Djumawa and Pleki, resembling two shadow figures, are in a secret meeting.

PROF. DJUMAWA — Pleki, I'm giving you this task. Make note of every event, in detail, that you witness. Don't leave anything out.

PLEKI — [*Stuttering.*] Y-yes, Professor.

PROF. DJUMAWA — You are doing this for the good of the institution. If all goes according to plan, then all will be successful. That includes your grades, even the ones that have been stuck in the mud.

PLEKI — Th-th-thank you, Professor!

PROF. DJUMAWA — The students will continue to study with full concentration and with a constructive attitude. The teachers will be able to continue their duties calmly and with dedication.

PLEKI — I und-d-derstand, Professor.

PROF. DJUMAWA — But you have to be careful. Use the most sophisticated methods so that your hands remain clean.

PLEKI — T-t-taken care of, Professor.

PROF. DJUMAWA — Go.

PLEKI — Y-yes, Professor. [*Exits.*]

Scene Seven

Classroom. Midday. The Students are waiting for their instructor.

AGUS — [*Entering.*] Good afternoon.

STUDENTS Good afternoon, miss.

AGUS Is this the psychology class?

STUDENTS Correct, miss.

AGUS I'm Dr. Santini's replacement starting today. [*The Students are silent.*] My name is Agustina, but you can call me Ms. Agus or Miss Agus. [*The Students remain silent.*] Or just Agus. Up to you. [*The Students are motionless.*] Okay, I'm not going to give a lecture today. [*The Students look at each other in confusion.*] What? You don't agree?

BONGGO Do you mean we are dismissed?

AGUS No, I just want to chat with you.

BONGGO Chat?

STUDENTS Chat?

PLEKI Ch-ch-chat?

AGUS Yes, chat. Don't you agree?

BONGGO Well, I agree. I don't know about the others.

SYENI I agree.

CIPING We agree. Yes? Yes? Yes?

Bonggo motions to his friends.

STUDENTS We agree!

AGUS [*Pleased because the Students are becoming involved.*] Now that we are all in agreement, let's change our seats so we can all see each other.

The Students look at each other in confusion. Finally Bonggo changes seats. The others follow.

Who wants to begin speaking? Don't forget to say your name and your year. Then say whatever you have wanted to say up until now but have been prevented from saying. Speak freely. There's no one here but us. There's no one who's going to monitor what you say, or do anything to you. [*No one is bold enough to start. Agus points to Fredrik.*] Come on! You start.

FREDRIK Me?

AGUS Yes, you.

FREDRIK Why me?

Bonggo goads Fredrik until he speaks.

Hmm . . . okay. My name is Fredrik. Usually I'm called Fred.

BONGGO He means Fredator! [*The Students giggle.*]

FREDRIK Shut up! [*Throws his eraser at Bonggo, but it hits Pleki.*]

PLEKI *Ow!* You j-j-jerk!

FREDRIK Sorry . . . sorry. [*The Students laugh.*]

AGUS Continue, Fred.

FREDRIK I'm in the class of '98.

BONGGO A senior—like my dad!

SYENI A veteran student! [*The Students laugh.*]

CIPING Hold on . . . hold on . . . hold on . . . okay. Yes? Yes? Yes?

AGUS Tell us why you chose this major.

FREDRIK Because I wasn't accepted into Electrical Engineering.

PLEKI S-s-stupid! [*The Students laugh. They've never laughed so freely in a classroom.*]

CIPING Be quiet. Yes? Yes? Yes?

AGUS Continue, Fred.

FREDRIK So I registered for this major, uh, and was accepted. The test was easy.

SYENI If it's so easy, why don't you graduate?

PLEKI S-s-stupid!

FREDRIK You're stupid! [*The Students erupt in laughter.*]

CIPING Hey . . . shut up, guys, will ya?

AGUS Do you feel this is the right major for you?

FREDRIK So far so good.

AGUS Is there anything else you'd like to say?

FREDRIK No, that's all. Thank you.

AGUS Let's clap our hands for Fred. [*The Students merrily clap their hands.*] What about you others? Does anyone want to speak?

SYENI I do. My name is Syeni.

CIPING I'm Ciping.

BUJEL | Bujel! I'm Bujel.

All the Students clamor to speak. The class, usually so formal, has become relaxed. From somewhere outside the classroom, the Instructors observe Agus and the Students.

MR. TEDJO | What does she want exactly?

MR. DAR | She's so daring.

MR. TEDJO | Only a few days at work and she's already showing off.

MRS. ATIKA | Acting so smart.

MR. MUS | But it looks like she's succeeding.

MRS. ATIKA | Succeeding at what?

MR. MUS | Well, it looks like she's leading a discussion. Almost all the students are speaking. Listen.

AGUS | In this era of democracy, speaking is the most important thing. We have to have the courage to speak, my friends. Don't be afraid to say whatever you want in order to better the educational system. It's a democratic matter.

MR. DAR | Democracy, democratic. Bah! She talks like a politician.

MRS. ATIKA | She probably thinks of herself as Aung San Suu Kyi.

MR. TEDJO | This can't continue. It's already gone too far. A snot-nosed youngster audacious enough to go over the heads of her seniors.

MRS. ATIKA | It's true, we've been stepped over. Think about it. She just started and already has a good position, replacing Dr. Santini and taking over her office. It's all because of the connection between her old dean and Professor Djumawa.

MR. DAR | We can't keep this quiet. We have to report this to Professor Djumawa.

MR. TEDJO | Right. If we keep quiet about this, we could be the ones the Professor blames. The best thing to do is to report this to the Professor right away.

MRS. ATIKA | I agree. Before it gets messy.

MR. TEDJO | Before she gets big headed.

MR. MUS | Come on!

INSTRUCTORS | [*Yelling while exiting.*] Suspect! Report! Prevent! Agreed! Okay! Do it!

AGUS — Now, my friends. In the future, we'll use this method of dialogue in response to my lectures. I hope that you will all be active participants in each dialogue we hold. That's enough for today. Thank you and have a good afternoon. [*Exits.*]

STUDENTS — Good afternoon.

Scene Eight

Prof. Djumawa's office. Afternoon. Prof. Djumawa, Dr. Santini, and Pleki are meeting there.

PROF. DJUMAWA — [*Reading Pleki's report.*] Good work, Pleki. This will reflect well on your grades.

PLEKI — Th-th-thank you, Professor.

PROF. DJUMAWA — Keep up with this work of yours. Don't let anything slip by your surveillance.

PLEKI — Y-y-yes, Professor.

PROF. DJUMAWA — Do this quietly. No one can know about it, not even the instructors. Only me and Dr. Santini. Understood?

PLEKI — Und-d-derstood, Professor!

PROF. DJUMAWA — Go now!

Pleki exits.

INSTRUCTORS — [*Entering.*] Good afternoon, Professor. [*Prof. Djumawa only nods in their direction.*]

MR. TEDJO — We would like to report—

PROF. DJUMAWA — I know already. No need to go over it again.

MR. DAR — What action should we take, Professor?

PROF. DJUMAWA — Nothing for now. I can take care of it myself. Tell her to come see me at once.

DR. SANTINI — Mr. Dar, please tell Agus to come here.

MR. DAR — Yes, Dr. Santini.

INSTRUCTORS — [*Yelling while exiting.*] Suspect! Report! Prevent! Agreed! Okay! Do it!

DR. SANTINI — So, we're not taking action against her?

PROF. DJUMAWA — As I just said, nothing for now. Better not move too quickly, Santini. Let's see what this child wants first.

AGUS [*Entering the office.*] Good afternoon, Professor, Dr. Santini. Mr. Dar told me that you'd like to meet with me. Is there—

PROF. DJUMAWA There is! I've said several times: don't bypass procedure. Don't bypass procedure. How can this institution remain stable, calm, and peaceful if we bypass established procedure? Following procedure is most important. As the new person, you cannot just act as you please.

AGUS Professor Djumawa, all I want to do is help the students. My simple method is dialogue—and at the root, empathy. Isn't that what Freud, Jung, and Rogers used with their clients? In this case, I consider the students my clients also. They're my friends, and I'm their partner. We work together and support each other with the hope of becoming more compassionate. Free subjects, bright minds, and clear souls.

PROF. DJUMAWA What a heartfelt speech. Unfortunately, I'm not moved at all. Your hopes are my hopes, too. And here, under my leadership, we've tried all methods of producing young, sensible generations ready to meet future challenges. In this institution there's a certain way to present the educational material effectively, without minimizing efficiency. You will have to understand, Agus, that here we use only the following principle: "Listen! Make note! Memorize!" Period!

AGUS But, Professor.

PROF. DJUMAWA My method has been praised by many people. Although this achievement is the product of my tireless efforts, I often feel that I'm not worthy of such high praise. I always tell whoever teaches here not to get trapped by the students' stupid questions. When we are with them, we must remember that we are the teachers and they are the students. There's a hierarchy. We're not partners.

AGUS Professor—

PROF. DJUMAWA That's why we need strict discipline. And correct behavior. For example, don't cut me off before I'm finished speaking.

AGUS Please forgive me.

PROF. DJUMAWA And this correct behavior includes, among other things, not showing off by listing names of psychology's forefathers that I haven't thought about for over thirty years. Here, there's only me, Professor Djumawa, and I employ an efficient teaching method based on my vast experience. As the senior here, I forbid you to critique my methods. Everything I do is part of a program. Don't talk about it with other instructors, and especially not with the students. Enough. Reread the rules I gave you. Or, if you don't agree, please leave.

DR. SANTINI Remember, you've been given the best facilities in this institution, ones that you'd probably not get anywhere else.

AGUS Yes, thank you. I still want to work here. I love my work.

DR. SANTINI Then you must understand what you can and cannot do.

AGUS Yes.

PROF. DJUMAWA This meeting has gone on long enough. Good day.

AGUS Good day, Professor, Dr. Santini. [*Exits.*]

DR. SANTINI You shouldn't have been so quick to accept her.

PROF. DJUMAWA It's nothing. Don't worry. I can take care of everything. Don't you think I can?

DR. SANTINI I always believe in you.

PROF. DJUMAWA Come here. [*Hugs Dr. Santini.*]

Scene Nine

Agus's office. Dusk. Agus is alone. Father and Mother begin to move in the frame of the portrait that exists only in her imagination.

MOTHER If you don't obey your parents, then who will you obey?

FATHER Your father and mother know what's best for your future.

MOTHER Why is it so difficult for you to understand this? We've served you your future on a platter; you just need to accept it. What's so hard? Just take it.

FATHER Everything we've done is for your future. Daughters usually obey their parents. Why don't you?

AGUS Black and white, right and wrong. The difference is slight.

MOTHER I'm embarrassed to see Pandu's family. Twice he's come asking you to marry him. But you turn him down. You say you want to reach your goals first. Now, Pandu's starting a relationship with another girl. You'll cry from a broken heart. It's all your own fault.

AGUS Who can determine—

FATHER Forget about your aspirations. Comply with our plans. For the sake of your future.

AGUS — Which is more sensible? To take a stand because it's right, or to be obedient even when it's wrong?

MOTHER — [*As the lights on the portrait begin to fade.*] Agus, don't be silent. Answer us, Agus. Answer.

FATHER — Agus, you're stubborn. Like a rock.

AGUS — I will never surrender. Is there still meaning if I fail?

MOTHER — Agus! Agus! Agus! [*The lights on the portrait fade out.*]

AGUS — Is there still meaning if I fail?

Scene Ten

Classroom. Midday. Agus and the Students are engaged in dialogue.

AGUS — No, I don't see a reason why you have to be forced into silence and confusion. You're not sheep to be herded along. You're students, future intellectuals, heirs to the nation. I want to find an honest way to exchange ideas—an open debate in which we are free to agree or disagree.

SYENI — But we're scared.

FREDRIK — We're afraid.

The Students all express their fears and worries.

AGUS — Why does fear censor our thoughts? Why do we let worry replace free thought? Threats and punishment are only successful in the military world.

BONGGO — Miss Agus, you want a change. Isn't that the same as wanting Professor Djumawa to step down?

AGUS — Professor Djumawa's system makes it seem like we have no power, not even to defend our own rights as free human beings. Everything becomes dependent on him. It's clear the Professor has a warehouse of experience. I'm not downplaying that. But that doesn't mean he can do whatever he wants, as if his is the only right way. It's fine to hold the seat of power for an extended period of time, but come on . . .

CIPING — There's a limit. Yes? Yes? Yes?

STUDENTS — Yes!

BONGGO — What do we need to do, Miss Agus?

AGUS — As long as criticism is only permitted through official channels, and as long as the general consensus of this institution is to forbid questions and debate, the only possible outcome is a power monopoly. We cannot continue to keep silent about this.

FREDRIK — Yeah, we can't remain silent!

BONGGO — We have to speak up!

SYENI — Right makes might!

CIPING — Whoever's afraid is a coward. Yes? Yes? Yes?

BUJEL — I'm no coward!

The Students all express their eagerness to oppose the system.

AGUS — Okay, my friends, raise your voices! Don't be afraid! Make noise! Come on, speak up!

STUDENTS — We are the generation of leaflets and slogans
Born from a generation of arrogance
Free thought has been suppressed by obedience
The freedom to take action has been shackled by
  restrictions

We are the generation produced in factories
Designed by a system
Our view of life comes from what we learn in school
Not from life itself

We are the instant generation
Swiftly molded by the machines of power
We haven't succeeded in answering the challenges of the
  times
And stutter when asking questions

Are we the generation that has lost culture?
Are we to become merely tools?

Scene Eleven

Prof. Djumawa's office. Afternoon. Dr. Santini is there with Prof. Djumawa, as usual. Pleki is in a corner of the room, obediently awaiting orders.

DR. SANTINI — Have you heard that the students are planning something big?

PROF. DJUMAWA — Yes. My informant here has already reported what's going to take place.

DR. SANTINI — They're only puppets. Agus is the puppeteer.

PROF. DJUMAWA — Just a bunch of sheep bleating. I admit Agus is charismatic.

Unfortunately, her uncontrolled ambition makes her less introspective. Her fate will be nasty. Tragic. A bitter end.

DR. SANTINI — What do you mean?

PROF. DJUMAWA — We must put an end to this before her head gets any larger.

DR. SANTINI — How?

PROF. DJUMAWA — Come closer so I can whisper it to you. [*Whispers in Dr. Santini's ear.*]

DR. SANTINI — But—

PROF. DJUMAWA — Santini, we've known each other for a long time. We have a relationship like mutual symbiosis. You're not only my assistant at this institution, but also my most loyal dean. We have to keep each other's secrets, right? I know everything you've done for as long as we've worked together. I know you've accepted bribes from the students, but I said nothing. As your director, I brought no action against you.

DR. SANTINI — But this plan is extremely dangerous.

PROF. DJUMAWA — Santini, next month I'm planning to raise the director and assistant director's base salaries four hundred percent. Do you agree?

DR. SANTINI — Yes, I agree completely. Okay, I will follow your plan.

PROF. DJUMAWA — As long as we keep each other's secrets, the plans will proceed smoothly. Pleki, come here! [*Pleki approaches. Prof. Djumawa whispers his plan to Pleki.*]

PLEKI — Y-y-yes, Professor.

PROF. DJUMAWA — Make sure no one finds out.

PLEKI — W-w-will do, Professor. [*Exits.*]

Prof. Djumawa gazes at Dr. Santini. He then passionately embraces his secret love.

Scene Twelve

A secret location. Midday. The Students are quietly engaged in an underground meeting. Sarman hides nearby, watching nervously.

BONGGO — This is the moment, my friends. We have to make our move now.

CIPING — Have you thought this through carefully?

BONGGO — What do you mean, Ping?

CIPING What happens if we don't succeed?

FREDRIK We'll have to take that chance. Agreed?

STUDENTS Agreed!

SYENI I also agree, as long as it doesn't lead to anarchy. I'm against the use of force.

BONGGO What matters is that we demonstrate in our own way. Fred, is everything ready?

FREDRIK Everything is ready. The demonstration location and the signs. Bujel is in charge of gathering the demonstrators.

BUJEL A bunch of demonstrators from other universities will be joining our group.

BONGGO Great! Professor Djumawa's system has to be reformed, and Professor Djumawa has to step down. It's been thirty years, and now is the time for us to make a change.

FREDRIK We demand total reform.

BUJEL Let's start now. I can't wait any longer.

SYENI But no anarchy. Right, friends?

BONGGO Let's do it!

The Students leave for the demonstration. Pleki quietly goes in a different direction.

SARMAN [*Coming out of his hiding place.*] Oh no, disaster! Disaster! The kids want to demonstrate! Miss Agus needs to know this. The kids need to be stopped! [*Takes off running to look for Agus, who enters at that moment and bumps into him.*]

Disaster! The world's been thrown off its axis. The kids are heading to disaster!

AGUS What's up?

SARMAN There's an uprising.

AGUS What kind of uprising?

SARMAN The students. They're making moves.

AGUS Making moves?

SARMAN Yes, ma'am. They're making moves in the parking lot.

AGUS I don't understand.

SARMAN The students want to demonstrate!

AGUS Demonstrate?

SARMAN Yes, ma'am. They want to force Professor Djumawa to step down from his post. They're also demanding changes to the campus. Total reform! That's what they're saying! You must go there right now. If not, a great war will take place, like the epic Bharatayudha in Kuruksetra.

AGUS Okay, I'll go there right away, after I put these books in my office.

SARMAN Quickly. But I want to remind you to be careful. I have a hunch this will become a big issue.

AGUS Okay, thank you. [*Exits.*]

SARMAN The earth has been thrown off its axis! Uprising! Disaster! [*Exits to the demonstration area.*]

Scene Thirteen

Parking lot. Midday. Bonggo leads the Students in a demonstration. Some hold signs saying TOTAL REFORM, DJUMAWA STEP DOWN, DEMOCRACY OR DEATH, *etc. One student reads poetry. His friends shout out slogans. Secretly, Pleki enters and pours gasoline around the demonstration area, then lights a match. He joins with the demonstrators and encourages them to throw rocks at Prof. Djumawa's office. Others then throw rocks, too. Chaos ensues. Sarman sees everything from a distance, but is unable to do anything. Fire begins to spread around the demonstration area.*

SYENI Wait, is that smoke?

BONGGO Yes, there's smoke! Where is it coming from?

PLEKI Sm-m-moke!

The Students, unaware of what has happened, look toward the fire.

Fire! Fire!

BONGGO Fire! Fire!

CIPING Fire? Fiiiirrrre!

The Students scatter to protect themselves. Agus arrives at that moment. The fire has spread everywhere. She finds the gasoline container and picks it up, confused. The Instructors enter and see her holding the container. They surround her and shove her off to the side.

INSTRUCTORS Suspect! Report! Prevent! Agreed! Okay! Do it!

Scene Fourteen

A university conference room. Afternoon. Agus, Prof. Djumawa, Dr. Santini, the Instructors, the Students, and Sarman have gathered for a meeting about the fire. The university's Board of Trustees is also present.

DR. SANTINI Honored ladies and gentlemen, please allow me, as senior faculty, to make some comments before a decision is reached regarding our colleague Agus. It may be that Agus is a gifted teacher. It may be that she has discovered a new, innovative teaching method to replace our older, conventional method. It may be that she's an exceptional person, that she can become a friend to the students. It may be that the freedom of opinion she touts will help develop a greater sensitivity to social conditions and the community beyond the students' own. They may be more empowered to express themselves, healthier in spirit, likelier to interact with one another, and so on. However, such freedom would instead produce an unjustifiable deviation. The students would become wild, and anarchy would ensue—a democracy out of control! Therefore, we ought to question Agus's presence in this institution. As both a teacher and a psychologist, she has questionable self-control. If a teacher, without weighing the consequences, leads a riot like this one, we can then estimate how slight her dedication, how superficial her moral values. Therefore, I and the other instructors propose that Agus be terminated from her post as soon as possible. The reckless freedoms she has allowed our students are irresponsible and have smeared the good name of our institution, which has for years enjoyed a high degree of discipline. And since we are downsizing, it is time for Agus to be dishonorably discharged from our institution. Please take my comments and recommendations into consideration, and please let us know your decision as soon as possible.

PROF. DJUMAWA Honored attendees, Dr. Santini has presented an irrefutable argument. Everything has been clearly articulated. There is also a witness whose testimony confirms it was Agus who emptied the gasoline container. As director of this institution, I second Dr. Santini's remarks. This institution hereby dishonorably discharges Agus. I will also write a letter to the Psychologists Association asking them to revoke her professional certification. We will then hand Agus over to the authorities. As for the students who demonstrated yesterday in the parking lot, they will all receive the penalty of D.O.! Drop out!

AGUS — Wait! Am I not going to be given a chance to defend myself? I've been slandered. I would never do something so despicable. If there truly is, as Professor Djumawa says, a witness who saw me encourage the students to set fire to the parking lot yesterday afternoon, I would like to know who it is.

DR. SANTINI — Pleki, please step forward.

PLEKI — Y-y-yes, D-D-Dr. Santini. [*Steps forward as the witness.*]

AGUS — Oh my God—Pleki?

STUDENTS — Pleki?

PROF. DJUMAWA — Is it true that you witnessed Agus encouraging the students to start a fire in the parking lot yesterday afternoon?

PLEKI — Y-y-yes, Professor. I s-s-saw it with my own eyes. Miss Agus told Bonggo to pour the gasoline there, then Bonggo lit a match and the fire started.

BONGGO — No, I didn't do that.

CIPING — None of us started the fire.

SYENI — I'm a pacifist. I would never let my friends do anything like that.

BONGGO — Miss Agus didn't know we were going to demonstrate. She couldn't be involved with what happened. [*To Agus.*] Please forgive us for not letting you know we were planning to demonstrate. We didn't want to jeopardize your position in the institution.

FREDRIK — This is definitely just one of Pleki's lies.

PROF. DJUMAWA — [*To Pleki.*] Are you lying?

PLEKI — There's n-n-no way I would dare lie to you, Professor, and this honored Board. I am t-t-telling the truth.

PROF. DJUMAWA — And will you stick by your story with the authorities?

PLEKI — I w-w-will, Professor.

The Students protest Pleki's testimony.

PROF. DJUMAWA — [*Banging a gavel to silence the Students.*] The witness has given his account of what he saw yesterday. [*To Agus.*] You can't deny it any longer.

AGUS — I'm being falsely accused. This charge against me has no merit. I arrived there after the fire started. I'd like to call a witness who can verify that.

PROF. DJUMAWA Fine. I will allow you to call whomever can testify that you arrived after the fire started. Do you have a witness?

AGUS [*Looks around the room, hoping for a witness to support her.*] If anyone witnessed me arriving after the fire started, please step forward and give your honest testimony.

SARMAN [*Stepping forward.*] I will.

AGUS It's true, right?

PROF. DJUMAWA Sarman?

SARMAN Yes, Professor. I am positive that Miss Agus didn't start that fire.

AGUS Please recount honestly what happened.

SARMAN Earlier today, I was secretly spying on the underground student meeting where they were planning the demonstration. I then reported the matter to Miss Agus, who knew nothing about the students' plans. Miss Agus wanted to stop the demonstration, but she didn't go straight there because she wanted to put her books away first. I was so afraid that I ran straight to where the students were demonstrating. And there I saw Ple—

DR. SANTINI Professor and esteemed Board, do you believe Sarman, a mere houseboy? Someone whose loyalty can be bought for a few cents?

SARMAN But I know for sure that Miss Agus is not guilty.

PROF. DJUMAWA You have worked here as long as I have. You have the heart to betray the institution that has given life to you and your family for decades?

SARMAN But, Professor—

PROF. DJUMAWA [*Points to Agus.*] You would choose this person, someone who has only worked here a few months, over us, whom you've known your whole life?

SARMAN But, Professor—

PROF. DJUMAWA Or are you working for Agus?

SARMAN No, Professor.

PROF. DJUMAWA Well then, please get back to work. Clean all the rooms. Make tea and coffee. Don't get involved in things that are none of your business.

SARMAN	Yes, Professor. [*Looks at Agus and whispers.*] Please forgive me, Miss Agus. [*Exits.*]
PROF. DJUMAWA	Please disregard that small interruption. As head of the Board of Trustees, I have come to the decision to fire Agus and to expel all students involved in yesterday's demonstration. [*Bangs gavel three times.*]
AGUS	I refuse to accept this unfair decision.
DR. SANTINI	The director has announced the decision and banged the gavel three times. What more do you want?
AGUS	Everyone has conspired to ruin me. Why? Because you're afraid that the students have taken the initiative to speak out! Because you're afraid there will be big changes and that the old system won't be accepted anymore! Is that why I have been brought down so disgracefully?
MR. DAR	But we found you at the fire with the gasoline container in your hand.
MRS. ATIKA	While you were teaching, we often saw you encouraging the students to challenge the law and the legal system.
MR. MUS	As a teacher, you overstepped the boundaries.
MR. TEDJO	Without considering the risk of it turning out as it did.
AGUS	But I didn't mean for the students to demonstrate. I just wanted them to have the courage to express their opinions, to agree or disagree.
BONGGO	Forgive us, Miss Agus. We know you're not guilty.
SYENI	How can Pleki slander you like this?
FREDRIK	We just wanted a change. We didn't want to be oppressed any longer.
CIPING	We wanted healthy dialogue. We no longer wanted to follow a system that obstructs freedom of speech and thought.
BUJEL	We didn't start the fire. Miss Agus never encouraged us. I swear.
SYENI	We're pacifists.
PROF. DJUMAWA	Silence! All this empty talk serves no purpose. It has already been decided that whoever disturbs the peace of this institution shall be disposed of by whatever means necessary.

AGUS — [*Giving up.*] I accept my dismissal, but please, give the students a chance to defend themselves, for the sake of their futures. Please, Professor.

PROF. DJUMAWA — [*Pays no attention to Agus.*] This meeting is officially over. [*Immediately exits the room with Dr. Santini and the Board of Trustees.*]

AGUS — Please! I beg you!

The Students shout in protest against the unfair proceedings. They move to attack. The Instructors form a line, blocking the Students' way and forcing them out of the room.

INSTRUCTORS — Suspect! Report! Prevent! Agreed! Okay! Do it!

Agus collapses. She weeps hopelessly.

Scene Fifteen

Prof. Djumawa's office. Nighttime. Prof. Djumawa and Dr. Santini are celebrating their success.

PROF. DJUMAWA — You acted so official.

DR. SANTINI — Really?

PROF. DJUMAWA — [*Imitating Dr. Santini.*] "The reckless freedoms she has allowed our students are irresponsible . . ."

DR. SANTINI — [*Laughing.*] That's how officials speak, isn't it?

PROF. DJUMAWA — Pretty much.

DR. SANTINI — You think I could become an official?

PROF. DJUMAWA — Of course, my dear . . . Come on, let's celebrate our victory. [*Pours champagne into Dr. Santini's glass.*]

Scene Sixteen

Agus's room. Nighttime.

AGUS — How am I going to bear this? How must I answer all the unanswered questions? I've lost. I'm defeated.

Black and white
Right and wrong
The difference is slight

Which is more sensible
To take a stand because it's right
Or be obedient even when it's wrong

I will never surrender
Is there still meaning if I fail?
Is there still meaning if I fail?

Agus ties a cord around her neck. Mother and Father enter.

MOTHER Oh my God, Agus!

FATHER [*Unties the cord around her neck.*] Why are you so headstrong?!

MOTHER [*Crying.*] Agus! Agus!

Scene Seventeen

Examination room in a psychiatric hospital. Evening. Agus sits shackled to a chair. Father, Mother, and Prof. Djumawa observe her with pity.

MOTHER Professor, I ask that you help cure our daughter. You are a leading psychologist. I believe that with your help our daughter will recover her mental health faster.

PROF. DJUMAWA Yes, by all means I will help.

FATHER I said repeatedly that there was no way she could heal a sick world on her own. But she was always such a stubborn child. She did whatever she wanted, even though she didn't have any authority.

PROF. DJUMAWA That's the spirit of youth. Impatient and reckless.

MOTHER That's why I've asked for our child to be placed under your direct care, treatment, and handling, Professor.

PROF. DJUMAWA I will treat Agus with my special method and apply all of my resources.

FATHER Thank you, Professor. You are much needed in the fight against the mental difficulties of our only daughter.

MOTHER We don't know who else to ask for help, besides you.

PROF. DJUMAWA You two have come to the right person with the right method.

Father, Mother, and Prof. Djumawa exit. Agus sits shackled to the chair. Her eyes are vacant, without expression. Everything that has happened passes silently through her mind. There are only the following lyrics:

VOICE-OVER A small bird flies high
Breaks through the atmosphere
Reaching for the tip

Of the crescent moon
Hope hanging
Over yonder . . .
The heavens radiate and shine
Shooting rays of light
The bird's feathers burn to a crisp

The small bird free-falls
Piercing the clouds
Carried by the wind
Lies flat on the earth
Silently
Silently
Silently

Lights out.

Translation by Cobina Gillitt

About the Contributors

Michael H. Bodden is a professor of Pacific and Asian studies at the University of Victoria, in Canada. A scholar and translator, he has translated plays by Mohammad Diponegoro, Usmar Ismail, Saadah Alim, Armijn Pané, and Sanusi Pané; poetry by Saraswati Sunindyo, Nurhidayat Poso, and Afrizal Malna; plays and short stories by Putu Wijaya; and short stories, plays, and essays by Seno Gumira Ajidarma. His books include *Resistance on the National Stage: Theater and Politics in Late New Order Indonesia* (2010) and *The Lontar Anthology of Indonesian Drama Volume Two: Building a National Theater* (2010).

Kathy Foley is a professor of theater at the University of California, Santa Cruz, and the editor of *Asian Theatre Journal.* A scholar and international performance artist, she is also a master puppeteer (dalang) of Sundanese *wayang golek* and has performed numerous times at the Indonesian Wayang Festival (Pekan Wayang Indonesia). Her recent work is on Islamic *wali* (saints) and *wayang.* In the spring of 2014, she was a senior Fulbright fellow at the University of Malaya, where she worked on politics, language streams, and theater. She has translated and adapted numerous Indonesian plays.

Cobina Gillitt is an assistant professor of theater and performance at Purchase College, SUNY. Her scholarly work on contemporary Indonesian theater has appeared in *Antigone on the Contemporary World Stage* (2011), *The Lontar Anthology of Indonesian Drama Volume Three: New Directions, 1965–1998* (2010), *The Senses in Performance* (2007), and numerous journals. In addition to her translation work, she is a performer and has been a member of Jakarta-based Teater Mandiri since 1988.

Barbara Hatley is emeritus professor of Indonesian in the Asian languages and studies program at the University of Tasmania, Australia, and adjunct professor of the School of Languages, Literatures, Cultures and Linguistics at Monash University, Australia. Her books include *Javanese Performances on an Indonesian Stage: Contesting Culture, Embracing Change* (2008), *Performance in the Asia Pacific: Regional Modernities in the Global Era* (2013), and an edited volume on performance in post-Soeharto Indonesia, *Performing Contemporary Indonesia: Celebrating Locality, Constructing Community* (2015).

John H. McGlynn is an American living in Jakarta. In 1987, he established the Lontar Foundation, and now serves as chairman of its Board of Trustees. He is also a trustee of AMINEF, the American Indonesian Exchange Foundation, which oversees the Fulbright and Humphrey scholarship programs in Indonesia. McGlynn has translated dozens of full-length literary works, and through the Lontar Foundation, he has edited and overseen the translation and publication of more than two hundred Indonesian authors. He also started Lontar's film documentation program, which to date has produced twenty-four films on Indonesian writers and more than thirty films on Indonesian performance traditions, and has subtitled more than a hundred Indonesian films. He serves as *Mānoa*'s corresponding editor for Indonesia.

Rita Matu Mona was born in North Sumatra in 1959, and is an actress, director, and playwright. As an actress, she has performed in such plays as *Time Bomb*, and plays by Bertolt Brecht, Georg Büchner, Arthur Miller, and George Orwell. In 1999, while helping to stage Brecht's *The Threepenny Opera*, she recruited and trained more than twenty street children for the performance. When *Make Note!* was staged in 1999 in Jakarta, the students were played by street children, twelve to sixteen years old, who had worked as prostitutes.

Armijn Pané (1908–1970) was born in Muara Sipongi, Tapanuli, Sumatra. He briefly attended medical school in Jakarta before turning to writing. He graduated with a degree in Western classical literature and worked as a language teacher and journalist. In the 1930s he published his first plays, and in 1940 *Belenggu* (Shackles), his controversial novel. Similar to *A Portrait of the Times*, the novel concerns urban, Western-educated characters who struggle to find their roles in a changing society, ending up alienated and doomed to fail. Pané also published collections of poetry and short fiction. He continued writing plays during and after the years of Japanese occupation. The Republic of Indonesia honored Pané for his work in literature in 1969 just months before he died.

N. Riantiarno was born in Cirebon, West Java, in 1949. He moved to Jakarta in 1967 to study at the National Theater Academy, developing an interest in the plays of Tennessee Williams, Arthur Miller, and Bertolt Brecht. In the 1970s, he began working in the style of early twentieth-century Malay "operas," which were traditionally performed by itinerant troupes in local vernaculars and used improvisation, dance, music, slapstick, and satire. Combining Malay and Brechtian theater styles, he wrote plays that were both sympathetic to the exploited and powerless underclass, and critical of the hypocrisy and corruption of government and society. *Time Bomb*, published here, is part of a trilogy about the character Julini.

Ratna Sarumpaet was born in Tarutung, North Sumatra, in 1949. She moved to Jakarta as a teenager and attended the Catholic University. Inspired by a performance of W. S. Rendra's play *The Barzanji Chant* (*Kasidah Berzanji*) in 1969, she studied in Rendra's Workshop Theatre as an actress. In 1974, she founded her own theater company, directing plays by Shakespeare and other European playwrights that incorporated Batak cultural elements. In 1993, she began writing plays that called attention to crimes against humanity. The play in this volume, *The Prostitute and the President*, is about child sex trafficking and was written in 2006 at the request of UNICEF. The following year, she adapted the play and directed a film version, titling it *Jamila and the President*. The film won the NETPAC Award in Rome, and the Youth Prize and Public Prize in France.

Iwan Simatupang (1928–1970) was born in Sibolga, North Sumatra. He studied anthropology in Leiden and Western philosophy in Paris. After he returned to Indonesia, he worked as a journalist and editor. In 1957, he began publishing plays. He also wrote novels, short stories, essays, and poetry. As an actor and director, he was associated with Theater 2000, an avant-garde dramatic company influenced by surrealism and existentialism. Like other playwrights in this volume, he was concerned with individual freedom and the social condition of marginalized, poor, and disenfranchised people. *No Address, No Name* takes place under a bridge, where outcasts survive by begging, scavenging, and prostitution.

Luna Vidya was born in Papua and began working in theater in 1984. She co-founded the Makkunrai Project in 2007, which raises awareness of gender issues in Indonesian society through plays and literature. In the last four years, she has concentrated on writing and producing monologues, occasionally in collaboration with other artists. *The Kitchen* is one of two scripts she adapted from short stories written by Lily Yulianti Farid, co-founder of the Makkunrai Project. *The Kitchen* has been produced in Australia, Paris, Tokyo, Singapore, Jakarta, and Makassar.

Kurniadi Widodo was born in 1985. A freelance photographer, he is currently based in Yogyakarta, Indonesia. In 2010, he and seven other photographers founded Cephas Photo Forum, a community group that promotes a critical approach to photography through sharing and discussion. (cephasphotoforum.org) kurniadiwidodo.blogspot.com

Putu Wijaya was born in Bali in 1944. He obtained a law degree in 1968 and also studied painting and dramatic arts. One of Indonesia's most prolific and celebrated writers, he is the author of thirty novels, forty plays, and a thousand short stories, essays, and film and television scripts. He has been a journalist, movie director, and actor, and has founded theater companies. His 1973 play *Aduh*, translated here as *Ought*, was the first in what he called his Stupid Theater style (*Teater Bodoh*). As in traditional Balinese drama, the plot is fantastic and minimal, the characters stylized, and the central issue unresolved.

Permissions

Rita Matu Mona. *Make Note!* Translated by Cobina Gillitt. Reprinted with permission from *Three Plays by Three Indonesian Women Playwrights*. Jakarta: Jakarta Arts Council, 2006.

Armijn Pané. *A Portrait of the Times*. Translated by Michael H. Bodden. Reprinted with permission from *The Lontar Anthology 2: Building a National Theater*. Edited by Michael H. Bodden and John H. McGlynn. Jakarta: The Lontar Foundation, 2010.

N. Riantiarno. *Time Bomb*. Translated by Barbara Hatley. Reprinted with permission from *Time Bomb and Cockroach Opera*. Edited by John H. McGlynn. Jakarta: The Lontar Foundation, 1992.

Ratna Sarumpaet. *The Prostitute and the President*. Translated by Kathy Foley. Reprinted with permission from *Three Plays by Three Indonesian Women Playwrights*. Jakarta: Jakarta Arts Council, 2006.

Iwan Simatupang. *No Address, No Name*. Translated by John H. McGlynn. Reprinted with permission from *Square Moon and Three Other Short Plays*. Jakarta: The Lontar Foundation, 1997.

Luna Vidya. *The Kitchen*. Adapted from the short story by Lily Yulianti Farid. Translated by John H. McGlynn. Printed with permission.

Putu Wijaya. *Ought*. Translated by Cobina Gillitt. Reprinted with permission from *The Lontar Anthology 3: New Directions, 1965–1998*. Edited by Cobina Gillitt and John H. McGlynn. Jakarta: The Lontar Foundation, 2010.

About the Lontar Foundation

Founded in 1987, the Lontar Foundation is an independent, nonprofit organization based in Jakarta, Indonesia. Lontar's purpose is to promote greater appreciation of Indonesian culture by supporting the development of Indonesian literature; making Indonesian literature accessible to an international audience; and preserving Indonesia's literary record for future generations. It accomplishes this through two major activities: publications, and research and documentation.

Before Lontar was established, there was virtually no place where a reader could regularly obtain translations of Indonesian literature. Today, Lontar is the only organization in the world that promotes Indonesia through the publication and distribution of literary translations.

The Lontar Publications Division has produced more than a hundred books on Indonesian language, literature, and culture. The Research & Documentation Division has produced twenty-four documentaries on Indonesian writers and thirty-two videos on Indonesian oral traditions. Lontar is now an integral part of the country's cultural scene and an active participant in a wide range of cultural activities in Indonesia and abroad.

Supporters of Lontar's goals include the following:

Donors: corporations and donor agencies that have provided Lontar with financial assistance.

Partners: institutions that have partnered with Lontar on the implementation of programs or have provided the Foundation with in-kind support.

Individual Friends: persons who have provided Lontar with either financial or in-kind support.

At Lontar's Web site, http://www.lontar.org/en/home, visitors may:

Purchase Lontar books and other products. Groups that purchase ten or more copies of each new Lontar book will receive them at a substantial discount.

Offer to work with Lontar on one of the Foundation's projects.

Provide direct financial assistance. Queries about making a bank transfer to one of Lontar's accounts can be sent by using the Contact Us link. American donors will receive a tax benefit by giving through Give2Asia at www.give2asia.org.